Advance Praise for Stewart Baker's
Skating on Stilts: Why We Aren't Stopping Tomorrow's Terrorism

"Stewart Baker's provocative book draws on his experience as a top homeland security official to raise important questions about the balance between security considerations and privacy concerns. This is a 'must read' for all concerned with striking the right balance."

U.S. senator Susan M. Collins, ranking member of the Homeland Security and Governmental Affairs Committee

"With penetrating intellect, pragmatic perspective, and broad counter-terrorism experience, Stewart Baker provides chilling insights into the terrifying threats presented by ever-more-high-tech terrorism, the maddening inadequacy of our defenses, and the lobbies responsible for this inadequacy. He recounts in vivid detail how the same entrenched business interests, bureaucratic turf wars, and anti-American Euro-bureaucrats that helped pave the way for 9/11 have continued to oppose policies that would make us safer. Especially devastating is Baker's portrayal of the deeply misguided "privacy lobby" who insist on perpetuating security dangers in order to avert highly improbable governmental abuses. This despite the exponentially increasing likelihood of cyber-attacks "that could leave us without power, money, petroleum, or communications for months" and biological attacks "equivalent to a nuclear detonation."

Stuart Taylor, Jr., *National Journal* columnist, *Newsweek* contributor, and Brookings Institution nonresident senior fellow

"Stewart Baker makes a cogent, vivid, and persuasive case that we should protect privacy by auditing the government's use of data about individuals and punishing misuse—but most definitely not by treating such data as private property nor by building walls around it, as we did before 9/11, that bar government-wide cooperation in fighting terrorism. This book will fundamentally change the terms of the technology-privacy debate."

R. James Woolsey, Director of Central Intelligence and head of the Central Intelligence Agency, 1993–1995

"If you have time to read only one book on the sorry state of our homeland security—make it this one. Free from political correctness, extremely well-informed, and written with great flare—by a high-ranking former government official, who has seen it all."

Amitai Etzioni, author of *Security First*, 2008

"Policy meets reality. No post-9/11 official spent more time trying to figure out how to keep America safe, free, and prosperous at the same time than Stewart Baker. His story offers important lessons for battling terrorism in the future."

James Jay Carafano, coauthor of *Winning the Long War* and director of the Heritage Foundation's Douglas and Sarah Allison Center for Foreign Studies

"Too much commentary about our efforts to prevent another 9/11 is based on prejudice, fear, disinformation and willfull disregard of the threats we face. Stewart Baker has courageously written an open and honest history of our recent efforts—rare in government memoirs—that no serious homeland security policymaker can ignore."

Ambassador John Bolton, former U.S. ambassador to the United Nations

"I don't agree with all, or even most, of the perspective Stewart Baker brings to the modern security debate. But I am very glad to have read what he has to say, both for the inside details on how security policy evolved after 9/11 and to engage with the argument he makes. The book is trenchant and well-written, and anyone who cares about the balance between privacy and public safety should be familiar with it."

James Fallows, national correspondent for the *Atlantic*

"Stewart Baker offers the perspective of a warrior in the trenches and frames the world of exploding information and data at that terrible intersection between perseverant, cunning bad guys and vulnerable, fatigued good guys. His mix of wrenching personal life stories and policy debates challenges us to recognize the complexity of the post 9/11 security challenges."

Admiral James M. Loy, Deputy Secretary of Homeland Security (2003–2005)

"*Skating on Stilts* is both a memoir and a guidebook. Baker takes us through the challenges of his days at DHS, and presents a framework for action that will stand the test of time."

John Hamre, former Deputy Secretary of Defense and president, Center for Strategic and International Studies

"A frightening and enlightening book—a must-read for anyone who wants to seriously discuss privacy, security, liberty, and control in today's exhilarating but dangerous technological environment."

Eugene Volokh, Gary T. Schwartz Professor of Law, University of California at Los Angeles School of Law

SKATING ON STILTS

SKATING ON STILTS

Why We Aren't Stopping Tomorrow's Terrorism

Stewart A. Baker

HOOVER INSTITUTION PRESS
Stanford University Stanford, California

The Hoover Institution on War, Revolution and Peace, founded at Stanford University in 1919 by Herbert Hoover, who went on to become the thirty-first president of the United States, is an interdisciplinary research center for advanced study on domestic and international affairs. The views expressed in its publications are entirely those of the authors and do not necessarily reflect the views of the staff, officers, or Board of Overseers of the Hoover Institution.

www.hoover.org

Hoover Institution Press Publication No. 591

Hoover Institution at Leland Stanford Junior University,
Stanford, California, 94305–6010

First printing 2010
16 15 14 13 12 11 10 9 8 7 6 5 4 3 2 1

Manufactured in the United States of America

The paper used in this publication meets the minimum Requirements of the American National Standard for Information Sciences—Permanence of Paper for Printed Library Materials, ANSI/NISO Z39.48-1992. ♾

Cataloging-in-Publication Data is available from the Library of Congress.
ISBN-13: 978-0-8179-1154-6 (cloth)

ISBN-13: 978-0-8179-1156-0 (e-book)

To Frank M. Coffin (1919-2009)

Frank M. Coffin served in Congress, in the executive branch, and for four decades on the U.S. Court of Appeals for the First Circuit. A year as his law clerk showed me that public service, affection, high standards, and good humor could be the core of a great career in writing, law, and government.

Contents

PART FOUR The Privacy Problem

Foreword

In the years following the September 11 attacks, America's struggle against Islamic extremism and transnational terror has given rise to many novel and difficult legal questions. To address some of those questions, the Hoover Institution launched the Koret-Taube Task Force on National Security and Law, which was made possible by the generous support of the Koret Foundation, the Taube Family Foundation, and the Jean Perkins Foundation. The task force, which is guided by Hoover's staunch commitment to the protection of rights under law and an acute appreciation that liberty depends on security, brings together an outstanding array of leading thinkers. Hoover convenes the group regularly, providing a forum in which they can think independently and benefit from the criticism of, and collaboration with, their distinguished colleagues.

On issues ranging from the detention, interrogation, and prosecution of enemy combatants at home to the use of unmanned aerial vehicles to conduct targeted killings in Afghanistan and Pakistan, task force members have produced a steady stream of influential op-eds, essays, law review articles, and books aimed at the broad public; provided important congressional testimony; and offered expertise to Capitol Hill lawmakers. In addition, the task force has reached out to scholars and former government officials wrestling with national security questions, both to benefit from their knowledge and experience and to give them access to task force deliberations.

We were especially delighted when Stewart Baker, a distinguished lawyer and public servant, agreed to join task force members at Hoover to present the arguments that culminated in *Skating on Stilts*. Baker's book draws on his extensive government experience and, in particular his recent service as the first assistant secretary for policy at the Department of Homeland Security. It explores a variety of grave threats presented by today's transnational terrorists and examines the steps we must take, consistent with constitutional principles, to bolster our defenses. In addition, it is concise, lucid, and compelling. We are therefore proud to include *Skating on Stilts* among the growing body of task force contributions to the crucial debate over national security law.

Peter Berkowitz
Tad and Dianne Taube Senior Fellow;
Chair, Koret-Taube Task Force on National Security and Law

Acknowledgments

I could not have written this book without the help of many others. John Hamre and the Center for Strategic and International Studies provided crucial support (including the thing I needed most—a quiet office with blank walls and no windows), enabling me to take the book past the point of no return in the first half of 2009. My partners at Steptoe & Johnson have been endlessly patient with me in the months since then. My son, Gordon, sacrificed a couple of great hiking trips with me so that I could finish this book. My former colleagues at the Department of Homeland Security encouraged and corrected me in equal measure. Both the Department of Homeland Security and the National Security Agency conducted a professional and prompt review of a draft of the book for classified material. And I will always be grateful to Secretary Michael Chertoff and President George W. Bush who made possible the achievements—and forgave the failures—described in this book.

I owe special thanks to Paul Rosenzweig, who served with distinction as my deputy and alter ego at the department and whose contributions to this book and the thinking behind it were profound. He did a first draft of more than one chapter, and he read and edited drafts of the rest. Most of all, in the drafting as in government, he gave me wise counsel and loyal assistance beyond any reasonable expectation.

Stewart Baker
Great Falls, Virginia

PART ONE
THE ROAD TO 9/11

Introduction | The Gift

A cold drizzle is falling on the Pentagon parking lot. The memorial for those who died here on 9/11 was dedicated in 2008—just a year ago—but it's almost deserted. In nearly four years at the Department of Homeland Security (DHS), I never managed to visit any of the 9/11 memorials. Now that I'm out of office, along with the rest of the Bush Administration, I have time to pay a quiet visit.

I don't like the place. Flat and unadorned, it feels like an extension of the vast Pentagon parking lot. The trees are scrawny, and the grounds are a utilitarian expanse of gravel and rain-slick paving stones. Beyond the sparse vegetation and a concrete wall, traffic hisses and thrums on a highway.

I think I know what the designers had in mind. They wanted everything understated and austere. There's a bench and a lighted pool of water for each victim who died here. Each bench bears a victim's name. The benches and the paths trace the course that Flight 77 must have taken—smack into the massive west wall of the Pentagon that looms nearby, gray in the rain.

The site is all about good taste and minimalism. Security is tight. The grounds look as though they're swept clean each night to remove any trace of the day's visitors, their litter, their mess, their grief.

But I'm not in the mood for good taste. The place feels cold and runic. Some benches arc toward the building; others arc away. Some of the pools have names in them; most don't. The benches are arranged by year, from 1998 to 1930.

I've come for a memorial; instead I've found some kind of puzzle.

I practice law for a living, but off and on I've spent years in government. This last tour has been a tough one. DHS was a startup, begun in the wake of disaster and assembled on the fly. Two years in, DHS suddenly realized that it needed a policy office, and I got the job. A startup within a startup, the office had to be built from scratch.

Everything was up for grabs—policies, procedures, authorities, personnel. I knew that wouldn't last; slowly the demand for routine would crowd out innovation. So in the midst of chaos—uncertain budgets, borrowed staff, no backup—I felt the pressure to push new ideas and policies into place as quickly as possible. Early on, what matters is how good your ideas are. Later, what matters is whether your ideas have been vetted with every office that thinks it has a stake in the decision.

So all at the same time, I had to build the office, recruit great people, solidify the budget, and put a solid policy structure under much of what DHS did.

I did that. Now I'm tired. I need time to clear my head.

So here I am, thinking about the people who died a few yards away—the people whose deaths drove me back into government. I am taking stock of what I've actually managed to do for their memory.

The place is nearly deserted. A handful of other people wander the paths. Two youngsters skip up to me. They want to know where the broken limestone is.

I look around. The place is as sterile as a French park. There's no place for anything broken.

"It's here somewhere. We have to find it for our class."

Great, I think. A puzzle and a scavenger hunt. I try sitting on one of the benches. It's sopping. My pants soak through. I stand.

That's enough. Time to go.

But the puzzle nags at me. The dates are easy enough. They're birth years. The benches arcing toward the building are for the passengers on Flight 77. The others are for victims who died in the Pentagon.

I look for my birth year—1947. Eleven dead. More than any other year. That seems fitting. By 2001, we baby boomers had shaped the

United States to reflect ourselves. We were what the attackers hated. This is our fight.

I'd known that from the start. On the day of the attacks, I looked out of my law office window and saw the smoke rising from the Pentagon.

I felt at least a bit of responsibility for our failure to stop the attacks.

In the 1990s, after a term as the National Security Agency's top lawyer, I spoke out in favor of keeping a wall between spies and cops. The idea was simple enough. Agencies like the National Security Agency (NSA) gathered intelligence on a global scale, and they rarely observed the legal constraints that applied to domestic policemen. To protect the civil liberties of Americans, it only made sense to separate intelligence gathered in that way from evidence assembled in a criminal investigation. With a wall between the two, criminal investigators from agencies like the Federal Bureau of Investigation (FBI) would be forced to observe the legal restrictions that went with criminal investigative tools. They wouldn't be tempted to take the shortcut of using intelligence that had been gathered with less attention to civil liberties.

That was the theory, anyway. In practice, the wall crippled our last, best chance to catch the hijackers before September 11, 2001. In August of that year, the wall kept the FBI from launching a full-scale criminal search for the hijackers—even though all of our security agencies were expecting an imminent al Qaeda attack, and even though both the FBI and the Central Intelligence Agency (CIA) knew that two dangerous al Qaeda operatives had entered the United States. The failure to track those operatives down wasn't a matter of incompetence or a failure to communicate, at least not in the last weeks. FBI criminal investigators spent the last part of August begging for a chance to track the terrorists. They were shut down cold—by lawyers who told them the wall simply could not be breached.

I wasn't the most enthusiastic proponent of the wall. I thought that the civil liberties dangers it was supposed to ward off were probably more theoretical than real. But I saw no harm in building in an extra margin of protection for civil liberties. If nothing else, the wall would reassure privacy advocates in the courts, in the newspapers, and on Capitol Hill that intelligence would not be misused. It was insurance, not just for civil liberties, but for the intelligence agencies themselves. For both reasons, I thought, it was best to keep the wall high.

It made eminent sense inside the Beltway.

Until the world outside the Beltway broke through, just a few yards from where I'm standing.

Slowly, as I wander back and forth among the rows of benches, the puzzle starts to fall into place. The oldest passenger was seventy-one; the youngest was three. The names of family members who died together are engraved in each other's reflecting pools. Husbands died with wives. Parents with children. Most of the passengers, though, died alone. Which would be worse, I wonder, facing death without a hand to hold or knowing that your spouse will die with you?

Close to the entrance is a knot of benches for children—two girls traveling with their parents and three eleven-year-olds without family. What was the hijacking like for these youngsters, I wonder, imagining the chaos as the passengers were forced into the back of the plane. At that age, I'd just assumed that adults were in control. They were the ones who made the rules, the ones who could always protect you when things got bad. For the first time, and the last, all those comfortable childish assumptions about the world had broken down.

The birth-year arrangement means that a long barren stretch of gravel separates the eleven-year-olds from the twenty-two-year-olds who worked in the building. Bereft of flowers and personal touches, all of the benches seem a little lonely; off by themselves, the children's benches seem lonelier still.

In the wake of the attacks, I recanted my support for the wall. I testified to the 9/11 Commission about the risks of overprotecting civil liberties. But that didn't seem like enough. I wanted to do more. I seized a chance to work for the Robb-Silberman Commission that investigated our intelligence failures in Iraq; I helped make recommendations about how to keep weapons of mass destruction out of terrorists' hands.

And finally in 2005 I joined the brainy, hard-charging Michael Chertoff at the Department of Homeland Security (DHS).

Wiser career decisions have been made; at the time, DHS was being widely mocked as disorganized and obsessed with duct tape and color schemes for terrorist warnings. But I've never turned down a chance to work in government with someone I respect, and bringing order to DHS policy was a chance to undo some of the harm that the wall had caused.

I had to decide where DHS policy could make the most difference. One place where the Department of Homeland Security had sole responsibility was the border. In fact, the one unquestionably good idea at the core of DHS was uniting border responsibilities that had been split among three cabinet secretaries. Neglected by all three, border security had collapsed under the weight of ever-increasing jet travel. Border officials were waving more and more visitors through our immigration and customs checkpoints with only a cursory look.

Al Qaeda sent twenty hijackers to carry out the 9/11 attacks. All but one got past our border defenses. Even stopping that one hijacker took an act of courage on the part of the border agent; in those days, keeping a Saudi traveler out of Orlando could easily trigger complaints about discrimination and lost tourism.

We had to rebuild those defenses—but without discouraging international travel. That would require clarity and determination. Already, the toughest measures were being stalled.

Civil liberties groups, far from feeling abashed at the role their doctrine had played in 9/11, were loudly fighting DHS's new security measures. They had an eager audience abroad; in fact, our allies in Europe had already forced DHS to rebuild the wall between law enforcement and intelligence, at least as far as border data was concerned. The Europeans had threatened to withhold data on transatlantic travelers unless DHS promised to keep that data from intelligence agencies—and even from other parts of the department.

I am beginning to see the appeal of this austere, cerebral memorial. I don't know most of the victims, and neither will others who come here. The memorial is not meant for memory but for connection. It tells us nothing but the names and the birth dates of the victims, but I see now that those are enough to build a web of connections. Just those facts drain some of the anonymity from the dead. They are all that's needed to pull us out of airy sentiment and make us feel instead the concrete loss the victims and their families suffered.

It's not much, in fact it's sadly impersonal, but it's more than most memorials can convey.

With Secretary Chertoff's full support, I fought back against the determined resistance of airlines, foreign governments, and civil liberties groups; we put in place a coherent border inspection strategy despite them. We hadn't won every battle when I left, but we were winning, and it looked as though the new Secretary and the new administration would keep up the fight. That was satisfying.

But satisfaction was not what I was feeling. I've never understood political memoirs that are a long tale of successes. In my experience, government rarely offers clear victories. The more ambitious your goals—if you want to do more than enjoy the limo rides, if you want to solve problems and reshape policies—the more likely you are to fail. In ways that hurt so bad you'll never forget them.

Maybe other government memoirists are better at putting their failures behind them. But I can't, maybe because I fear that my failures will end up costing the country as much as the failures that led to 9/11.

The same exponential changes that undercut border defenses are at work elsewhere. Moore's Law, which has predicted decades of exponential growth in computer capabilities, is creating scary new vulnerabilities here at home; soon a host of criminal and military organizations will be able to leave individuals bankrupt and countries without power or a financial system. Similar exponential changes in biotechnology will empower a generation of garage hackers who may or may not end up curing cancer but who will certainly end up making smallpox at home.

Unlike jet travel, these technologies have not yet been misused on the scale of 9/11. And without three thousand dead, business, international, and civil liberties groups have been ferocious in opposing any action that might head off disaster. I struggled to sound the alarm, to prepare the country for computer network and biological attacks, but I failed more often than I succeeded.

That's over now. I've been relieved. The new administration has embraced civil liberties rhetoric with enthusiasm. Some of them seem convinced that they have a mandate to roll back any security measure that reduced privacy or inconvenienced the international community. I don't think that will happen with border security, but the new administration's deference to privacy groups and international opinion will make it far harder to do anything about the new threats.

Maybe, I think, they're right not to pick those fights. Maybe Americans are tired of battle, tired of remembering 9/11, tired of its lessons. Perhaps the fight against the new threats will just have to wait until something bad happens.

The rain is growing heavier. The low clouds are darker. The lights in the pools have begun to glow. I'm ready to leave.

Passing a bench, I see something: a tiny dot of color in the vast, sterile park.

It's a bit of glass, like a clear blue marble left in the kiln too long and melted into an oblong. It's easy to miss. I've already walked past it once. But it wasn't dropped at random.

It sits centered at the end of one bench. In this scrubbed, cerebral monument, it looks almost defiant, an act of personal rebellion against the clean lines and uniformity.

The name on the bench is Ronald Hemenway, electronics technician first class. He died at work in the Pentagon. He was thirty-seven—the right age to have a wife and young children still feeling the pain of his loss eight years later.

I imagine mother and child sitting together on the bench. They glance carefully around and slip the blue stone from a pocket. A child's hand centers it at the end of the bench, just so.

A gift of memory. For a father. For a family.

For all of us.

It is memory that will save the changes DHS has made at the border. We remember what weak defenses cost us.

But the memory of 9/11 may not save us from the new threats. When catastrophic terrorism returns, the terrorists will use weapons that have already been deployed—by governments, by business, by all of us. Like jet travel, the weapons will be technologies we value. If we do nothing, these technologies and the new powers they confer will eventually be used against us in shocking new ways.

I tried my best to manage those new risks as aggressively as we were dealing with border security. But with the new technologies, that was a lot harder; privacy groups, business, and the international community resisted change with fervor. And too often they won, blocking our efforts to head off the greatest risks.

Those are the failures I most regret. The lesson I learned from the wall and 9/11 was simple: The civil liberties advocates of the time did not know where to stop. They only stopped campaigning for the wall after it had killed three thousand Americans (and some didn't stop even then). They couldn't see the line between reasonable protections and measures that crippled our effort to fight terrorism. And they still can't. They and their allies in business and international organizations are natural conservatives, opposed to any change that might help government fight terrorism in new ways.

I'd chosen not to fight these entrenched interests in the 1990s. When I left the National Security Agency, I'd written a long article that endorsed a wall between spies and cops. I've spent years undoing that mistake.

Now I am leaving government again, and writing again—and hoping to keep others from making the same mistake.

Call it a gift of memory.

1 Skating on Stilts

In a way, all truly popular technologies resemble the bicycle. A bicycle is an implausible thing. To see how implausible, take it out in the street and stand it up. Now let go.

It falls over.

Stand it up in the street and put a man on it; it falls over faster, and he's likely to skin his knee. The thing is utterly unstable.

So who would imagine that the way to solve the instability is to put a man on it and roll the bicycle down a long hill?

Nobody. It defies common sense that something so unstable could become more stable when it's moving. Perhaps that's why nobody imagined the bicycle, at least not for a couple of thousand years after it became perfectly possible to build one.

It took a lot to make the bicycle imaginable. In 1815, the Battle of Waterloo brought an end to nearly twenty years of European war. At the same time, the largest volcanic explosion in recorded history occurred, at Mount Tambora in what is now Indonesia.

The next year, summer never came. Snow fell in every month. Crops failed. Without the crops, pack animals died.

Everyone in Europe cast a wary eye on St. Helena, where Napoleon was imprisoned, and wondered how they'd fight a war without pack animals.

The following year, in 1817, a German official named Karl von Drais showed them how. He invented the bicycle. He demonstrated that soldiers could carry heavy weights quickly over long distances by riding and pushing a crude bicycle. His model weighed nearly fifty pounds, was built of wood and had no pedals. But once he showed that it worked, others improved the design until by the turn of the century the bicycle as we know it was everywhere.

The Romans—perhaps even Alexander the Great—could have built a bicycle like Karl von Drais's, something with crude bearings and no pedals.

They didn't, though. Why not? Here's my theory: The whole idea was simply implausible. Who could imagine traveling at high speeds on a vehicle that can't even stand upright by itself?

But moving forward is the key to the bicycle's stability. A bike moving at one mile per hour is a lot more stable than a bike at rest, and at five miles per hour it's more stable still. At even higher speeds, the bike can adjust faster and roll over obstacles that will bring it to a dead stop at lower speeds.

Go faster and feel safer. We all remember discovering this amazing rule as kids. If 5 mph is good, 10 should be better. And it is! We remember how it ends, too. Fifteen mph is better still. And twenty. Everything is better on a bike when you go faster. Until, quite surprisingly, it's not.

That's when you discover that falling off a bike at 30 mph means something a lot worse than a skinned knee.

And suddenly the Romans don't look quite so dumb.

Lots of technology is like the bicycle. It seems implausible at first. As Arthur C. Clarke once said, "Any sufficiently advanced technology is indistinguishable from magic."[1]

Once we relax and learn to trust it, it really does give us new, nearly magical powers. It gets better and better, faster and faster.

Then it starts finding new ways to kill us.

In a way, that's what happened on September 11, 2001.

Technology—cheap commercial jet travel—made the attacks possible. In fact, it made attacks like September 11 more or less inevitable.

It may be hard to remember now, but air travel was once seen as the great technological achievement of the twentieth century. Futurists marveled at how it would change our world.

In 1907, as heavier-than-air flight was just becoming a reality, Alexander Graham Bell declared that it would not be long until "a man can take dinner in New York and breakfast the next morning in Liverpool."[2]

By the 1920s and 1930s, airplanes and air travel were to young men what computers became in the 1970s and 1980s—a way to revolutionize society, make a better world, and find a fortune. After World War II, the youngsters of the twenties and thirties set about building their dreams, and they succeeded.

As late as 1958, European flights were still a special event. That year, *Life* magazine ran a feature story "Off for Paris in Jet Time," describing a Pan American flight from Idlewild (not yet Kennedy) Airport in New York. Actress Greer Garson was in "deluxe" class, along with forty other passengers paying $909 for their round-trip tickets. Another seventy-one economy passengers, attired mostly in suit and tie, or dresses, also made the trip.[3]

Fifty years after Bell envisioned transatlantic travel, it was still remarkable enough to deserve a gushing feature in the preeminent magazine of the era.

That ended in 1959, when Boeing introduced its 707. The new jet cut flying time between New York and London from twelve hours to six. In an instant, international air travel went from luxury to commonplace. By 1965, 95 percent of transatlantic travelers were crossing in the fast jets of Pan Am and European airlines such as British Overseas Air.

In the seventies, Boeing introduced the jumbo jet. By then, jet travel had lost any resemblance to magic and had acquired an unfortunately close resemblance to, well, bus travel. Yet jet tourism kept growing. In 1950, air travelers flew about 28 billion kilometers. By 2000, that number had grown to three trillion.

In those years, international air travel had roughly doubled every five years. That's fifty years of exponential growth.

Any technology that grows so fast is going to have some unexpected effects. As it grew, jet travel brought a slow revolution to the border.

The U.S. border agencies now at the heart of the Department of Homeland Security were confronted with exponentially increasing international travel. As they watched, a rising tide of travelers slowly overwhelmed their 1950-era security measures.

Border checkpoints and searches, travel visas and printed passports—these things had changed little since the nineteenth century. Some were even older; written safe conduct passes for travelers go back to 1414 in England and the oldest, existing passport was issued in 1641 by King Charles I. Even the name "passport" reveals its antiquity. Passports were used to pass through the gate (the *porte*) in a medieval city wall. By the 1980s, though, the walls were down and the gate was open.

Border controls that depended on a serious inspection of individuals, their passports and their luggage, simply could not keep up. Security officials could not spend much time with each traveler. The lines at the border were getting too long.

By the 1980s, governments had begun to vie with each other to dismantle these border security measures. U.S. Customs abandoned individual inspection of travelers, allowing those with nothing to declare simply to stroll through the Green Lane. The United States also adopted the Visa Waiver Program (VWP). That program abolished our single most important restraint on foreign visitors entering the United States—the visa.

Visas are travel permits. Issued by a country's embassy or consulate abroad, they authorize the visa holder to travel to that country. The process of issuing a visa can be quite simple or quite elaborate, but it typically requires at a minimum that the applicant go to the embassy of the country he wants to visit to provide whatever information the consular official requires.

As a control mechanism, the visa is highly flexible. To discourage illegal economic migration, nations may grant very few visas in poor countries—and those only to the well-to-do. They may also deny visas to potential troublemakers, criminals, or terrorists. They may insist that the local government vouch for the visa applicant. They may require that applicants fill out detailed forms, or provide fingerprints, to help in the clearance process.

These control mechanisms worked pretty well in the first half of the 20th century. But a flood of commercial jet travelers turned visas into costly barriers to casual travel—barriers that soon began to fall.

In 1988, the United States stopped requiring visas for nationals of Japan and the United Kingdom, and these governments did the same for Americans. The United States was certainly not alone. If anything, other countries moved further and faster. In 1985, for example, most members of the European Union began simply abolishing controls at their borders with other member states. In countries like Belgium, border inspectors were deployed only at international airports. Everywhere else, travelers were free to enter and leave the country without a glance from officialdom.

By the end of the 1980s, even the world's most notorious border barrier had fallen. The fortified iron curtain cutting Eastern Europe off from the West was broken—by governments and by crowds of citizens from East and West.

Soon, the retreat from border control measures became a rout. Thirteen years after admitting two countries to the VWP, we had opened our doors to two dozen. By 2001, half of all the foreign visitors to the United States—a million a month or more—were coming without visas. No American official laid eyes on these travelers, or even knew they were coming, right up to the moment they reached the immigration booth at LAX or JFK.

Even when visas were required, they were streamlined to eliminate the hassles, as well as the safeguards. In Saudi Arabia, for example, the U.S. State Department launched the Visa Express program in June 2001. The program allowed applicants to obtain a visa by submitting a two-page application to their Saudi travel agency instead of going to a U.S. consulate to provide visa information.

Commercial jet technology had triumphed. It had made mass international travel possible, empowering millions. And almost without noticing it, these millions of empowered travelers were eroding a system of border security that had existed for decades.

Border officials noticed, of course, but they could not resist the onslaught. If they insisted on the old controls, tourism and foreign investment would lag behind the rest of the world. As they saw it, they had only one choice: surrender the old control system or watch their country stagnate.

So they surrendered.

We all know what happened next.

Four years after the 9/11 attacks, I joined the Department of Homeland Security. Secretary Michael Chertoff asked me to create and run a policy office that would let DHS lift its head above the scrum of daily crises and think about its biggest challenges.

DHS was still a startup, barely two years old, and it had spent those two years getting organized, finding desks and office space—and at the same time frantically trying to build defenses against an unseen enemy. No one had had much time to think about the future. That was one of the reasons we needed a policy office, or so I thought.

I wanted to think about 9/11 in a new way. It seemed to me that it was an event driven as much by technological change as by evil men and government errors. Sure, there were evil men, and there were errors. But we had to get beyond the immediate mistakes and focus on the long-term trends that had made the attacks possible in the first place.

When we started tracing the roots of the 9/11 attacks, we realized how jet travel and a growing flood of travelers had wrecked our traditional border defenses. That's when we began to ask what other technologies might have in store for us.

Technologies like jet travel are seductive. That's why we flock to them. They give us more choices and more reach. Commercial jets allowed us to work or play on any continent in a matter of hours. More recently, computers and the Internet gave us instant access to knowledge that once was available only to a handful of librarians. Biotechnology, a new, explosively exponential technology, gives us the power to create and design life itself.

Giving individuals the opportunity to use these tools, with the choices, reach, and power they confer, is a great thing—much of the time. It's like skating on stilts that get a little longer each year. Every year we get faster and more powerful. Every year we're a little more at risk. We are skating for a fall, and the fall grows worse every year we put it off.

Technologies that empower ordinary individuals also empower people like Osama bin Laden and Unabomber Ted Kaczynski. Commercial jet technology had been around for nearly half a century before nineteen men were able to use it to kill three thousand. But the possibility of something like 9/11 was inherent in the technology from the start.

The 9/11 Commission (formally known as The National Commission on Terrorist Attacks upon the United States) criticized officials for a failure of imagination in the run-up to the attacks. Even those who knew al Qaeda was planning an attack did not imagine domestic jet hijackings that ended in suicide attacks on national symbols. I resolved when I joined DHS to keep that failure in mind. Where else was our imagination failing us?

Once I began to look for other emerging threats, I realized that jet travel is not the only technology that puts Americans at risk. Computer technology and bioengineering are more recent. Their power to change our lives is still growing, and their future is harder to predict. But if we wanted to get ahead of tomorrow's terrorism, DHS had to begin thinking about future risks as well.

Based on my own experiences, I knew of two that were bearing down on us fast.

For decades, information technology has been driven by Moore's Law. One version of the law holds that the number of transistors that can be cheaply placed on a chip doubles every eighteen to twenty-four months.

As chip capacity grows, the cost of computer power falls. A computer that cost $1 million in 1970 could be duplicated for $500,000 in 1972 and for $10,000 in 1984. By the end of the 1980s, personal computers were giving individuals capabilities that were once available only to government and the Fortune 500; electronic spreadsheets, word processors, contacts files, and email began expanding the capabilities of all.

Surely one of the oddest results of going to work for NSA was my initiation into the vanguard of this trend. The agency controlled encryption, and especially exports of encryption technology to other countries. But as cheap home computers made the Internet a potential source of mass electronic commerce, Microsoft and other software companies wanted to build encryption into their products. They rightly saw a need for more security if computer networks were going to carry large transactions.

"We're going to put encryption in your toaster," one Microsoft representative told me, invoking a day when every kitchen appliance would have its own Internet address.

To defend NSA's encryption policy, I had to understand this Internet thing and the changes it would bring. While I never fully accepted the techies' encryption policy proposals, I came to believe that they were right about the Internet. A revolution was coming. After leaving government I built a law practice around that insight. I represented dozens of Silicon Valley firms, including Netscape in the days before its IPO helped to launch the Internet revolution.

So I had a ringside seat as Moore's Law worked its magic. By the late 1990s, computing power that had cost $1 million in 1970 could be had for a hundred dollars.

Cheap computing and telecommunications (not to mention a gradually softening policy on encryption exports) did indeed create a mass market Internet. We were able to search the accumulated wisdom and folly of humanity in seconds. We could download books, music, and movies—what we wanted when we wanted it. We could bank, play games, trade securities, salute friends, trash enemies, gossip, build businesses, lose and find lovers—all online.

Oh, and a few more things: we could be defrauded, robbed, extorted, and blackmailed—with stolen secrets—online, too. The industry push to incorporate strong encryption into their products turned out to be a red herring. Government did get out of the way, but even the strongest encryption didn't provide the security the techies thought it would. Crooks easily found ways around it.

But, as with commercial jet travel, the bad news about information technology arrived late—long after the technology had become indispensable. We were up on our stilts and skating hell for leather before we even noticed there might be a problem. It wasn't until the 1970s that some of the first hackers discovered they could obtain free phone service by fooling AT&T's computers, and it took until 1988 for the first computerized "worm" to clog the Internet. Computer viruses also emerged in the 1980s, passed from disk to disk. They were an annoyance, but little more. Most were written simply to show off the skills of the author.

But as we moved our lives online, criminals followed. Hackers discovered that there was money in compromising other people's computers. Spammers could use those machines to send messages without fear of being shut down. Online networks allowed foreign criminals to reach across borders without leaving home as Nigerian spammers learned to defraud gullible men and women in the United States and Europe.

Networks of compromised machines were marshaled into vast zombie armies that could attack a single website together, knocking it off line. For some sites, being off line even for an hour was so costly that they'd pay extortionate fees to stop the attack.

Exploiting computer security holes wasn't the cyberspace equivalent of spray-painting graffiti on subway cars anymore. It was a new form of organized crime. It paid well enough to attract real talent. And that talent found new ways to make computer hacking pay.

Compromising the computers of credit card processors and merchants allowed identity theft and credit card fraud on a massive scale. Sending booby-trapped emails to known individuals, in contrast, might only compromise a single machine, but it would allow the criminal to steal every name and password used on the machine—and to empty the bank account of the victim.

As the criminals demonstrated what could be done online, governments followed their example. Governments didn't steal money, though. They stole secrets. Protected from prosecution and motivated by patriotism, government hackers turned out to be even more effective than the crooks. Countries that depended on computer networks began to wonder whether they had any secrets left.

Bad as it was to lose secrets, that wasn't the worst threat from government hacking. Once a system has been compromised, the attacker can choose its fate; he can keep the system alive and milk it for its secrets; or he can kill it—shut it down for as long as he likes. This was great for government attackers; they could exploit their adversary's systems for intelligence purposes for years, and then, in a crisis, they could shut the systems down.

The tools to infiltrate information systems grow more sophisticated every year. The United States is the most at risk. It is probably among the top five intelligence targets of every government on earth. Why? Because our unique global military reach means that no government on earth can safely ignore the likely U.S. reaction to its actions. Put another way, every tin-pot president-for-life who wants to attack a neighbor has to worry first about whether he can beat his neighbor and second about whether the United States will choose to stop him. So every government wants to know how we will react to what it does, and ideally it wants a weapon that can persuade us not to get in its way.

For many governments, hacking U.S. information systems serves both purposes. Hostile nations can gather intelligence about our view of them while they plan attacks on a neighbor. And once the attack is launched, if the United States interferes, the code that was used to spy on us can be deployed to shut our systems down. Electricity, aviation, communications, and banking can be disrupted, perhaps even sabotaged irreversibly. Without a shot being fired, without even a clear sense of who the attacker is, much of the United States could find itself living in post-Katrina New Orleans, but without hope of a rescue anytime soon.

How effectively this weapon could be deployed today is in dispute. But there is little dispute that the attackers have been gaining on the defenders by leaps and bounds. Two nations, Estonia and Georgia, have already suffered serious, coordinated cyberattacks originating in Russia during disputes with that country. The attacks were effective, but not crippling. So perhaps foreign nations cannot use information technology to kill or harm Americans on a large scale today. But it seems likely that they will have that capability soon. Just as it took decades for terrorists to figure out how to cause catastrophic failures in the air transport system, so it may take decades for attackers to find and exploit the most damaging holes in our information networks. So far, there is no sign that the spies and the crooks who are trying to do that are running out of ideas or money.

And what are we doing as this threat gathers?

More or less what border officials were doing in the 1980s. We are embracing information networks with the same enthusiasm we have displayed since the 1970s, and doing very little to close the security holes this technology opens.

We are up on the bike and flying downhill. Only now, as the scenery begins to blur, are we starting to understand that maybe this technology, too, will find a way to kill us.

If jet travel and computers were the ghosts of technologies past and present, biotechnology is a specter that haunts the future. It became my personal nightmare while working for the Robb-Silberman Commission. The United States agreed to give up biological weapons in the 1970s, and stopped all work on them at that time. The Russians signed the same treaty but, if anything, they expanded their biological weapons programs, continuing to make ever more loathsome and unstoppable diseases. Little wonder then that their client states and allies, like Iraq, also had biological programs.

Most troubling from an intelligence point of view, our spies had little or no insight into these programs in Russia or in Iraq, at least not until defectors revealed them. It was just too easy to hide them, in medical or insecticide factories, say, or in anonymous laboratories on the outskirts of obscure cities.

The death and demoralization that biological weapons cause can be equivalent to a nuclear detonation. That makes it crucial that we do a better job of tracking foreign governments' illicit biological programs, as the Robb-Silberman Commission recommended.

But that wasn't the scariest part of what I learned while serving the commission. What scared me most was how rapidly the ability to make biological weapons is being democratized. Biotechnology is growing as fast as jet travel and computers. The cost and difficulty of biological engineering is being reduced at an exponential rate.

This means that scientists' ability to build dangerous organisms is also increasing exponentially. In 2005, that progress allowed scientists to rebuild the deadly 1918 flu virus from scratch. Worse diseases can be revived in the same way. Although smallpox has been eradicated in the wild, it has become more dangerous to humankind than ever now that vaccinations have stopped. It has not been synthesized, at least not that we know of. But the failure to recreate smallpox is now a matter of choice, not capability. Larger and more complex organisms than smallpox have already been created, and the cost and difficulty of assembling such DNA sequences keeps dropping.

In fact, the current state of the art has moved from viruses to bacteria. In 2008, scientists assembled the entire DNA sequence for a small bacterium that causes urinary tract infections. It was substantially larger than the sequence for smallpox.

Of course, you have to be really sophisticated to assemble a sequence that large. Only a handful of labs can accomplish that feat today. But Moore's law will do soon for DNA synthesis what it did for mainframes. DNA experiments that were once the province only of big institutions with sophisticated staffs will in a few years be the playground of smart high school kids.

Indeed, that's the dream of a lot of influential and wealthy industry leaders. The people who grew rich from the information revolution would like the biotech revolution to be a straight replay—complete with DNA hackers operating out of their parents' garage, DNA synthesis IPOs, and "open source" DNA coding languages. Those who advocate a "wet" replay of the information revolution are not concerned that biotech and synthetic DNA haven't really delivered big improvements in human health yet. Massively democratizing computer power was good for all of us, they say, pointing to the results of the personal computer and the Internet. Why shouldn't the mass democratization of DNA synthesis also produce an outpouring of creativity, playfulness, and unexpected progress? Besides, they conclude, it's going to happen whether we like it or not, so we might as well get on the bandwagon.

But you don't have to be Cassandra, or Ned Ludd, to see that a world where millions of people can make smallpox from scratch might turn out to be a dangerous place.

That's not just a future that might kill you by mistake; that's a future that could kill you in a fit of adolescent pique.

As the risks of future misuse emerged, a failure of imagination started to look pretty good compared to actually, you know, *having* an imagination. At least a lack of imagination lets you sleep at night. Because the question for DHS was what were we going to do about these risks now that we saw them.

I knew one thing. We couldn't call time-out. We couldn't turn our backs on the technologies and walk away from the harm they can do.

Tokugawa-era Japan is famous for giving up firearms in the early 1600s, a hundred years after guns had been introduced by the West and widely adopted throughout Japan. For the next 250 years, it is said, Japan was ruled, and wars were fought, by the sword, even though guns were acknowledged to be more effective weapons.

But Tokugawa Japan is famous because its story is so uncommon (indeed, some say it isn't true). Certainly no other nation is known to have denied itself an important technology for so long and survived. That's especially true for technologies like synthetic DNA. Manmade diseases wouldn't stop at our borders just because we decided to discourage biotechnology. We could let other countries take the handlebars, of course, but we'd all take the same fall in the end.

If we couldn't give up the latest technologies, we knew, we would have to find ways to manage their risks. We'd have to begin now to think about how to guide the rising curve of exponential change, how to steer it away from the most deadly consequences. Could we do that? We weren't sure. But we started with travel—the technology whose exponential adoption had already caused so much death on September 11, 2001.

The problem of jet travel, at its heart, is that everything happens so fast—life-and-death decisions are a matter of seconds.

And not just while the plane is in the air. When international flights arrive at our airports, DHS can spend no more than thirty seconds with each traveler. In those thirty seconds, we have to decide who should be waved through and who should get more detailed attention. Indeed, thirty seconds is probably longer than we can afford to spend; anyone who has experienced the lines at JFK or Dulles when many international flights arrive at the same time knows that they are dehumanizing and exhausting—not exactly a welcoming ceremony.

Our solution was to use information about the traveler more effectively. First, we had to find out, in advance, who was coming here. We sought information from the airlines about the passengers they were carrying; and in the end we asked all international travelers, even those for whom visas weren't required, to provide information about themselves before they traveled.

We also needed more information about risky travelers if the system was going to work. We had to knock heads in the bureaucracy to ensure that each agency was contributing to a single list of known or suspected terrorists. More importantly, we needed better data to help decide who was risky. And not just from other U.S. government agencies. We needed information from other countries; if you want to know who the terrorism suspects are in Hungary, chances are that the Hungarian authorities have better sources than the Federal Bureau of Investigation or the Central Intelligence Agency.

We also needed information that would help us spot new recruits who hadn't yet come to the attention of the authorities. Aussie ranchers call their unbranded calves "clean skins." Their intelligence agencies have borrowed the term to describe terrorists who don't yet have a record. They are every terrorist group's dream and every government's nightmare. But no terror recruit is perfectly clean—with the right information, subtle clues often reveal connections that identify risky travelers, even if we've never seen them before.

That was the heart of the solution. If we got data in advance, we could identify the tiny fraction of suspicious travelers who should be pulled aside for additional screening. The thirty-second interview in the booth was no longer our only chance to find bad guys. Instead, it would become a backstop—a chance to double-check work that had been done in advance.

In theory, that should have been enough. If you know whom you're worried about and who's coming, you can do the sorting on that basis. But terrorists aren't always so obliging, or so stupid. If the government screens travelers based on who they are, then the terrorists will try to defeat the system by changing identities.

So we had to lock travelers to a single identity, and we did, raising security standards for passports around the world and recording travelers' fingerprints so that terrorists couldn't use different passports to enter the United States. Even if they managed to fool another country into issuing a passport in a false name, they wouldn't be able to fool us.

At this point, some readers must be wondering what the fuss is about. Surely this approach to border security is obvious. There's nothing especially groundbreaking or high-tech about a passenger-screening program that uses data to improve decision making.

Well, yes and no.

Yes, it's easy to *imagine* such a border control system. It was easy to imagine such a system in the 1980s, too. But governments didn't implement it. They did the opposite. They surrendered to the tide of travelers.

Why, we wondered, did they make a choice that seems so foolish now? We soon found out that we would have to fight for our new border strategy. And it wasn't at all clear that we would win—even though the new approach moved most travelers as fast as before, and even though the old approach had produced a disastrous failure and left three thousand dead.

It didn't matter. We were in for a bruising political and diplomatic battle with powerful groups that weren't used to losing. To them, our new approach was a threat greater than terrorism. They had defended the border status quo against past efforts to improve security, and they didn't think the unfortunate events of 9/11 were a reason to change course.

The first and most obvious opponents of change were the businesses whose profits depended on the status quo. Our new strategy was going to shake things up. For example, in the old days, to encourage travel, the United States had told a number of countries in the Western Hemisphere that they could come to the United States without a passport. That put a big hole in our security strategy, but when we filled it by requiring that all international air travelers have passports, industry howled.

Tourism, travel, and airline executives wanted to keep riding the exponential growth in jet travel. They didn't want innovations in government security on the border. The industry couldn't be sure that the measure would improve security, but if the measure made travel less attractive, they knew they'd be hurt. So the safe course for industry was to always advocate less control, not more. And that's what they did. We had to jam the requirement through over their resistance.

The second opponent of change was the privacy lobby. In the United States, left-leaning groups like the American Civil Liberties Union (ACLU), the Electronic Frontier Foundation, and the Electronic Privacy Information Center (EPIC), joined with right-leaning libertarian groups like the Eagle Forum and Americans for Tax Reform. In Europe, the privacy advocates were government agencies—privacy bureaucracies. They could usually count on support from journalists who shared their views. Throughout our tenure at DHS we faced claims from all of these groups that using data to screen travelers was somehow an abuse of personal information. Privacy watchdogs in the United States and Europe didn't like it when government got access to any information for any purpose. If the data was collected at all, they agreed, its use must be restrained in the most stringent manner. They wanted suffocating controls on what we gathered and how we used it.

I started to believe that some of the privacy groups just objected in principle to any use of technology that might help catch criminals or terrorists. The example I remember best was when the police at Logan Airport got handheld computers. The computers were connected to public databases so they could check addresses and other information when they stopped someone. It was pretty much what any businessman could do already with a Blackberry or iPhone.

The American Civil Liberties Union went nuts. The executive director of the Massachusetts chapter called the handhelds "mass scrutiny of the lives and activities of innocent people," and "a violation of the core democratic principle that the government should not be permitted to violate a person's privacy, unless it has a reason to believe that he or she is involved in wrongdoing."[4] Another ACLU spokesman piled on. "If the police went around keeping files on who you lived with and who your roommates were, I think people would be outraged," he told *USA Today*. "And yet in this case, they're not doing it, but they're plugging into a company that is able to do it easily."[5]

Remember, the handheld computers only tied to public databases that any citizen could search. "It's nothing we don't have access to already," Lieutenant Thomas Coffey told the *Boston Globe*. "Instead of me having to go down to the registry of deeds in a particular county, I can now access this information via a BlackBerry," he added.[6]

If the ACLU considered that a civil liberties disaster, I remarked, we'd better not tell them that we also have access to the White Pages.

Still, "no" was the privacy community's default answer to any improvement in law enforcement technology. The rest of us can use Blackberries, Google, and Facebook all we want to gather information about our friends, our business associates, and even our blind dates. But the ACLU seemed to think that law enforcement should live in 1950 forever.

So it's no surprise that privacy groups challenged our passenger screening time and again, in the press and on Capitol Hill. Each time, they found sympathetic ears in the establishment media. They forced us to justify our plan over and over again. Without the strong, consistent support of Secretary Michael Chertoff, a superb policy advocate in his own right, and his willingness to take on the *New York Times* and the ACLU, our strategy would have been chipped away bit by bit.

Business and privacy groups are conservative by choice in this debate. The third player—the international community—is conservative by nature. Other countries just don't like it when the United States changes policies. And our new border strategy was a change. The Canadian ambassador to the United States was vocal in questioning our plan to require passports for all travelers, questioning whether we were really ready to carry out our plan, and predicting disaster if we did. He pressed us many times to postpone the requirement, and the Canadian government would have been delighted to see it delayed forever.

It makes a kind of sense that other nations would line up against change. After all, the travel and tourism businesses are often multinationals, as are some of the privacy groups. If new U.S. border measures make Americans safer but put a burden on Lufthansa, European officials may feel it's their job to represent the interests of Lufthansa.

Sometimes it's hard to separate that motive from a less attractive one. Unfortunately, anti-Americanism is now an institutionalized part of the politics of most Western nations. Practically all developed democracies, particularly in Europe, have a party that is anti-American and a party that is not.

There are a lot of reasons for this. They may blame us for changes in the world that aren't exactly our responsibility. (We blame Hollywood for the skewed values taught by the movies; Europeans blame us. We blame globalization for the excesses of the market; Europeans blame us.) Europeans may also have felt slighted or ignored as the United States put its post-9/11 policies together. Certainly President Bush's moral certainty after 9/11 did not wear well abroad; he was cast as a trigger-happy cowboy in a tale of American unilateralism and disregard for world opinion.

Even with a new president, and a Nobel Peace Prize-winner at that, I don't expect much change in this institutionalized anti-Americanism. Saying "no"—or "yes, but"—to the United States is the diplomatic default position of virtually every foreign ministry across the globe.

And that is indeed what the diplomats of the European Union said when DHS began to implement a data-based screening system. Borrowing arguments from both their travel industry and their privacy advocates, European officials set out to thwart DHS's new policy and to roll back the clock, to take us back as close as they could get to the old, failed status quo.

As we'll see, they very nearly won.

Even if al Qaeda disappears tomorrow, the temptation to terrorism will not go away. And tools that can give new power to terrorists are being improved every day. Terrorist attacks using these technologies are completely foreseeable.

But I also know now just how hard it is to head off foreseeable disasters. Anything government does to steer the course of an exponential technology, any suggestion that we apply the brakes or put on a helmet will face diplomatic, privacy, and business resistance.

These constituencies will fight for the status quo. It's a strange kind of status quo that they want—constant, exponential acceleration. But acceleration can feel very stable.

For a while.

I'm proud of what DHS was able to do about terrorism at the border. It was a revolution. It took years of hard fighting to put in place security solutions that worked with new technologies instead of against them. Truth be told, it took three thousand deaths, too. Without those deaths, not much would have changed at the border, even today.

I'd like to think that we can apply that lesson to other technologies. Maybe this time we can change course a few degrees before we suffer a catastrophe. I'd like to think we can build prudent, imaginative security measures into information networks and biotechnology, just as we did with our border procedures. I'd like to think that we can do that before there's been a disaster.

But, really, I'm not sure we can.

That's what the rest of this book is about.

2 Atta's Soldier

If you want to understand how difficult it can be to change security policy in the face of privacy, international, and business opposition, the best place to start is in the months before September 11, 2001.

The entire government knew an attack was coming—somewhere. And yet so entrenched were civil liberties and international interests that it took an act of individual courage to keep even one hijacker out of the United States in the months before the attack.

Worse, that kind of courage was missing when the time came to look for known terrorists within the United States.

For years pockets of the FBI had waged a stubborn insurgency against the civil liberties strictures created by the court that administered the Foreign Intelligence Surveillance Act, or FISA. Unlike most agencies, the FBI had both intelligence and criminal authorities, and its agents often shared information with each other without much regard for the court's effort to build a wall between the intelligence and law enforcement. But in August 2001, just as sharing was needed most, the FBI's resistance was finally stamped out, and the last chance to stop the attacks was lost.

It's a long flight from London to Orlando, and in August it only takes a touch of Florida's afternoon heat and humidity to leave jet-lagged passengers slumped and rumpled in the line for immigration control. But in early August 2001, there was nothing slumped about Mohamed al Kahtani. He was a small man, but he stood in the line like a soldier.

That's what he was. He had come to Florida on a martyrdom mission for al Qaeda. At that moment, Mohammed Atta was waiting upstairs, on the other side of border control, talking to al Qaeda's man in Dubai on a pay phone, demanding to know where the new arrival was.

But Atta's soldier had a problem. When he strode to the immigration booth for what should have been a thirty-second interview, Kahtani told the officer he spoke no English. He left his customs and arrival form blank. Little things, but they made the officer suspicious. In four years at Orlando airport, this was the first Saudi she'd encountered who did not speak at least a bit of English.

She sent him to secondary inspection, where an experienced border official would be able to ask a few more questions.

That's when Kahtani met Jose Melendez-Perez.

Melendez-Perez is a quiet man with glasses and a mustache. He'd been in the military himself—twenty-six years as an enlisted man in the Army before starting a second career as a border inspector.

Melendez-Perez called Kahtani into the interview room. The man was "well groomed with short hair, thin mustache, black long-sleeved shirt, black trousers and black shoes," Melendez-Perez remembers.[1] Kahtani stood about five-feet-six and was in "impeccable shape . . . He had a military appearance," Melendez-Perez told the 9/11 Commission.[2] As soon as they made eye contact, though, Kahtani began behaving oddly. He gave the inspector a long stare with more than a hint of arrogance in it. Kahtani wasn't happy. He'd been cooling his heels in secondary inspection, and he was already impatient. As he sat down for the interview in a windowless room, the temperature in the room seemed to drop. Kahtani was giving off an air of menace.

Melendez-Perez launched into the interrogation, waiting for the translator on the speaker-phone to repeat the questions in Arabic. (In this book, conversations that are paraphrased or reconstructed from paraphrases are marked with dashes rather than quotation marks.)[3]

—Why don't you have a return ticket? Melendez-Perez asked.

Kahtani showed anger. He resented the question. And the finger he waved in Melendez-Perez's face didn't require translation.

—Where are you going when you leave the United States? Melendez-Perez asked, unfazed.

—I don't know; a friend is coming to the U.S. to travel with me. He is making the travel arrangements.

—And when will the friend arrive? Melendez-Perez asked.

—In three or four days, said the Saudi.

—And what is the purpose and length of your visit?

—I'll be here for six days. I'll travel around the United States with my friend, said Kahtani.

Melendez-Perez thought the whole thing was fishy. Why wait around for his friend for three or four days if the whole stay is just six days?

"It was clear that he was upset," Melendez-Perez recalled to me later. "He didn't have answers to my questions, so he started to get aggressive."[4]

The Saudi's anger and sense of entitlement were unusual.

"This was the first time anyone had done that in a secondary interview," Melendez-Perez told me. "Usually, you know, people try to stay calm and persuade you they're good people who should be admitted."[5]

Melendez-Perez kept pressing.

—And where will you stay?

—At a hotel.

—Won't it be hard to stay at a hotel if you don't have a reservation and don't speak the language? Melendez-Perez asked.

—I've got a friend upstairs waiting for me, Kahtani told him.

—And what is your friend's name? Melendez-Perez asked.

—Actually, I'm going to call my friend once I've found a place to stay.

Kahtani's story was changing.

—So, what's your friend's phone number, then? Melendez-Perez pressed.

—That's none of your business, said Kahtani. It's personal; there's no reason for you to contact him.

—How are you going to pay for your hotel and your travel and your flight home? Melendez-Perez asked him.

Kahtani had $2,800 in cash and no credit cards. A return ticket would use up most of that.

—My friend is going to bring me some money, Kahtani said.

—Why would he bring you money?

—Because he is a friend, said Kahtani.

—How long have you known this person?

—Not too long, said Kahtani.

By now, Melendez-Perez had spent more than an hour with Kahtani, growing less and less comfortable with the hostile and evasive Saudi. It felt to Melendez-Perez almost as though Kahtani had received counterinterrogation training.

Kahtani must have known that his answers weren't satisfactory, but he didn't seem to care. In the end, he expected to be admitted no matter what he said. After all, his papers were in order. A search of his luggage had turned up empty. Melendez-Perez had nothing concrete, just a bunch of answers that he didn't like.

That would have been enough to turn most travelers away. But Kahtani was a Saudi. And as far as Melendez-Perez knew, no Saudi had ever been turned away by a border inspector.

The Saudis who came to the United States "knew they were going to get taken care of," Melendez-Perez told me.[6]

"When I started work in Miami, I got instructions about arriving flights with Saudi passengers. We were told 'Don't do anything to offend Saudi passengers.' When a flight with a lot of Saudis would arrive in Miami, the line supervisors would get nervous. They would tell the officers, 'Make sure you treat these people well and follow protocols for them.'"[7]

In Orlando it was the same.

"Even the supervisors were nervous about how Saudi passengers are greeted," Melendez-Perez said.[8] The special treatment could be seen as simple cultural sensitivity. For example, if a female passenger accompanies a male, and the man doesn't want her to show her face to the male officer, the female would be sent to secondary to be seen by a female officer.

But the supervisor's nervousness sent an informal message, too: "No one was into refusing Saudis," says Melendez-Perez.[9]

If he had any doubt about that, it didn't last long. Melendez-Perez stepped out of the interview room to check Kahtani's computer records. And to warm up. Just being in the room with the Saudi was chilling his blood. He'd been in there a while. The whole office must have realized what was happening.

As he stood by the computer, one of his coworkers walked by, a stack of immigration forms in hand.

"Hey, you're trying to refuse a Saudi? Are you crazy? You'll get in trouble for that," his colleague said without breaking stride.[10]

"He gave me the wrong answers. I can refuse anyone for that," Melendez-Perez retorted.[11]

But he knew that wasn't true.

"I didn't really have the authority to refuse Kahtani. But I could recommend refusal. The question was, 'Would that fly?'"[12]

The problem wasn't the inspector's instincts. "I had a good record. Sometimes officers recommended refusal and it didn't stand up, but I had built up credibility."[13]

The problem was the nationality of the man he was trying to send home. The United States wanted Saudis to feel welcome when they came to the country. They were good for business; and anything that made them uncomfortable would provoke criticism from the tourism industry. And they had clout. Saudi Arabia had paid much of the cost of the first Gulf War. Its diplomats were wired in Washington, and unhappy Saudi tourists were quick to call the embassy. In fact, Washington had already made the front-line border supervisors nervous about anything that hinted at cultural insensitivity or discrimination.

Melendez-Perez was determined, though. This guy was bad. He took the problem to his supervisor, who had the authority to approve his recommendation. Listening to Melendez-Perez, the supervisor must have wondered how he'd justify the refusal if the Saudis—or the U.S. ambassador to Saudi Arabia—decided to complain.

He'd say, "Well sir, my inspector's intuition told him the guy was up to no good. He didn't like the way Mr. Kahtani stared at him and Kahtani's answers to his questions seemed arrogant and strange." Could the diplomats make that sound like ethnic prejudice, or cultural insensitivity, or just an arbitrary bureaucratic power trip? Sure they could. He had no grounds for excluding Kahtani that would stand up to second-guessing.

The supervisor was willing to back his inspector, but only if he could find someone to back *him*.

—Let's take this higher, the supervisor said.

He put in a call to the assistant director of the port. Melendez-Perez listened nervously as his supervisor laid out the case to the assistant director. Then the supervisor fell silent. He handed the phone to Melendez-Perez.

The assistant director wanted to talk to Melendez-Perez directly. He had a lot of questions. He wanted to know why Melendez-Perez was pushing the issue so hard.

—When he looks at me, said Melendez-Perez, I feel a bone-chilling cold. The bottom line is, he gives me the creeps.

Now it was the assistant director's turn to squirm. The call was his. And so was the blame if the decision blew up into a diplomatic mess. He needed something more, a clear bureaucratic line of defense, not all this talk about Kahtani's "chilling" demeanor and unconvincing answers.

But the assistant port director had an idea. He quoted the Immigration and Nationality Act: "An applicant for admission may be required to state under oath any information sought by an immigration officer regarding the purposes and intentions of the applicant in seeking admission to the United States."[14]

"Put him under oath and ask the questions again," the assistant director ordered. "If he won't answer, he's in violation of the law. Then you can refuse him."[15]

The stakes were high as Melendez-Perez walked back to the windowless room where Kahtani was waiting. If Kahtani refused to answer, he would be on the next plane home. But if he just repeated what he'd said before, Melendez-Perez's boss—and his boss's boss—would be in a tough spot.

Melendez-Perez administered the oath. And he began asking the same questions Kahtani had already answered. Kahtani could see what was happening. They were covering the same ground all over again. The officer wasn't even trying to disguise the repetition. Kahtani had had enough. He balked. He was sick of the whole thing.

Melendez-Perez breathed a sigh of relief. That was it. They wouldn't have to rely on his intuition if they were called on the carpet. Kahtani had blundered into a flat violation of the law. Now he could be sent home.

Ninety minutes later Melendez-Perez and another inspector were on the jetway of a Virgin Atlantic flight to Heathrow with Kahtani between them. The plane was empty. Kahtani would be boarding before anyone else.

Before boarding, though, Kahtani had one more thing to say. He was standing erect, almost cocky, in the door when he turned to the inspectors.

"I'll be back," he said.[16]

For the first time all day, he spoke in English.

He was right. He would be back. But not in time to meet Mohammed Atta, who left the airport that day without his soldier.

And not in time to meet the other hijackers, either. Five weeks after Kahtani was sent home, Flight 93 took off with four hijackers on board. Every other hijacked flight that day had a team of five. As it turned out, the missing man made all the difference. Organizing quickly, the passengers attacked the shorthanded crew of hijackers. Unable to keep the passengers out of the cockpit, the hijackers were forced to crash the plane in an empty field near Shanksville, Pennsylvania. It never got near its likely target, the Capitol in Washington, D.C.

When Kahtani did return, it would be in shackles. He was captured in Afghanistan as an enemy combatant in 2002.

There's a good chance that the Capitol was spared thanks in part to the determination and imagination that Jose Melendez-Perez and his superiors showed. Melendez-Perez turns aside praise for what he did.

"That's why I was getting paid," he says.[17] But, in fact, he managed to do his job in part because he and his bosses found a way to protect themselves from bureaucratic second-guessing.

A few months earlier, though, in New York and Washington, it was second-guessing that triumphed. As a result we lost our best chance to save the World Trade Center and the Pentagon.

3 | To the Wall

March 9, 2001, was cold and gusty in Washington. No one without a clearance even knew that Royce Lamberth, the chief judge of the Foreign Intelligence Surveillance Court, had sent a letter that day to John Ashcroft, the recently confirmed Attorney General of the United States.[1]

But almost immediately, the letter set off the worst turmoil ever experienced in the clubby world of foreign intelligence wiretaps. For the first and only time in its history, the FISA court was disciplining an FBI agent, singling him out by name and barring him from any appearance before the court. Even papers that he signed would be rejected. Why? Because the court no longer trusted his assurances that the FBI was observing the elaborate set of rules that the court had erected to protect the civil liberties of terrorist suspects.

This could not be tolerated. The court was determined to bring the FBI to heel; this ruling would show just how seriously the court took its civil liberties procedures.

Widely described inside the FBI as a contempt order, the ruling looked like a career killer. Indeed, the court's letter seemed to accuse the agent of making false statements to the court, a felony under federal law. That's how the attorney general saw it. The Justice Department's Office of Professional Responsibility was called in to consider what other sanctions might be proper.

This was the beginning of a years-long nightmare for the agent. But in the secret cloisters of intelligence law, it would not be his nightmare alone; it would spread and spread, like ripples on a still lake.

It sent a chill of fear first through the FBI counterterrorism machinery in Washington, then deep into the warrens of the National Security Agency at Fort Meade.

In August, though, the chill had not yet engulfed the FBI counterterrorism squad in New York. They were champing at the bit, having just learned that an al Qaeda terrorist had recently entered the United States. They didn't know for sure that he was planning an attack, but they'd been hearing all summer that a big one was coming. If a major-league terrorist was in the United States it might be real trouble. They geared up to go looking for him.

That's when the nightmare reached them, too. They shouldn't have the information, they were told, and were forbidden to act on it. They could end up like the other agent, censured for breaching the civil liberties protections erected by the court. They were stopped in their tracks.

A few days later the nightmare became America's.

Spies and Cops

The letter Judge Lamberth sent John Ashcroft on March 9 was a long time in the making. In fact, it marked the climax of a decade-long undercover battle over civil liberties and intelligence wiretaps. The basic story can be teased out of official documents, particularly a staff report of the 9/11 Commission that was not declassified until 2009 and a Justice Department Inspector General report from 2004, and many of the participants are now willing to talk about those events.

The March 9 letter had its roots in the difference between law enforcement and intelligence wiretaps. Law enforcement wiretaps are heavily regulated. They can only be initiated if other investigative techniques have failed; they can only be carried out for a limited time. They require constant supervision and review. They are approved only for specific kinds of crime. Wiretaps that don't keep producing new criminal evidence must be halted. And once a criminal case begins, the defendant can see transcripts of the wiretaps and challenge their legality. If the law enforcement agencies have gone beyond the law, the courts will exclude the evidence, and the defendant will likely escape justice. Everyone in criminal justice understands that and conducts himself accordingly.

Intelligence wiretaps are different. They don't have to pay off right away, and they can be renewed repeatedly. Sometimes they're left in place for years before they reveal something useful. And they aren't triggered by suspected criminal activity. Any representative of a foreign government is fair game for an intelligence tap. The rules that apply to law enforcement taps just aren't appropriate for intelligence wiretaps. So, in 1978, when the United States embarked on the experiment of putting intelligence wiretaps under judicial oversight, it wrote a special statute for them. FISA sets much more flexible rules for wiretaps aimed at agents of a foreign power than the law sets for law enforcement wiretaps.

Once Congress had created two parallel wiretap statutes, civil liberties conflicts were nearly inevitable. Usually, there wasn't much overlap between the two. Law enforcement wiretaps were for organized crime and politicians. Intelligence wiretaps were for foreign spies and the like.

But espionage is both a crime and an intelligence matter. We usually expelled foreign government spies without prosecution, but we could prosecute Americans when we caught them spying. Which raised the question whether the suspected spy should be wiretapped using FISA or the law enforcement wiretap law.

Civil libertarians and judges had nightmares about such cases. They feared that law enforcement agencies would game the system, picking and choosing the wiretap law that gave them the most latitude. If they couldn't persuade a court to grant a law enforcement wiretap, they'd just use a FISA wiretap instead.

The intelligence agencies had a similar nightmare. What if they found an American spy while conducting an intelligence wiretap and Justice decided to prosecute? As soon as the accused spy got in front of a judge, he would claim that his privacy rights had been violated.

He'd claim that the government had played a shell game, using a FISA tap to catch him when it should have used a law enforcement tap.

If the court agreed, the wiretap could be declared illegal. The spy could go free—but first, he'd likely get a chance to read transcripts of all the government's wiretaps and to figure out how they were done. Years of intelligence gathering could be put at risk.

Even worse, there was no way of knowing when the line had been crossed. It might take years before an intelligence wiretap was put at issue in a criminal trial. By the time a judge told them the intelligence agencies were out of bounds, it would be way too late to fix the problem.

They had to know where the line was. But the law was sparse. The courts had given a few hints. They seemed to say that a proper intelligence wiretap would morph into an improper law enforcement wiretap when the primary purpose of the tap shifted from intelligence gathering to building a criminal case. If the main reason for the tap was gathering evidence, the prosecutors would have to get their own wiretap and live by the rules that the law set for those intercepts.

So if the intelligence agencies wanted to stay out of court and out of legal trouble, all they had was a rule of thumb: The less contact the better between the agencies running the intelligence taps and the prosecutors and investigators handling the criminal case. That reduced the chances that the courts would think that there'd been a shell game in progress. Or, to put it in terms the *New York Times* might have used, the less contact there was between prosecutors and intelligence wiretaps, the less likely it was that American liberties would be eroded by the misuse of FISA for criminal justice purposes.

For a while, the concern was mostly theoretical. When FISA was adopted in 1978, no Americans had been prosecuted for espionage since Julius and Ethel Rosenberg more than a quarter-century earlier. But 1985 turned out to be the Year of the Spy. A dozen Americans were caught spying for foreign governments. They were legitimate FISA counterintelligence targets. They could also be arrested and prosecuted.

But if the authorities were getting ready to prosecute someone, shouldn't they use ordinary wiretaps with all their built-in privacy and civil liberties protections? Suddenly the intelligence agencies' nightmares seemed to be coming true. A solution had to be found. And it was. The two investigations would be kept separate. FISA taps could be used to keep track of likely spies for years, waiting for their tradecraft to slip. When it did, if criminal prosecution looked like an option, the case could be handed off to the prosecutors, who would have to meet all the usual criminal standards if they wanted to carry out wiretaps or other searches. The two things would be independent of each other. The prosecutors didn't need the details of the intelligence. All they needed was a tip that they should begin a separate criminal investigation.

The first course of the wall had been laid, but it seemed to work. The Department of Justice successfully prosecuted several of the spies caught in 1985. America's spies and cops had found a way to live together.

Until the wheels nearly came off.

It was 1993. Janet Reno had taken the helm at Justice as attorney general. She had not brought a contingent of loyalists with her to the department. But she did bring Richard Scruggs, once her boss in Miami, who had come north to handle national security matters for her. Reno was comfortable relying on the career professionals. At first. But within months of arriving, she'd relied on them in approving a raid on the Branch Davidian compound at Waco, Texas, that had gone badly wrong. Dozens of cult members died in a fire, and later investigation cast doubt on much of the advice she'd been given before the raid.

Now it looked as though the career professionals had let her down again. Scruggs could barely contain his disbelief. Shortly after the Waco disaster, he and the attorney general had been briefed on the worst espionage case the United States had seen in a generation. Aldrich Ames, a CIA operative with intimate knowledge of the agency's Soviet sources had sold them all to the Soviets for several million dollars.

To move its investigation forward, the FBI asked the attorney general to personally approve a physical search of Ames's home. Because the search was done for foreign intelligence purposes, the FBI told her, no court-ordered warrant was required. It felt odd to tell the police they could break in to an American's home without going to court for a warrant, but she had relied on the professionals. This wasn't a criminal matter.

Or was it? Scruggs had heard a rumor, and he wanted the truth. He called the two top criminal division prosecutors in national security cases to his office.

—Has the FBI been briefing you about the fruits of their foreign intelligence search of Ames's home? Scruggs demanded to know.

They had.

Scruggs exploded.

—And how are we going to explain that at trial? he asked. How can we tell the court that the attorney general personally authorized the FBI to break in to an American's home without a court order and that the evidence was then turned over to the prosecutors?

It was a debacle, and a civil liberties windfall for Ames. Almost as soon as he was arrested, in early 1994, his lawyers began making precisely the argument that the intelligence agencies and Scruggs had feared. Ames had betrayed the identities of nearly a dozen men. They had almost certainly paid for his treason with their lives, and he could have faced the death penalty if his case had gone to trial. Instead, he was able to negotiate a quick plea for himself and his wife that kept him alive and allowed her to leave prison in 1998.

The Ames case opened a chasm in the little community that understood intelligence wiretaps. For the intelligence agencies, the case was a bullet dodged. The plea deal had kept the courts from deciding whether intelligence techniques violated civil liberties when they were used to help prosecutors. But the intelligence agencies didn't think they could dodge many more bullets like that one. The rules of the road had to be clarified so they could steer clear of retroactive second-guessing by the courts.

As NSA's top lawyer, I was part of the intelligence community at the time, and I shared its concern about privacy claims. In 1994, after I left NSA, I argued in a *Foreign Policy* article[2] that intelligence and law enforcement should be strictly separated. The privacy risks that came from blurring the lines between intelligence and law enforcement might be more abstract than real, I thought, but they had to be taken into account: "However theoretical the risks to civil liberties may be, they cannot be ignored."[3] Foreign intelligence gathering is intrusive, harsh, and deceitful—and should be. I didn't think the courts would or should tolerate the application of these qualities to ordinary criminal defendants. And so I argued for an approach that "preserves, perhaps even raises, the wall between the two communities."[4]

I had plenty of allies in that little world. The FISA court had its own reasons for wanting strong civil liberties protections. Since its creation, it had been incessantly attacked by civil liberties groups as being too secretive and too friendly to the government. It was called a rubber stamp court because it almost never turned down a wiretap application.

The slurs hurt. "I have struggled with the perception for years that we did whatever the government wanted and were rubber stamps," said Judge Royce Lamberth, who became chief judge of the FISA court in 1995. "That was not and is not true."[5]

But making that case was an uphill fight. The court's proceedings were so highly classified that the judge could do little to rebut the charge. Perhaps he felt he had a little more to prove than most. A Republican appointee and a former prosecutor, Lamberth was a colorful, aggressive judge. When not on the bench he sometimes attended sober Washington events in a cowboy hat. A tribute to his Texas roots, he says. Truth in advertising, say some of the lawyers who've appeared before him.

Whatever the truth, Judge Lamberth didn't want anyone to mistake his court's commitment to civil liberties. That was Job One. "We worked to protect civil liberties while protecting the country itself. The judges asked themselves: Are we going to lose our liberties if we approve this kind of surveillance?" Lamberth told one reporter. "We knew that the country has not always done things right."[6] But those days were over; the FISA court was on the job.

In its mission to head off civil liberties objections, the FISA court had an ally—an obscure but powerful Justice Department office. The Office of Intelligence Policy and Review (OIPR) was the liaison between the court and the executive branch. No paper was filed and no word was spoken in the FISA court without the approval of the intelligence review office. As the guardian of intelligence wiretaps, OIPR wanted to make sure there were no civil liberties abuses on its watch.

When I was at NSA, I had worked with Justice's intelligence review office. It was a small office, and for a generation it had been run by a legend. The counsel for intelligence policy was Mary Lawton, a tiny, tough-talking, hard-smoking spinster with a fine legal mind. She had taken over soon after the intelligence scandals of the 1970s. She believed strongly in the intelligence mission, and especially in her boys at the FBI. She usually found a way to justify the wiretaps and other operations they wanted to carry out.

But she had sharp elbows and a keen sense for the politics of survival. No one talked to her court but her. She was almost as effective at keeping others from talking to the attorney general about classified matters. In government, there's almost nothing that can't be accomplished if you're the only person in the room with the decision-maker, and Lawton knew that.

She also knew how to deal out punishment for bureaucratic offenses. From time to time, someone would cross a line with Lawton. FBI agents would complain to the director about a ruling. Or I'd raise doubts about her refusal to make a particular argument to the FISA court.

The punishment was always the same. She'd stop taking our calls. We'd be referred to her deputy, Alan Kornblum. Bald, bullet-headed and energetic, Kornblum meted out the punishment. He would demand endless rewrites of the same documents. They were never good enough. He wouldn't send the applications to the court without changes. And the changes weren't good enough either. Finally, desperate at the prospect that we'd miss the deadline and have to drop an important wiretap, I'd call Mary and surrender. Then she'd help us get our paperwork filed in time. Lesson learned. It was a small world, but she ruled it absolutely.

Then, in 1993, Lawton died suddenly. Shaken by the near miss in the Ames case, Attorney General Reno asked Richard Scruggs to take over. Scruggs decided immediately that the tension between law enforcement and intelligence could not be allowed to fester any longer.

He wanted tough new civil liberties guidelines, including a "Chinese wall" between criminal prosecutors and investigators on the one hand and intelligence operations on the other. There would be no more casual mixing of investigations like the Ames case. Instead, the informal understanding would become formal. If the intelligence agencies found a spy, they could use FISA to watch him for as long as they liked, identifying his contacts and drawing a bead on what he had compromised. But they'd have to do all that without any help from the prosecutors.

At some point, the intelligence community would see no value in continuing to watch him, or the case would begin to look like something that could lead to an arrest. Then they could tell the law enforcement agents what they knew. The prosecutors could seek a law enforcement tap and use it to gather the evidence they'd use to prosecute. The earlier work by the intelligence agencies would stay out of the case; no one could say the prosecutors had misused a FISA tap they barely knew about.

Scruggs's relationship with the attorney general was strong. She was determined to avoid another civil liberties debacle of the sort that only a plea bargain had avoided in the Ames case. And he had the solution—a wall in time between intelligence gathering and criminal investigation. It seemed to the lawyers of the intelligence review office, and of the intelligence community, that we had found a safe place to stand, protecting both civil liberties and intelligence sources.

But no sooner had we taken a stand than the ground began to slip from under our feet, like sand in a withdrawing tide.

We had reckoned without the determination of al Qaeda—and the machismo of America's prosecutors.

Prosecutors and Terrorists

While the lawyers argued nice points of civil liberties doctrine in Washington, Islamic extremists had begun to target New York City. We had granted an immigrant visa to a vicious Islamist ideologue. Omar Abdel-Rahman, also known as the blind sheikh, was allowed to stay as a "religious worker" spreading his faith. And spread it he did, preaching death to Americans with enthusiasm and to great effect.

Shortly after his arrival, his allies and acolytes had killed the radical Jewish activist, Meir Kahane. The case was handled by FBI agents and prosecutors based in Manhattan. These offices saw themselves as a criminal justice elite, the center of criminal justice excellence in the country. The U.S. attorney for the Southern District of New York only occasionally accepted guidance—and certainly never direction—from Washington, where the office was known as the "Sovereign District" of New York. The FBI office in Manhattan had a similar esprit. In Washington, agents made coffee; in New York, they made cases. Big ones.

But they had booted the Kahane case, wrapping it up quickly in a trial that portrayed the shooter as a lone nut. In fact, he was part of the blind sheikh's Islamist circle, and the blind sheikh was planning on much more than a one-off murder.

Indeed, his acolytes were just getting started. Soon, they would set off a huge car bomb in the World Trade Center, hoping to bring the whole complex down. While the elite of federal law enforcement was struggling with that case, the blind sheik's allies planned an even more ambitious attack. Their scheme was eerily similar to the assault on Mumbai that would take place in 2008. Bombings on the bridges and tunnels to Manhattan would isolate the island one evening; in the confusion, several luxury hotels would be seized by terrorists disguised as kitchen workers. Mass executions would follow.

The first plot succeeded, though the buildings did not fall. The second plot failed; it was thwarted by an informer. But the plotters' contempt for the authorities was plain. The cream of federal law enforcement had overlooked the blind sheikh's organization the first time. Now they took the new attacks personally.

The commitment today of the Obama administration's Justice Department to prosecuting terrorists like common criminals in civilian courts can be traced back to those early years. Prosecutors were riding high. They had indicted a sitting head of state, Manuel Noriega of Panama, in 1988, and the country had invaded Panama to bring him to justice. Prosecutors are to the Justice Department what fighter pilots are to the Air Force. The most talented ones have a bit of a swagger, and there's nothing they think they can't do.

Islamic terrorists, the Southern District's prosecutors believed, had messed with the wrong people. Southern District prosecutors and investigators weren't afraid of international conspiracies. They had convicted over a dozen Mafioso in the "pizza connection" cases of the 1980s. Now, spurred by a mix of shame and outrage, they marshaled their full resources against the terror plotters.

And they delivered. By 1995, nearly fifty extremists were on trial for the Mumbai-style plot.

But this wasn't the Mafia, playing by well-understood rules. In the middle of the trial, the hunted became the hunter. The judge, prosecutors, and witnesses all received death threats. The prosecutors put criminal wiretaps in place. They came up dry. Mary Jo White, the ambitious head of the Southern District, called for FISA wiretaps to keep the coverage up.

Now the fat was in the fire. It was too late to follow the old practice of closing any intelligence taps before opening a criminal case. There were several ongoing criminal investigations into Islamist terrorism in New York. Worse, law enforcement wiretaps had already been tried and failed. It looked as though the prosecutors were doing exactly what civil libertarians and the intelligence review office has always feared—using FISA because criminal wiretaps weren't producing enough information.

Scruggs's OIPR offered a simple solution that would protect defendants' rights fully. If Mary Jo White wanted intelligence taps, all she had to do was drop the criminal case. Either that, or she could stop asking for intelligence taps in a case that had clearly gone criminal long ago. If FISA taps were launched now, the FISA court would think that its broad authorities were being hijacked to serve the prosecutors of the Southern District. To protect against civil liberties objections, the court would reject the wiretap applications. Or, worse, it would grant them, and the whole thing would come crashing down later, when the wiretaps were reviewed by the trial court in the middle of a high-stakes terrorism prosecution.

But the fighter jocks of the Sovereign District weren't used to taking orders from a no-name intelligence aide like Scruggs, no matter how close he might be to the attorney general. The prosecutors wanted intelligence wiretaps, right now, and they wanted to know everything the taps were producing. After all, if the intelligence community couldn't go looking for a foreign conspiracy to kill American officials, what good was it?

They argued for the greatest possible sharing of intelligence and the narrowest possible view of the civil liberties problem. They wanted anything that might help them make a case.

And what about civil liberties? The prosecutors were used to the claim that they were violating defendants' civil liberties. That's what practically every criminal defendant says these days. The prosecutors could take the heat, and they expected to win in the end. The intelligence guys, they thought, were being nervous nellies. They should just grow a pair.

OIPR's effort to save FISA from civil liberties attack was suddenly at risk.

The Intelligence Review Office Takes on the Prosecutors

In the spring of 1995, Richard Scruggs went to New York to face off with Mary Jo White. Scruggs took Alan Kornblum, who remembers that White was assisted by a well-regarded junior prosecutor named

Patrick Fitzgerald. Fitzgerald would eventually become famous in his own right as the man who prosecuted both Scooter Libby, Vice President Cheney's chief of staff, and Illinois Governor Rod Blagojevich.

White rejected Scruggs's demand that she choose between FISA taps and her criminal case. Kornblum says White wanted a new kind of procedure that would keep the intelligence and criminal cases technically separate while permitting information to slip across the boundary. The intelligence review office rejected the idea but, as he remembers, Deputy Attorney General Jamie Gorelick forced the two sides to agree on something close to White's proposal: An intelligence investigation, complete with FISA wiretaps, would be opened. But to ensure that the wiretap did not become an end run on the civil liberties protections that applied to law enforcement taps, the prosecutors would have no control or direction over the intelligence investigation. Intelligence memoranda would only be given to prosecutors with the permission of the intelligence review office. A single prosecutor would have full visibility into the intelligence "take," but no say in shaping the operation.

Most fateful was the way the deal treated the FBI. The bureau's investigators were divided into criminal and intelligence teams; the criminal team would not be allowed to influence the course of the intelligence investigation.

The wall had arrived. What had been a wall in time—first do the intelligence investigation, then do the criminal investigation—was now a wall between investigators.

The deal made sense as a way to protect civil liberties. Without it, there was a risk that intelligence taps would be influenced by the evidentiary needs of the criminal investigators and prosecutors. If the government was serious about making the criminal investigators turn square corners, there had to be restrictions on how they dealt with the intelligence gatherers.

But it made no sense in terms of countering terrorism. How could two sets of federal agents hunt the same Islamic terrorists without working together? No one was entirely happy. In OIPR's view, the wall would only protect civil liberties if it were strictly enforced. The procedures sounded good. In theory they kept intelligence intercepts separate from criminal investigations.

But the intelligence review office feared that the prosecutors might win the fight in practice. After all, a prosecutor would see everything the intelligence agencies turned up as soon as it was gathered; he could talk to the intelligence side freely, and if he were as good as Fitzgerald was rumored to be, he'd have no trouble giving the agencies hints about how to improve the criminal case. In the same vein, there were separate FBI teams for intelligence and criminal work. But they all worked for the same bureau; it would be impossible to keep them from talking to each other. The prosecutors were surely counting on exactly that.

Who had won depended on how strictly the wall was enforced. The intelligence review office soon began to fear that it would lose the enforcement battle. The deal with the Southern District only resolved matters for that office. In July of 1995, Deputy Attorney General Gorelick released department-wide guidelines for cases where intelligence and criminal investigations ran parallel. The basic rules were hard to argue with. Prosecutors could have information from the intelligence operation but no control over it. Prosecutors were expressly prohibited from exercising any direction or control over intelligence taps that intersected their criminal investigations. If the intelligence taps turned up evidence indicating the commission of "a significant federal crime" it had to be reported to the Justice Department's Criminal Division.[7] These guidelines were adopted by the attorney general in July of 1995.

But the details made the intelligence review office antsy. Its lawyers feared that the prosecutors wouldn't really respect the wall that was supposedly protecting the rights of defendants. Sure, everyone agreed that prosecutors could not control or direct intelligence taps. And the intelligence officials knew that, like every federal employee, they were obliged to report evidence of a crime to the Justice department.

But the attorney general's guidelines went well beyond reporting of crimes. They didn't just call for a report; they required a detailed description of the facts and circumstances of the crimes, and ongoing consultation. This seemed to stretch "crimes reporting" to the point of artificiality. ("Hello, Justice? CIA here. I'm calling to report a crime. You won't believe it, but al Qaeda is *still* plotting to kill Americans in gross violation of federal criminal law. Here's today's detailed evidence of exactly how they're planning to do that.")

Sure, the guidelines said that prosecutors couldn't direct or control the intelligence tap, but the temptation to cheat would be strong. The intelligence review office and the intelligence community's lawyers all feared that prosecutors would ask questions that were really hints about what the intelligence agents should do next. And that eager-to-please intelligence agencies would turn the informal guidance into their own direction. The FBI criminal investigators, many of whom were experienced lawyers in their own right, could informally lobby their intelligence colleagues to shore up the weak spots in the criminal case. Everyone would get along famously, chiseling away at the wall and the rule that criminal defendants can't be wiretapped without intense judicial supervision.

It would all be good—until the music stopped. Then some judge would put everyone under oath and pull the whole story out of them. At which point the intelligence wiretaps would be held to violate the defendants' civil liberties, with incalculable consequences.

Then the prosecutors who had boasted of their *cojones* would stand before the judge like naked men in an arctic gale.

Or, even worse, when the risk of a bad ruling became clear, the prosecutors would turn against the intelligence agencies, displaying the mix of self-righteousness and flop-sweat that replaces the prosecutors' swagger in the weeks before trial. Nothing would be more important to them than winning the case. Not classified information, not future intelligence operations. Nothing. Suddenly, to ensure victory, the prosecutors would become fierce internal advocates for whatever civil liberties rules they thought the judge was likely to want.

The only way to avoid this, the lawyers of the intelligence review office thought, was to keep the wall high from the start. That meant putting them in the middle. They had to act as chaperone and gatekeeper, overseeing the exchanges between intelligence collectors and prosecutors. Before anything could get across the wall, the intelligence office would have to approve it. The office, after all, was exquisitely responsive to the FISA court and the civil liberties risks. If it could police the wall, it would keep overeager prosecutors and over-cooperative agencies from sliding into forbidden territory.

The only problem was that the attorney general's guidelines didn't give the intelligence review office a chaperone's role. They left the wall in place as a technical matter, but they didn't give OIPR the tools to enforce it.

The attorney general had made her decision. But as far as OIPR was concerned, that was just the beginning of the fight.

Within two years, the attorney general's decision was a dead letter. Whatever the guidelines might say, the FBI was refusing to share intelligence wiretap information with criminal prosecutors without the permission of the intelligence review office.

How did that happen? Put simply, the office had outmaneuvered the prosecutors.

It had the FBI over a barrel. All of the bureau's FISA wiretaps had to go through the intelligence review office, which controlled their drafting and filing. They were always on a tight time frame. And Alan Kornblum had learned one lesson well. Delay was OIPR's trump card.

If the intelligence review office said the documents weren't ready for filing, then they wouldn't go to the court. That meant the wiretaps would lapse, or never be set up. The targets, who might be extraordinarily dangerous terrorists or spies, would escape surveillance. OIPR could punish any FBI agent who talked too much to the criminal division by threatening to wreck his investigation.

But wasn't that a violation of the guidelines? Couldn't the FBI go to the attorney general and object? Sure, if the intelligence review office was dumb enough to say that it was punishing the bureau for too much cooperation with prosecutors. But FISA filings are immensely complicated. If the intelligence office thought an FBI unit needed disciplining, it only had to send the applications back at the last minute with a host of research to do and changes to make. The unit would have to work nights and weekends and still might lose the tap. If it complained, the intelligence review office could simply say that the office had done an unprofessional job of preparing the application. There was no recourse.

Proud as it was, the bureau had to capitulate. And it did. No one would be allowed over the wall without a chaperone.

The prosecutors soon realized what had happened. They sent complaint after complaint to the attorney general; report after report declared that the guidelines were being flouted. If the intelligence review office and the FBI wouldn't provide information more freely, the prosecutors argued, then the guidelines needed to be revised. A drumbeat began, from the Southern District to the Criminal Division. The guidelines would have to be rewritten to take the intelligence review office out of its "babysitter" role. The prosecutors had to have access to FISA information, free from OIPR's oversight.

This was serious. Prosecutors didn't usually lose battles in front of the attorney general, who was after all the nation's chief prosecutor.

In 1998, the prosecutors showed their power by cutting the intelligence review office's Kornblum down to size. He had turned down several FBI requests for applications to conduct surveillance of Wen Ho Lee, a suspected Chinese nuclear spy at Los Alamos National Laboratory. He didn't think they met the legal standard under FISA, and he knew they'd likely end up being challenged if Lee were arrested and tried. True to type, he had sent them back time and again for more work, never quite saying no. Eventually, the agents shelved the requests. Later, when the government's lethargic handling of the matter blew up into a political scandal, they managed to tag Kornblum with much of the blame.

Also in 1998, the intelligence review office got a new leader. Frances Fragos Townsend (later George W. Bush's homeland security adviser) came from the prosecutor's side of the house. She had spent time in the Criminal Division and the Southern District of New York. When she arrived, she quickly pushed the wounded Kornblum aside, taking him out of the direct line of communication to the court and bringing in a new deputy to handle FISA applications.

Now OIPR's back was to the wall. It seemed only a matter of time before the wall had been eroded as a practical matter. But once again, the wall's defenders had a hidden trump card, and it was time to play it.

As designed by Mary Lawton, the relationship between the FISA court and the intelligence review office was uniquely tight-knit. FISA judges were appointed to seven-year terms from the ranks of existing federal judges around the country. Most had no intelligence background whatsoever before being appointed. They had no familiarity with the immensely complex statute governing intelligence wiretaps. There were no reported cases to read and evaluate. Everything was classified. They were deeply dependent on the OIPR lawyers who guided them through the applications. They thought those lawyers "were top-notch, very impressive," says Judge Lamberth, remembering his first impression.[8] The intelligence review office, in turn, worked hard to earn the court's trust by not taking a traditional litigator's approach to the court.

"Historically," Fran Townsend remembers, "we had more a comfortable than an adversarial relationship with the court."[9] So it was only natural that Chief Judge Lamberth would have been fully briefed on OIPR's fear that the prosecutors would never be satisfied until they had undone the intelligence review office's strict view of what civil liberties required.

And so, as the prosecutors circled, the FISA court itself began to stir.

The FISA Court Stages a Coup

The issue came to a head in 1998. Al Qaeda's bombing of two U.S. embassies in East Africa had put the Southern District's latest criminal investigation of the group into overdrive. But it also put the wall front and center. As with other al Qaeda cases, the criminal investigation was practically inseparable from the ongoing intelligence monitoring. So what rules would govern this investigation?

The intelligence review office did not want to return to New York for another chest-bumping showdown over the wall. The prosecutors were winning. If the guidelines had to be reworked for the East Africa cases, the intelligence review office would go into battle with half the department arrayed against it.

Staring defeat in the face, the intelligence review office finally played its trump card—the FISA court. Judge Lamberth remembers Kornblum suggesting that the guidelines be turned into FISA court orders. "He felt, and we agreed, that if you have rules, you should follow them," says the judge.[10]

The idea had understandable appeal from a civil liberties viewpoint, too. Unlike the attorney general, who was, after all, a prosecutor at heart, the court would be an honest broker. It could give the rights of defendants their due weight, without a conflict of interest and without yielding to the importunings of the prosecutors. And so it was done. The FISA court simply annexed the attorney general's guidelines, making the wall a matter of court order.

It was as simple as that; a quiet coup on the top floor of the Justice Department. From now on, the court would decide what was needed to prevent misuse of FISA taps, and the rules it settled on would simply be imposed as a condition on any antiterrorism wiretaps approved by the court.

For the prosecutors it was check and mate. The FISA court had the department over a barrel. The government had to keep the wiretaps up; an attack could occur at any time, and the government could not afford to be deaf to the planning. If the department wanted the taps, it had to accept that the FISA court was making the rules.

In theory, this court order could have been appealed. There was a pretty good reason to think that the court's action was inconsistent with the law. The Justice Department did at last appeal the wall orders in 2002, when the FISA court insisted on keeping them in place despite the investigative debacle they ultimately caused. The department won easily. The review court was scathing in its assessment of the legal basis for the FISA court's judicial coup, saying that the FISA court had "mistakenly categorized" the 1995 guidelines as statutorily required procedures "and then compelled the government to utilize a modified version of those procedures in a way that is clearly inconsistent with the statutory purpose."[11]

At the time, though, Justice didn't utter a peep. The intelligence review lawyers had no interest in overturning their own bureaucratic triumph, and they controlled all appearances before the court. But even the prosecutors must have seen that an appeal would be a nightmare for Justice. The prosecutors would have had to ask the intelligence review office to assemble the first appellate review panel in FISA history, something that would not have been done quietly. The appeal would have turned into a major civil liberties *cause célèbre*. The newspapers would have treated it as an effort by Justice to cut back on the protections for defendants created by criminal wiretap law. One can imagine the headlines turning the FISA court into an unlikely civil liberties hero: "Revolt of the Rubber Stamp Judges" might have been among the milder ones. Many in Congress as well would have seen the issue through a civil liberties lens, and hearings could have been expected, perhaps even legislation to write the wall into law. Civil liberties groups would have filed amicus briefs, as indeed they did in 2002. And, in the end, there was no certainty that the appeal would succeed, at least in the atmosphere that prevailed before 9/11.

Once the applications had been signed and the opportunity for appeal had passed, the wall was law. Neither the attorney general nor the Sovereign District of New York could defy or modify a court order.

There was a new civil liberties sheriff in town.

For advocates of defendants' rights, the court orders were a triumph. The wall was now far beyond the reach of the prosecutors. But salvaging the wall was only half the battle. The real key was making sure that the wall was enforced. The FBI had been forced to accept the intelligence review office as the gatekeeper between its intelligence agents and the prosecutors, but how could the court be sure that the FBI itself was enforcing the wall between the intelligence and criminal teams that were both pursuing al Qaeda? The members of each team were FBI agents and analysts, after all; it only made sense for them to pool information and resources. But that process could allow criminal investigation motives to infect the intelligence wiretaps. And that would lead to disaster in a later criminal trial. It would look as though the wall had been honored mainly in the breach.

This was no idle worry. FBI agents are tough, proud, and tribal. To them, the intelligence review office was just another Justice office full of lawyers who didn't understand the street. The agents pursuing al Qaeda shared a common bond, and they needed each other's help. It was crazy, they must have thought, to deny information to each other. As long as investigative cooperation could slip cross the wall informally, from one agent to another, it would continue, no matter what the intelligence review office said. Bringing the FBI to heel would not be easy.

But now the civil libertarians had the FISA court in their corner. "If you have rules, you should follow them," Judge Lamberth believes.[12] Soon the FBI would learn just how firmly he held that view.

Several al Qaeda members had been arrested in the East Africa bombing cases, and by 2000, their trial in the Southern District of New York was drawing near. Patrick Fitzgerald was again at the center of the case.

As Fitzgerald prepared to defend the East Africa FISA intercepts against a suppression motion, he noticed something troubling. The FBI affidavits that led to the FISA orders had dutifully mirrored the FISA court's new guidelines, affirming that there had been no contact between the FBI's criminal and the intelligence teams. But Fitzgerald knew the investigators, and he knew that wasn't true. The FBI teams overlapped.

This was a big problem. There was no evidence of deliberate misrepresentation. The affidavits had described the world that the intelligence lawyers thought existed. But, stuck behind the wall, they had evidently not pressed for the actual facts. And in the end, deliberately or not, the affidavits described a world that didn't exist.

It was a nightmare not just for the intelligence office but for the prosecutors. The Sovereign District was on center stage with this latest prosecution of al Qaeda; but its case was suddenly at risk because of problems with the FISA orders. A suppression hearing loomed. The judge overseeing the criminal trial would have to be told of the mistakes. And the judge would surely ask whether the FISA court had been told of the false statements. According to Judge Lamberth, Fitzgerald eventually announced that the clock had run out; if the attorney general didn't tell the FISA court about the error by the end of the day, Fitzgerald would have to disclose it himself.[13]

In a way, it was just what the intelligence review office had always feared. A prosecutor with a case to protect was suddenly claiming that defendants' rights had been jeopardized by the FISA process and was forcing action that could disrupt the functioning of FISA.

The Wrath of the Least Dangerous Branch

Not long after, Judge Lamberth got an unexpected call.

It was Attorney General Reno.

—I'd like to come see you, she said. I need to tell you something.

—All right, Madam Attorney General, the judge replied, but I know you've got a busy schedule. Much more crowded than mine. I'd be happy to come see you.

—No, no, Reno said. My mama always told me that when you're in trouble, you're the one who goes to see the judge. And I'm in trouble. I'm going to come to you.[14]

Taking a seat in the judge's chambers a few hours later, the attorney general confessed to the errors. It was bad. As many as seventy-five orders had been affected by false affidavits.

Judge Lamberth was not a retiring sort of judge. When he thought the government was not living up to its obligations, the chief judge was relentless. In other cases, he has threatened to hold two Interior secretaries in contempt of court and accused federal officials of racism and bias. Whether he was called a straight shooter or a loose cannon, everyone who appeared before him knew that Judge Lamberth was heavy artillery—especially when he thought he'd encountered government wrongdoing.

He certainly brought out the big guns now. He demanded an investigation of the alleged failure to adhere to the wall. Justice's Office of Professional Responsibility was assigned to track down any evidence that the agents who prepared the applications had committed misconduct.

Judge Lamberth was assisted in his work by a new legal adviser. Alan Kornblum had grown tired of his isolation at the intelligence review office and had joined the FISA court as its first clerk in decades. He brought with him the old, uncompromising OIPR view that the only way to preserve FISA's value for intelligence gathering was to maintain a strict separation of criminal and intelligence functions. So, while the affidavit errors were an embarrassment for OIPR as an office, it might in fact serve the office's long-term strategic interests. This was a chance to make sure that the wall was enforced for real. At last even the FBI could be brought to heel.

The court and its new legal adviser set about constructing new enforcement mechanisms. In October, Judge Lamberth reinforced the court's oversight of who got to see FISA wiretaps. From that point on, every agent who had access to FISA-derived intelligence would have to sign a special certification, promising that none of the information would be conveyed to criminal investigators without the FISA court's permission.

The election of 2000 eventually brought George W. Bush to power and John Ashcroft to the attorney general's suite, but this did nothing to diminish the FISA court's clout or ambition. As a senator, the new attorney general had been notably supportive of civil liberties, playing to an antigovernment, libertarian strain of Republicanism that had grown strong in opposition to the Clinton administration's centrist support for more law enforcement authority. Attorney General Ashcroft had no interest in picking a civil-liberties fight at the start of his term. Quite the reverse.

According to published sources, Judge Lamberth met early with the new attorney general and gave him one piece of advice. If he wanted to mend fences with the FISA court, Townsend had to go.

She had lost the confidence of the court. Some say the problem was how close she was to the prosecutors, others that the affidavit fiasco had left her damaged.[15]

Not long afterwards, Townsend got word from the attorney general. Her services would no longer be needed. She departed, to head the intelligence office of the Coast Guard.

In early 2001, the FBI sat unknowing in a civil liberties bull's-eye. Many of its field agents were still doing what they had always done—informally sharing information about terrorists. They had a job to do and inside the bureau, at least, sharing with other agents was part of getting the job done.

But the ground had shifted. The FBI had no allies. The judicial coup that incorporated the wall into the FISA court's orders had forced the prosecutors to change sides in the fight over information sharing. Now the prosecutors were demanding that any assurances submitted to the FISA court be strictly accurate. So was the court. And so was the intelligence review office. The assurances looked like boilerplate, but they had become deadly serious, especially for the agents who signed them.

How serious soon became clear. In early 2001, OIPR told Judge Lamberth that it had found another group of investigations where the FBI had not observed the wall. These investigations had nothing to do with al Qaeda, so the FBI teams at work on them had not been touched by Fitzgerald's lash. Sharing across the wall had continued despite the flap in the Southern District. More than a dozen applications had been compromised by false assurances that the wall was in place.

It was the last straw for the FISA court—and for the FBI. The court would insist on an investigation, of course, but that would take months. Judge Lamberth's term would end in a year, and he was determined to strictly enforce the civil liberties protections he had put in place. The court's rules had been broken, and someone was going to pay. Now. Not months from now.

All seven members of the FISA court assembled and agreed. According to Judge Lamberth, one of the seven said, "If I discovered that an affiant in my court had made false statements, I wouldn't spend too much time worrying about whether the false statement was negligent or deliberate. I'd bar him from the courtroom immediately. Why don't we do that?"[16]

It made sense to Judge Lamberth. On March 9, 2001, he sent a letter addressing the attorney general in the bluntest possible terms. "I was disturbed to learn this week that we now have another series of cases in which the FBI affidavits contain information that is not true," he said.[17] The affidavits had been signed by a supervisory agent who was widely viewed as a rising star at the bureau. Not anymore.

At least not if the FISA court had anything to say about it. Effective immediately, Judge Lamberth declared, "the court will not accept any affidavits" from the agent.[18] (The agent was later identified by the *New York Times*, but when I tracked him down, he asked me not to use his name in this book, and I'm honoring his request.) Judge Lamberth also demanded that the intelligence review office "must immediately conduct an inquiry and verify the accuracy of the pleadings in these cases, and explain how such inaccurate information came to be presented to the court."[19]

In the end, Justice's Office of Professional Responsibility expanded its investigation to include the FBI agent's actions. Given the court's harsh language, the investigation wasn't likely to come out well for the agent. OIPR had already decided that the statements were false. The only question seemed to be whether the agent had deceived the court negligently or deliberately. Sanctions could be imposed either way, and if worse came to worst, the agent was at risk of a felony prosecution for making false statements to a federal official. (In fact, years later, after the wall had been discredited by the 9/11 attacks, the investigators would find that the misstatements were simple negligence.)

"The agent was crushed," Townsend remembers.[20] The bureau thought the order would put an end to the agent's career. So did the intelligence review office.

The effect on the FBI was immediate. It did all it could to undo the order. According to Judge Lamberth, "everyone was lobbying me to back off."[21]

The attorney general asked him to reconsider. Separately, FBI Director Louis Freeh "came over and begged me to rescind the order, everything under the sun that could be done about that order."[22] So did the head of FBI counterintelligence and other friends and colleagues of the agent. The disciplinary action was causing turmoil in the bureau.

But Lamberth simply dug in harder. He later told a reporter, "We never rescinded it. We enforced it. And we sent a message to the FBI."[23]

What message was the court sending? That the agents should "tell the truth"[24] about enforcement of the wall, said Judge Lamberth.

Maybe so.

But that wasn't the message FBI agents heard.

What FBI agents heard was a little more pointed and a lot more frightening: Nothing was more likely to end their careers than failing to observe the wall.

Caught between the prosecutors, the intelligence review office, and the FISA court, they had nowhere to hide. If they didn't follow the civil liberties protections set out by the court to the letter, they would be punished, and harshly. Whether the mistake was negligent or intentional "didn't really matter," in Judge Lamberth's words.[25]

Even after that message had been sent, the court was determined to underline it. In April 2001 the court decided to put every supervisory agent with responsibility for an intelligence team on notice. Each one was required to sign the FISA applications filed by their offices. They had to confirm all of the facts that the applications set forth. Assistant U.S. attorneys were required to do the same.

With the lesson of the disciplined agent still reverberating through the institution, the new requirement was a reminder. What the FISA court had done to the first agent it was quite prepared to do to the rest of them. The new requirement forced every agent and every Justice official to double- and triple-check their compliance with the wall. Any error, any misstep could lead to sanctions.

In the confusion, with new players having to flyspeck the massive FISA applications and triple-check their compliance with the wall, the government began to miss deadlines for submitting wiretap applications. The offices just couldn't process the bulky filings under the court's new civil liberties standards fast enough. For the first time since FISA was enacted in 1978, FISA taps had to be dropped, not for substantive reasons but simply because the old orders had expired before new ones could be requested and approved.

That meant lost coverage. Suddenly, known terrorists could make plans and exchange information without the government learning what was going on. The biggest impact, according to published reports, came in the cases that inspired the court to write the new protections—the investigations of al Qaeda.

As many as twenty al Qaeda wiretap orders were reportedly dropped in the year leading up to August 2001—just as preparations for the 9/11 attacks were reaching a crescendo. Honoring Osama bin Laden's right to be free from unlawful criminal wiretaps was turning out to be costly. Enforcement of the wall was protecting his operatives from scrutiny at a critical time, just as preparations for the September 11 attacks were at their most intense.

All through this period, the intelligence system was blinking red. Everyone feared and expected a spectacular al Qaeda attack. The director of Central Intelligence was urging greater effort to find out what al Qaeda was up to. Even the FISA court knew that something big was in the works.

But the FBI and other intelligence agencies had something more important to deal with. They were in the grip of a full-fledged bureaucratic panic. Law professors might call the judiciary "the least dangerous branch" of government; FBI agents had a different view.

"FBI personnel involved in FISA matters feared the fate of the agent who had been barred," says one declassified Joint Intelligence Committee report on the 9/11 attacks.[26] FBI intelligence agents "began to avoid even the most pedestrian contact with personnel in criminal components of the Bureau or DOJ [Department of Justice] because it could result in intensive scrutiny by [OIPR] and the FISA court."[27] If a star agent could be held in contempt, it could happen to anyone, they believed. The personal certifications were a constant reminder of the peril faced by anyone investigating al Qaeda.

The wall was getting higher every month.

End Game

On August 22, an FBI analyst named Donna got a call that could have stopped the looming attacks cold. The call came from an FBI detailee at the CIA. The detailee had discovered that a major al Qaeda operative entered the United States in July. This couldn't have been an accident. Something was up, and it was serious.

The last, and most promising, opportunity to halt the plot had opened up. Stopping it should not have been hard. Khalid al-Mihdhar had been living under his own name in California and could have been found there before September 11 if the bureau had moved quickly.

But Donna had a lot to do, and it wasn't until August 28 that she sent an alert about al-Mihdhar, including a related NSA report, to the FBI's New York office.

The NSA report was valuable, but it posed a complication. Less than a year earlier, NSA had begun adding a special "caveat" or legend on the face of reports derived from FISA wiretaps. The caveat said that information in it could not be shared with law enforcement unless special permission had been granted.

This rule, too, was part of the wall. NSA carried out fewer FISA wiretaps than the bureau, and it had always been more independent of the intelligence review office; still, it was dependent on both the office and the court. When those offices grew more demanding about policing the wall, NSA had to follow suit.

Donna wanted to stay within the rules set by the FISA court. She therefore sent the alert only to her intelligence contact on the bin Laden squad.

But as if to underscore the risk of unauthorized sharing that the court had been fighting for over a year, the intelligence investigator sent the alert to his supervisor, who ignored the NSA's caveat and sent the intelligence about terrorists in the United States to the entire criminal investigative team responsible for bin Laden.

One of the squad members, a criminal investigator by the name of Scott, was immediately galvanized. The team investigating the Cole bombing was already up and running. It had resources and manpower. He wanted to put those resources to work right away to find al-Mihdhar.

Donna was alarmed. She knew a violation of the new rules when she saw it. She insisted that Scott destroy the alert. It should not have gone to him under the rules as she understood them.

But Scott was not deterred. Known terrorists had entered the country. This was too important to leave to an undermanned intelligence team.

He argued that his criminal investigators could devote more agents to the search. The criminal investigators, he said, could use grand jury subpoenas and other law enforcement tools that were far quicker than those available to the intelligence side of the Bureau. They had all the resources they needed inside the United States. The intelligence guys didn't.

He was right. At this time, the FBI's intelligence arm was notoriously underfunded and sometimes even disrespected by the rest of the bureau.

Even so, Donna insisted, the resources could not be used. The wall prevented the mixing of criminal and intelligence investigations.

Scott must have been the bravest or the most clueless agent in the bureau. He ignored Donna's advice and kept pressing.

Donna appealed to the FBI general counsel's office for a ruling. That office knew the score. Its lawyers had seen the FISA court's crusade to reinforce the wall up close. The FBI's general counsel, Larry Parkinson, would later tell the 9/11 Commission staff that the disciplined agent's fate was "'a big deal' for a lot of people." It "spooked" them, and they "became less aggressive."[28]

Spooked, the lawyers certainly were. They sided with Donna. Scott was out of line. He was risking a civil liberties scandal that would put his career and theirs in jeopardy. The search would have to be done by the thinly staffed intelligence arm of the bureau. Scott and his resources were off limits.

Even after this definitive ruling, Scott refused to go quietly. He protested in eerily prescient terms: "Someday someone will die—and wall or not—the public will not understand why we were not more effective and throwing every resource we had at certain 'problems.' Let's hope the [lawyers who gave the advice] will stand behind their decisions then, especially since the biggest threat to us now, UBL [Usama Bin (sic) Laden], is getting the most 'protection.'"[29]

From Washington, Scott's fight to get criminal resources into the search for al-Mihdhar looks like an act of courage that borders on the foolhardy. He had already received intelligence in violation of the wall, and now he was kicking up a fuss, bringing in lawyers, drawing attention to the violation, and advertising his disagreement with the FISA court's rules.

It was as brave in its way as Melendez-Perez's decision to send Kahtani home based on little more than intuition. But unlike Melendez-Perez, Scott got no help from his higher-ups. The wall had become a maze of walls. And in the end, one agent's determination to do his job was not enough to overcome all the walls—the complex civil liberties rules, the harsh enforcement regime devised the intelligence review office and the FISA court, the lurking machinery of scandal.

Scott had nowhere left to go. He did what he was told. He left the job of finding al-Mihdhar to Donna and the understaffed FBI intelligence unit.

They were still looking when September 11 dawned, bright and crisp.

4 Never Again

It was the kind of day that made Melissa Doi want to dance. But then, most days did. At 32, she knew she'd never realize her dream of becoming a ballerina but Melissa was still a dancer at heart. "She would get happy and just dance," said a friend and former classmate. "Salsa, kick lines, everything."[1] And what a day it was for dancing—the first break from summer's muggy heat. Plus, it was Tuesday, and on Friday, Melissa was planning to take her mother to Italy.

There was a lot to do before then. She was already at work at IQ Financial Systems on the eighty-third floor of the World Trade Center when the plane hit.

She called 911; the transcript was released years later.

> Melissa: Holy Mary, mother of God . . .
>
> Operator: Hi there, ma'am how are you doing?
>
> Melissa: Is it . . . is it . . . are they going to be able to get someone up here?
>
> Operator: Well, of course ma'am, we're coming up for you.
>
> Melissa: Well, there's no one here yet, and the floor is completely engulfed. We're on the floor and we can't breathe . . . And it's very, very, very hot . . .
>
> Operator: Ma'am listen, everybody's coming, everybody knows, everybody knows what happened, okay? . . .
>
> Melissa: . . . It's very hot, everywhere on the floor . . . It's very hot. I see . . . I don't see any air anymore . . . All I see is smoke.
>
> Operator: Okay dear, I'm so sorry . . . stay calm with me . . .

> Melissa: I'm going to die aren't I?
>
> Operator: No, no, no, no, no, no, no say your, ma'am, say your prayers.
>
> Melissa: I'm going to die.
>
> Operator: You gotta think positive . . .
>
> Melissa: Please, God.
>
> Operator: You're doing a good job ma'am . . .
>
> Melissa: No, it's so hot, I'm burning up . . . Stay on the line with me please, I feel like I'm dying.[2]
>
> Melissa Doi didn't speak again.

I felt an almost personal sense of responsibility. After all, I had supported the wall. I'd done my best in government and in my writings to influence the tiny community of lawyers who had debated the issue over the years. I thought the risks to civil liberties were hypothetical, but I also thought it couldn't hurt to add a few extra safeguards to the process. I never imagined that it would end with three thousand deaths.

I saw things differently after that. The lesson of 9/11 and the wall was clear: It's foolish to write rules for government to protect against hypothetical civil liberties or privacy abuses, and even more foolish to enforce those rules as though they matter more than the security mission. Rules that restrict intelligence gathering are never cost-free; sometimes they impose very real costs in terms of lives lost.

I grew deeply skeptical of efforts to write new privacy limits on government in the absence of demonstrated abuses that required new limits. We should not again put American lives at risk for the sake of some speculative gain in civil liberties.

I thought that would be obvious to everyone. In the wake of a tragedy like 9/11, it would be unseemly and divisive to blame the people who helped create the wall for the failures that occurred in August of 2001. No one knew then what the cost of building such a separation would be. But we should know now, I thought; we can't prevent every imaginable privacy abuse without hampering the fight against terror, risking more attacks and more dead.

I thought then that everyone—from the privacy groups to the prosecutors and intelligence agencies—would join in a more realistic view of civil liberties rules after the attacks. And for a while it seemed to be so. Few people blamed the civil liberties groups for what happened on that day. The USA PATRIOT Act[3] was put together quickly to override the wall and to make a host of other small changes to the rules governing terrorism investigations. After detailed negotiations between the Bush Justice Department and the Senate Judiciary committee run by Sen. Patrick Leahy (D-VT), a compromise bill was taken to the floor. It was a modest set of changes in the right direction, and I thought it would set the tone for future civil liberties debates.

Boy, was I wrong. Within a year or two of passage, civil liberties groups began treating the USA PATRIOT Act as a symbol of overreaction. Privacy groups argued, without much evidence that I could see, that civil liberties had been put at risk by the response to 9/11. They began to attack new programs, like the TIPS program to encourage citizens to report suspicious conduct, or Admiral Poindexter's Total Information Awareness program, which would have developed new data analysis (and privacy protection) tools to identify terrorists. And they soon found success. TIPS was quickly canceled, and in January 2003, Sen. Ron Wyden (D-OR) attached an appropriations rider that dropped funding for Admiral Poindexter's effort.

It made me uneasy. I knew Poindexter. He was tone deaf to politics but smart about technology. What he hoped to do was exactly the kind of research that DARPA (the Defense Advanced Research Project Agency) had been doing for forty years—pushing the envelope of what was possible in the hopes of finding new solutions to hard problems. Understanding that a technology was possible was not the same as deploying it, and Poindexter was alert to privacy risks, which he also hoped to head off with new technologies. He even invited several privacy groups to an early briefing to reassure them of his good faith.

But the privacy groups were merciless. Immediately after they were given the conciliatory briefings, they leaked the story, putting the worst possible spin on its every aspect. This didn't seem like the new, more cautious civil liberties lobby, attentive to the importance of security as well as privacy, that might have been expected in the wake of 9/11.

Nor did it seem likely to create a new, more balanced atmosphere in the halls of government, where it did not go unnoticed that John Poindexter was the only person forced from government because of the events surrounding 9/11.

There was worse to come.

A key failure of August 2001 was the inability of an undermanned FBI intelligence unit to find the two hardened al Qaeda killers that they thought might be in the United States and planning a major operation. Yet all the data necessary to find the ringleaders, and most of their accomplices, was readily available in private computer systems.

If they had obtained access to the data in airline reservation systems, even Donna and the undermanned FBI intelligence team could have immediately found the two terrorists they were looking for. And they could have broken the rest of the plot wide open by finding the links between those two and the other hijackers.

For example, three other hijackers, including Mohamed Atta, the plot's operational ringleader, used the same addresses as the two known terrorists.

Another hijacker used the same frequent-flyer number as al-Mihdhar. And five other hijackers used the same phone numbers as Mohamed Atta. That's eleven out of nineteen—all linked by simple data from the airline reservation system.

The information necessary to prevent 9/11 was in plain sight. But there was no easy way for government to obtain reservation data on domestic flights, and certainly not *before* a crime had been committed. (Officials could also have found a twelfth hijacker in an INS watch list for expired visas, and the remaining seven could have been flagged through him by matching the addresses of people who lived with him or his co-conspirators.)

Just to make this failure particularly excruciating, that same reservation data was routinely gathered on a voluntary basis by customs officials for international flights, so the government had tools for analyzing passenger lists. It had simply never applied those tools to domestic flights.

The government was determined not to let that happen again. First the Justice Department and then DHS, after its creation, launched an ambitious program to gain access to domestic airline reservation data. The creaking air security regime was being overhauled. A system that simply looked for weapons and the handful of people on the "no-fly" list wouldn't cut it anymore. It was obvious that reservation data could help identify risky passengers for closer inspection. To build a system that would do this, DHS launched CAPPS II (the second-generation Computer Assisted Passenger Pre-Screening System).

Privacy groups quickly rose to the attack. It was less than eighteen months after 9/11, but the groups had already won two victories, and now they were shifting their targets. Instead of going after half-formed (and arguably half-baked) programs, now they would try to kill a program that responded directly to the failings of August 2001.

Buoyed by past victories, they spared no hyperbole. "This system threatens to create a permanent blacklisted underclass of Americans who cannot travel freely," an ACLU legislative counsel, told the Associated Press in February 2003.[4] Recalling Admiral Poindexter, the ACLU's Barry Steinhardt declared that CAPPS II would "give the government an opening to create the kind of Big Brother program that Americans rejected so resoundingly in the Pentagon."[5]

By June 2003 the organization had filed suit to block the program. The ACLU and other left-leaning privacy groups built an alliance with libertarian-conservative groups like the American Conservative Union, the Eagle Forum, and Americans for Tax Reform. "You name it, we've gone into bed with them," an ACLU spokeswoman told the press.[6] By August this left-right coalition was lobbying heavily against CAPPS II.

And by September, the privacy groups had won.

Congressional appropriators stopped the program dead in its tracks, prohibiting implementation of CAPPS II and any similar program until the General Accountability Office certified that ten strict conditions had been met. The professionally dissatisfied auditors at that office were unlikely ever to certify that the conditions had been met. The conditions seemed to be a prelude to killing the program entirely.

I was growing more and more disillusioned with the privacy groups. They seemed to have lost any sense of responsibility, either for past disasters or for future security. Supported by the *New York Times* and the rest of the establishment media, they were now opposing any new security measure as an intrusion on civil liberties—even if the risk to civil liberties was entirely hypothetical.

By December of 2003 when I testified before the 9/11 Commission, I was worried enough to make the point explicit:

> Perhaps it isn't fair to blame all the people who helped to create the wall for the failures that occurred in August of 2001. No one knew then what the cost of building that wall would be.
>
> But now we do know. Or at least we should. We should know that we can't prevent every imaginable privacy abuse without hampering the fight against terror. We should know that an appetite for privacy scandals hampers the fight against terror. And we should know that, sooner or later, the consequence of these actions will be more attacks and more dead Americans, perhaps in numbers we can hardly fathom.
>
> We should know that. But somehow we don't . . .
>
> [B]it by bit, we are again creating the political and legal climate of August 2001.
>
> And sooner or later, I fear, August will again lead to September.[7]

I still believed in protecting privacy and civil liberties. I had served on a task force created by the Markle Foundation to find ways to use technology and data to fight terrorism while protecting privacy. And I urged the 9/11 Commission to adopt the Markle task force's recommendations, which called for expanding both the use of data and the use of electronic audits to create accountability for any actual privacy abuses that might occur. (There's a longer description of my still-evolving thoughts on how to protect privacy without sacrificing security in Part Four of this book.)

I can't say that my testimony to the 9/11 Commission made many converts. When it came time to question me, Commissioner Ben-Veniste opened with a speech praising "those who are vigilant in protecting our constitutional rights and civil liberties against over-reaching in times of national crisis . . . because they are courageous in the face of what's seen to be a popular demand."[8]

Courageous? By then I'd had enough.

"I have a different definition of courage than Commissioner Ben-Veniste," I responded when it was my turn to speak. "I don't think it takes any courage in this town to agree with the *New York Times*."[9]

In 2004, determined to do more than simply manage a prosperous law practice while the government dealt with the terrorist threat, I accepted an invitation to become general counsel of the Robb-Silberman Commission.[10] The commission's first job was to investigate intelligence failures concerning Iraqi weapons of mass destruction. But it was also charged with determining how to avoid such failures—and how to improve our intelligence about WMD in the future. I was in charge of the drafting team, and I was happy with the final report, which represented a bipartisan consensus on the commission and resulted in numerous changes in government practice.

As the Robb-Silberman Commission was winding down in 2005, Michael Chertoff asked me to come over for a talk. He had just become the new Secretary of Homeland Security.

Created two years earlier, DHS had started with nothing—no offices, no furniture, no copiers. And from day one it had been in the spotlight. Its first secretary, Tom Ridge, had managed the remarkable feat of cobbling together a working agency on the fly, but occasionally the baling wire broke or the chewing gum gave out.

The first thing the Chertoff team did when it geared up was to conduct a review of how the department was working and what it needed. More than anything, they decided, it needed a policy office that could bring coherence to the department's sprawling components. They needed an undersecretary for policy, and Secretary Chertoff was offering me the job.

I went to DHS headquarters for the interview. The department was housed in an old girls school, and it still felt like one. "Salve Regina" said the carved stone lintel over the entrance to the secretary's suite. The building was in a nice neighborhood; across the street were the Swedish embassy and the campus of American University. But the place itself was a testament to the haste with which DHS was created.

The U.S. Navy had taken it from the headmistress of Mt. Vernon Seminary in 1941 (literally—they kicked the students out, moved in, and dared her to sue). They hadn't updated some of the dorms since then. When DHS was looking for space, it found that the navy was planning to move out, and they claimed the grounds. But the navy was in no hurry to move. So they gave DHS some of the less attractive space and kept the best offices for themselves.

Chertoff's office still had the worn couch and ragged industrial carpet installed for the GS-15 who'd occupied it before him. That unprepossessing office was symbolic in my mind of the department's plight. DHS had several huge components to coordinate. Agencies like the Coast Guard, Customs and Border Protection, and the Secret Service could trace their origins back more than a hundred years. Each had built for its leader an office that was far more impressive than the office of their new boss, the secretary of DHS. In the same way, the components' beefy, multibillion-dollar budgets and staffs allowed the components to set their own course with little risk of oversight by Secretary Chertoff's limited staff.

But Chertoff was not worried about his quarters. He was determined to make the department run, and to his cadence. A gaunt, intense man—a runner with a deep competitive streak—Chertoff had aced law school. (He was the model for some of the most intimidating characters in Scott Turow's first book, *One L*, about his experience at Harvard Law School.) Chertoff had clerked on the Supreme Court, prosecuted mobsters in New York and New Jersey, run the criminal division at Justice, and been appointed to a federal court of appeals. Exactly the career he must have hoped for when he was a law student.

But the federal bench is a slow place after all that action. The phone never rings. And Chertoff loves action. Now, after two years of judging, he was rested and eager to get back in the fray. DHS was a startup, a department with no tradition, and no one to say "we don't do it that way here." He was offering me a chance to join him in writing on that blank slate. The policy office would be brand-new—a startup within a startup. The good news was that the office could be whatever I wanted to make of it. The downside was that I'd have to assemble it from scratch.

I had a general idea how hard that might be. I had helped start the Department of Education for another federal judge, Shirley Hufstedler. Unlike private startups, government startups aren't created out of whole cloth. They're assembled from bits and pieces of other agencies, and their creation is supposed to demonstrate that their mission now has a new and higher priority. But the other agencies don't see it that way. For them, the new department is an interloper that is stealing a piece of the old agencies' turf. Since turf stealing is the bureaucratic equivalent of cattle rustling, the agencies that are losing bits and pieces of their organization show no mercy. The Health, Education, and Welfare leadership that contributed most of the Department of Education did its best not to leave us even working furniture, let alone a working agency or employees. It took years to build a functioning Education Department, even though the bulk of the Department was simply the "E" in HEW.

DHS was far bigger. (Today it is roughly the size of the Department of the Army, larger than Navy or Air Force, and in fact larger than any department other than Defense and Veterans Affairs.) And unlike Education, it had no core. Its seven main components came from four cabinet agencies. The Secretary and his staff would have to get these proud, independent agencies pulling in the same direction, using only the tools put together in two years by Secretary Ridge. My assignment would be the hardest government job I had ever undertaken. But also the most rewarding. Chertoff would turn out not only to be as smart as his résumé suggested, but also willing to make tough policy decisions and to stick with his people when those decisions turned out to be unpopular with the *New York Times* editorial board. Like me, he had lived with the wall and knew how a fear of hypothetical privacy concerns had crippled cooperation between agencies. He, too, was determined not to let Americans go unprotected again.

"When can I start?" I asked.

Just about the first order of business for the new DHS policy office was figuring out how the United States could control international travel. During the year before 9/11, twenty hijackers had slipped into the United States. And so had several hundred million other travelers. Finding twenty terrorists in a stream of hundreds of millions of entrants sounds impossible. In fact, our border officials did stop one of them, a remarkable feat given the technology and standards of the day.

But a 5 percent success rate in stopping terrorists is not a passing grade. We had to do better.

In the immediate aftermath of 9/11, the government tried going back to the methods of the 1950s and 1960s. Every car was stopped. Every air passenger was interviewed and searched. The results were predictable. Soon, the wait at the Canadian border was measured in hours and miles, not minutes and yards. At airports, the lines grew longer and crawled to a halt.

It became clear why these methods had been abandoned nearly everywhere by the 1980s. They required that we give up the benefits of modern travel. We simply could not inspect every person crossing the border. And bad as 9/11 had been, we weren't willing to give up travel because of it.

By the time I came on board, DHS had begun to feel its way toward that path. The department was playing by ear. But a solution was beginning to emerge. The role of my policy office was to crystallize it.

We knew we couldn't inspect every passenger at the booth. We didn't have time. But if we could get enough information in advance, and analyze it quickly, we could conduct a "virtual inspection" before the passenger had even arrived. We could use what we knew about travelers to separate the business travelers who crossed the Atlantic every Sunday from travelers who needed a much closer look.

We didn't need to find terrorists using their travel data. We just needed to identify those travelers who ought to get more attention. They would be sent for a "secondary" inspection that more or less resembled what everyone went through at the border in 1950. They'd be interviewed at length and, if necessary, their luggage could be examined. It was the secondary inspection of Kahtani that kept him out of the country and off American Flight 77. With a bit of information about who was coming, and a clear sense of whom we wanted to keep out, we could supplement our officers' intuition, flagging suspect travelers and waving through the rest. We could concentrate our inspectors' talents on a smaller pool of more likely prospects.

We'd be diverting the growth of jet travel just a bit. We couldn't bring back the old system, but we could use new technology ourselves to restore a measure of security.

This was new. In the first half of the twentieth century, we couldn't have screened passengers before they arrived. Border systems then relied on personal interviews, visas, and passports because they had to. But now information technology was doubling in capability even faster than travel volume did. Data once was costly to retain, store, and analyze, but now it was becoming cheaper and easier every day.

What's more, the airlines whose passengers were overloading the old border system were using new technology to identify and manage the travel of those same passengers. If we could use *their* data to identify the handful of risky passengers who needed an interview, we could do our screening while the plane was in the air.

What information did we need? We boiled it down to three things.

First, we needed to know in advance who was coming to the United States. In theory, we could wait until the passenger showed up at the front of the line and presented his passport. We could then run his name through our computer systems to see what we already knew about him.

But in the real world, that would never work. Computer systems are never instantaneous, and the more information they process the slower they run. Everyone understands this. None of us turn on our computers and sit with our fingers on the keyboard while Windows boots up. We go and pour a cup of coffee, and when we return, our data is ready.

DHS needed the same thing—time to let the computer run before the passenger showed up for inspection. We couldn't afford to add any more time to primary screening. After all, with 90 million passengers arriving by air each year, adding even ten seconds to the average interview would add ten thousand extra days of waiting into the system. We also needed to process information in advance to avoid mistakes. The fewer decisions we forced border officers to make in thirty seconds or less, the less risk there was of error.

DHS already had some ways to find out who was coming to the United States. For countries where the visa requirement still applied, we knew which travelers had been given visas. We could prepare for those travelers before they showed up.

Things were worse if the travelers were coming from one of the two dozen countries for which we'd abolished the visa system. For these "visa waiver" travelers, we didn't know they were coming at all until they showed up at the booth in JFK in New York or Dulles Airport in Washington. Since half of our overseas travelers were from visa-waiver countries, this was a big hole.

We filled it by tapping the information systems the airlines were already using. In addition to the passenger manifests for each flight, we wanted information from the system the airline uses to keep track of travelers' reservations. This system usually contains a bit more information—such as whom the passenger is traveling with, the name of his travel agency, emergency contact information, and payment details. The data is not especially sensitive (it had better not be, since it is shared widely among airline personnel). But as the example of the 9/11 hijackers showed, travel reservations could be crucial to making connections between the travelers we were already aware of and their accomplices about whom we know nothing.

That was our answer to the first question: Who's coming?

And that begs the second question: Who shouldn't come?

Again, in the aftermath of 9/11, much progress had been made in answering this question. The shocking lack of coordination among the agencies tracking potential terrorists had ended. The consular officials who issue visas had access to the same consolidated list of potential threats as the DHS border officials, the CIA counterterrorism agents, and the FBI investigators.

That's important. But really, if you wanted to know which French travelers posed the greatest risk, would you ask the CIA? Or would you ask the French security agencies?

The right answer, of course, is "why not ask both?" We did. Unfortunately, the French weren't talking. Although the United States had made concerted efforts after 9/11 to get agreements with other countries to share lists of suspected terrorists, practically none acquiesced. We had a handful of agreements with close allies, but even countries like France and Germany had not signed up.

Outside of information about terrorism suspects, cooperation was even worse. We had practically no information about criminals crossing our borders. If a thirty-five-year-old British man showed up with a ten-year-old boy who was traveling with him, and DHS officials became suspicious of the relationship, they had no way of finding out whether the man had been convicted of molesting children in the UK. The Brits didn't share that information with us. Neither did any of our allies, with the exception of the Canadians.

Oddly, the Canadians would not give DHS a list of suspected terrorists, not even those living minutes from our unguarded border. But, perhaps because Canadian troopers stop Michigan drivers for speeding every day and need to know whether they're wanted, Canada and the United States have long exchanged data on the criminal records of their citizens. That was our only international criminal data exchange.

Whether a traveler's crimes were raising funds for a terrorist organization or smuggling drugs or both, and no matter how relevant they might be for the scrutiny he should get at the border, the traveler left his crimes behind him when he boarded the plane to the United States.

We were going to need more. We didn't have to take as gospel everything foreign governments said about their citizens, but we did need to know what they thought. Because if *they* were worried about a particular traveler, that was reason enough to ask him some questions before letting him into *our* country. We could make up our own minds, but we needed to get the information first.

The hard question was how we'd do that. Other countries weren't firmly opposed to sharing information. After all, that would make their border officials more effective, too. But sharing information with the United States was bound to meet some political resistance at home. Our allies needed help in overcoming that resistance.

In theory, the answers to the two questions "Who's coming?" and "Who shouldn't come?" make a complete screening system: We know who's coming, and we know who shouldn't be let in without a close look. But we have smart, adaptable adversaries. If our defense depends on knowing the names of the bad guys, the first thing that bad guys will do is change their names.

That leads to our third and last question: How do we know who is who? How can we be sure that the name on the manifest list and the passport is the right one?

We could start with better passports. Congress had already started us down a path to more secure passports. After 9/11, it declared that countries would lose their visa-free travel privileges if they did not adopt passports with improved security features, including an electronic chip to hold biometric data securely. Countries were also required to promptly report the identification numbers of lost and stolen blank passports so we could watch for what would otherwise be perfect forgeries made from official blanks.

The deadline for meeting these requirements would occur on our watch. If we held firm, we could radically reduce the risk of identity fraud. That in turn would bolster the effectiveness of our identity-based screening program.

But Tom Ridge's team had gone one step further to attack the identity theft problem. They had begun fingerprinting foreign visitors to the United States. Initially, they took only two fingerprints, because the main purpose of the prints was to tie a person to his name and passport biometrically. We couldn't necessarily stop all identity theft with the prints, but we could guarantee that, once a traveler presented himself and his passport under one name, he'd never be able to use a different name or passport without setting off alarms.

On examination, this was the most solid of the three legs on which a new approach to border security would rest. The Ridge team had launched many good initiatives designed to lock travelers to a single identity. It was up to us to bring them home successfully. We had to press our allies to adopt better passport technology and to report lost and stolen passports, using the leverage of the visa-waiver program. And we had to implement the fingerprint program successfully at a time when some countries were taking umbrage at the very idea. (Brazil had announced that it would fingerprint Americans in retaliation and then had jailed an American Airlines pilot who offered his middle finger to the officers administering the process.)

We ended up expanding these identification programs in several ways. We switched to gathering ten prints instead of two. This didn't add to the protection against identity theft, but it did give us a new way to identify those whom we wanted to keep out of the country. The Defense Department had begun to gather fingerprints in safe houses and even from the remnants of roadside bombs in Iraq and Afghanistan. We didn't know exactly whose prints they were, but if anyone who left prints on a roadside bomb ever showed up in the United States, we were sure we wanted to talk to him.

And rather than simply play defense in other countries, we went on the offensive, urging other countries to adopt compatible fingerprint systems for screening purposes. The more countries there were who had locked a person to his passport, the harder it would be for him to take on a new identity. By the time I left office, Japan had already begun implementing its own prints-at-the-border system, the UK was using prints for asylum applicants and was testing a border fingerprint system, and the European Union had announced plans for a similar system. Implementation, meanwhile, went so smoothly that protests petered out as travelers realized how little the process resembled being booked for a crime.

When we finished constructing the new border strategy, we were pleased. Commercial jet travel had completely overturned the border control measures that the United States and other countries had relied on for much of the twentieth century. And by the 1980s, border controls were under siege, collapsing as international travel continued to double each decade. But we didn't have to abandon control of our borders if we used information technology prudently. We could build a screening system that told us who was coming and whom we should look at closely, and we could satisfy any reasonable privacy concerns.

In fact, we were well down the road, thanks to Congress and our predecessors. The "who's coming" measures were already online, and so were the measures to lock travelers to a single identity.

As long as we kept these two initiatives on course, we could devote our main effort to getting data that would allow us to identify suspect travelers. Of course, doing that wouldn't be easy. We'd be fighting all the defenders the status quo could muster.

In the end, it would take a massive diplomatic effort, multiple international negotiations, a harsh battle with other departments and the National Security Council.

And a game of chicken with the entire European Union.

PART TWO | FLIGHT AND FACTS

5 Europe Picks a Privacy Fight

Jonathan Faull was laying down the law. Trim and articulate, Faull was a director general in the European Commission—the highest-ranking career official in Europe's executive branch.

We sat opposite each other in an Arlington high-rise with striking views across the Potomac to the Washington Monument and the Mall. A phalanx of other European officials was arrayed across formica tables from their DHS counterparts.

It was the first meeting of the U.S.-EU Policy Dialogue on Border and Transportation Security since I had become head of policy for the Department of Homeland Security.

And it wasn't going well.

The policy dialogue was a fancy name for regular meetings between top officials at the Department of Homeland Security and the European Commission. It had been advertised as a good way to work with like-minded countries. Why go to twenty-seven European capitals, the commission had argued, when you can come to Brussels and talk to all of Europe? But we were constantly surprised at how contentious the dialogue seemed to be. Weren't we allies? Wasn't the fight against terrorism something we all shared? Somehow that didn't make the talks less combative.

Today, as so often recently, the contention focused on airline reservation data. The European Union, Faull said, had now completed its review of DHS's compliance with the rules for how to handle airline reservation data. European inspectors had sent DHS a questionnaire to complete, had reviewed DHS's operations in the field, and then had spent a day quizzing DHS officials about their practices.

The European Union was not completely satisfied. The inspectors had found substantial compliance with the rules, Faull acknowledged, but this compliance had come too slowly, and there was plenty of room for improvement in the department's handling of reservation data. Faull made it clear that the commission would be watching closely in future. And next year, he promised, there would be another inspection and another report.

Faull is a formidable man. He had served in important positions throughout the European Commission—overcoming by sheer ability the innate suspicion that all British officials must endure in Brussels, where Brits are viewed as not truly committed to the European project. Despite this handicap, Faull had risen to the top of the European Commission's fastest-growing directorate—the directorate of Justice, Freedom and Security.

That wasn't helping him today. Perhaps it was just his accent or the continental tailoring of his suit, but to the Americans it seemed that a whiff of condescension hung in the air.

DHS was being schooled. The department may have passed its midterm exam, but by European standards it was not a particularly good student. "The U.S. gets a B," the German who led the review told one DHS official. Europe would expect a better performance next time.

If the department did not meet European standards, Faull made clear, the European Commission could declare that United States privacy law was not "adequate." That in turn would cut off the flow of airline reservation data that DHS was using to keep terrorists out of a still-traumatized United States.

The threat was deadly serious.

The roots of this conflict could be found in the rubble of the World Trade Center. In the weeks after the attacks, Americans asked how we could have missed the evidence that attacks were being planned on American soil.

Our attention soon focused on the wall between the intelligence agencies looking for terrorists and the law enforcement agencies charged with investigating crimes. Appalled at the failure to connect the dots, lawmakers asked why the wall had been raised so high between investigators with a common mission. There was no evidence that the wall had ever done much to protect civil liberties, but evidence of the harm it could do was still smoking in two American cities.

Backed by Congress, the Bush administration immediately acted to tear down the wall. Three separate laws passed between 2001 and 2004 required the sharing of all terrorism data among intelligence and law enforcement agencies. After that, Congress must have thought, there could be no barriers left; information on terrorists would have to be shared throughout the United States government.

At the same time that the wall and its costs were being publicly debated, a second lesson from the attacks was circulating quietly through the administration. An analysis of the hijackers' airline reservations showed that the entire plot could have been broken up if authorities had simply gotten access to the airline's travel reservation systems.

Remember the two terrorists the FBI was looking for but could not find in August 2001? It turned out that they could have been found easily if the government had simply had access to airplane reservation data. And, once the two were found, reservation data would have exposed links to nearly a dozen of the other hijackers, who shared addresses, phone numbers, or frequent flyer numbers with the known terrorists.

Though this analysis was not widely discussed in public, it had an immediate effect on Congress. Less than two months after the September 11 terrorist attacks, in the Aviation and Transportation Security Act of 2001[1], Congress required all air carriers to provide airline reservation data for travelers flying into the country. The data, known as "passenger name records" or PNR, would supplement information drawn from the passenger manifest for each flight. (Airline manifests contain basic information on all passengers and crew on a particular flight.) By requiring that the airlines turn over PNR and manifest information for all passengers arriving from overseas, Congress ensured that border authorities would be able to perform the analysis that was not done in the days before September 11.

When DHS took over border management, it expanded the information systems used to screen arriving passengers. And we had made passenger travel data central to our new strategy. It told us two things: who was coming and who was risky. Knowing who was coming from Western Europe was especially important. Because no visas were required to travel from Western Europe, without the airline information we would be left in the dark until the passengers showed up at the customs booth. The data was also useful in figuring out who was risky. As the 9/11 hijacker data showed, we could sometimes find risky travelers because the reservation data exposed hidden connections among the passengers.

That's certainly what it did in June 2003.

It was an unseasonably cool day at Chicago's O'Hare international airport. DHS border inspectors were busy but not overwhelmed. The U.S.-led war to topple Saddam Hussein's Ba'athist regime in Iraq had been launched a little less than three months earlier. Fear of terrorism had kept some would-be passengers from the skies, but O'Hare was still operating at a fairly brisk pace.

A Jordanian man named Ra'ed al-Banna was among the throng of passengers who had just arrived on KLM flight 611 from Amsterdam. After waiting in line, al-Banna presented his passport to a U.S. Customs and Border Protection officer.

Without the computerized targeting system and data drawn from airline reservations and past travel, the officer would have had less than a minute's worth of information with which to make a decision about al-Banna. He could look at al-Banna's passport, and he could ask him a question or two. Unless there was something distinctly odd about the passport or the answers, al-Banna would be waved along, just like the mass of international travelers queuing behind him.

Al-Banna had a legitimate Jordanian passport; he held a valid visa that allowed him to work in the United States; and he had visited the United States before for a lengthy stay.

Short, dark, and good-looking, he was entirely comfortable in the West; he spoke English well and knew Nirvana from Nine-Inch Nails. On a quick look, there was no reason not to admit him; his paperwork was in order.

But on June 13, 2003, the data in the system called for a closer look. Al-Banna was sent to secondary inspection, where officers could inspect his luggage and documents and question him more closely. They asked him about his past travel to the United States, and the longer he talked, the less comfortable the officers became. They weren't satisfied that he was being completely truthful in his answers. They decided to refuse him admission. They took al-Banna's picture and fingerprints and put him on a plane back to Jordan.

So far it was a fairly routine day at the border. Not until nearly two years later did events in Iraq give it a new and troubling significance.

On February 28, 2005, at about 8:30 in the morning, several hundred police recruits were lined up outside a clinic in Hilla, a city in the south of Iraq. With no warning, a car drove into the crowd and detonated a massive bomb. One hundred thirty-two people were killed, and about as many were wounded. It was the deadliest suicide bombing Iraq had seen, and the death toll remains one of the highest of the war.

The driver was Ra'ed al-Banna. It wasn't easy to identify him. But when the authorities found the steering wheel of his car, his forearm was still chained to it.

A few days later, his father in Jordan got a short phone call from Iraq. "We congratulate you on the martyrdom of Raed," the caller said. To this day, the family insists that they had no clue when al-Banna decided to join the extremists.

The al-Banna case is the one DHS officials talked about most often, but it wasn't the only one. Every port of entry has a story about terrorist suspects turned away or smugglers identified using reservation data.

In Atlanta, for example, DHS officials at the airport spotted a member of a Pakistani extremist organization flying in from South America. The man had previously been identified conducting surveillance of the American ambassador to Argentina and trying to enter the U.S. Embassy under the guise of official business. That was a victory for the automated targeting system. Even better, the DHS officers found that the extremist's travel reservations linked him to two other travelers. Without that data, these previously unknown radicals would have entered the United States easily. With it, DHS officers quickly got them to admit that they were traveling together.

In Minneapolis, DHS officials acting on a tip from the unit that evaluates targeting data stopped a Qatari student with a valid visa. On inspection, it turned out that his laptop contained clips showing various improvised explosive devices exploding against soldiers and vehicles as well as a manual in Arabic on how to make the devices. Perhaps most troubling, the file also contained images of the student reading his will and quoting the Koran. Charged criminally based on his statements during secondary inspection, the traveler pleaded guilty to visa fraud.

In Newark, DHS officers noticed a woman returning from the Dominican Republic with her children. That didn't seem unusual until the officers examined her travel reservation data. Then they discovered that she hadn't taken the kids with her on the outbound flight. After more digging, they found that the woman had made many trips to the Caribbean island nation. Each time she left without children; each time she returned with them; and each time they were different children.

More research in the system uncovered links between this woman and other travelers. It turned out that many of them had the same travel patterns—they would leave the United States alone and come back with children. The travelers were members of an international child-smuggling ring, and reservation data was the key to taking it down.

The value of reservation data was well-established. And its privacy impact was small; this wasn't especially sensitive information, and it was already being shared by travel agents, airlines, baggage handlers, and the like.

So why, I wondered, was Jonathan Faull trying to put limits on its use to fight terrorism? How did Europe come to enlist in such an unlikely privacy crusade?

In the summer of 2002, less than a year after the 9/11 attacks, the last of the debris from the World Trade Center had just been removed. The final steel girder standing—the Stars and Stripes beam—had been cut down in a moving ceremony. The remaining recovery workers scrawled messages on it; some touched it as though it were a coffin.

But Europe's attention had already focused on how to roll back the measures the United States had taken to protect itself from repeat attacks. That summer, the European Commission approached the United States and lodged a formal objection to the gathering of travel reservation data on passengers flying from the European Union.

U.S. rules for handling the data were simply not "adequate," the European Union declared. Unless the United States accepted European limits on how travel information could be gathered and processed, Brussels said, European airlines would be forbidden to supply the information.

The Europeans had just fired the first shot in an international privacy war—a war between countries that ought to have been on the same side.

Oddly, the road to confrontation began with a moment of transatlantic convergence. In 1973, as computerized records began to spread through government, a U.S. government advisory committee recommended a code of fair information practices. The code prohibited secret data systems, gave all individuals the right to find out what information had been recorded about them and to correct erroneous records, and insisted that information obtained for one purpose must not be used for other purposes without the individual's consent.

In 1974, the U.S. Congress enacted the Privacy Act[2], which enshrined these principles and more in law. European nations were equally eager to regulate in the field. A British advisory committee recommended similar guidelines. Sweden, France, and Germany all enacted data protection laws in the 1970s, and all of them contained similar principles. By 1980, the Council of Europe and the Organization for Economic Cooperation and Development (OECD) had both recommended a similar set of guidelines to all developed nations.

The American policy initiative seemed to have sparked a remarkable confluence of laws across the Atlantic. It's the sort of thing that ought to make an internationalist's heart grow warm—the laws of nations gradually growing together as international dialogue produces transnational consensus.

No such luck. What these broadly parallel laws in fact yielded was three decades of bitter transatlantic conflict.

Part of the problem was cultural. Americans, with their suspicion of government, had been quick to apply the privacy principles to government databases but slower to apply them to the private sector. In Europe, where government was more trusted than the private sector, privacy laws were written more broadly to cover all personal data in private hands. To enforce the rules, privacy bureaucracies sprang up across the continent.

But the deeper problem was European unease about the growth of data processing, and the transfer of data across national borders. Labor unions in Europe feared that their jobs would move to the United States, where it was often cheaper to process data during the 1970s and 1980s. One French justice official saw even broader implications saying in 1977 that, "Information is power, and economic information is economic power. Information has an economic value and the ability to store and process certain types of data may well give one country political and technological advantage over other countries. This in turn may lead to a loss of national sovereignty through supranational data flows."[3]

Against this background, the new data-protection laws were a godsend for European policymakers. If U.S. law could somehow be characterized as inadequate to protect European data, then the data could not be sent to the United States. The data processing jobs would stay in Europe, as would the "political and technological advantage" the French justice official worried about.[4]

In the end, European authorities didn't have much trouble deciding that U.S. laws were inadequate. They focused on the limited nature of U.S. privacy regulations for the private sector. In Europe, to take one example, it was unlawful for companies to sell their customer lists to junk mail companies; in the United States it was not. So if those lists were sent to the United States, European authorities thought, no law would prevent them from being used to send junk mail to Europeans. To prevent such an end run on European law, the authorities declared, the data would have to stay in Europe.

The United States, in turn, saw the ban on exporting data to "inadequate" countries as simply a clever bit of protectionism. In a wide variety of international forums, the United States argued that personal data should be freely transferred among jurisdictions as long as the data-protection regimes were comparable. The debate festered for nearly twenty years.

Then in 1995 the European Commission stopped debating and acted; its new directive on data protection made the export ban official EU policy. No personal data could be transferred, the directive declared, to countries that do not provide an "adequate" level of protection. To be deemed adequate, countries would have to adopt laws that more or less parroted the language of the European directive. Everyone knew that the United States would not simply adopt laws written in some other capital. A confrontation seemed inevitable until, in 1998, the United States and the EU found a compromise. They agreed that, under a "safe harbor" arrangement[5], U.S. companies could promise to follow EU law even while processing data in the United States and that the United States would enforce the companies' promises. In return, Europe agreed to allow "safe harbor" companies to transfer their data freely across the Atlantic.

From a European point of view, this was a great symbolic victory. The EU had branded the United States an inadequate defender of personal data, and it had used a combination of economic clout and moral suasion—European soft power—to make the charge stick. Europe's "adequacy" requirement was gradually forcing countries and companies around the world to adopt European privacy standards. Perhaps the EU could hear a faint echo of the old days, when statutes written in a European capital automatically became law in many distant lands. That one of those distant lands might be the United States seemed particularly satisfying. The EU liked how the privacy conflict was playing out.

All of the conflict had so far centered on regulation of the private sector. For good reason. The United States had not been slow to apply privacy principles to government. Indeed, its enthusiasm for imposing privacy limits on government exceeded that of the Europeans. And there was no history in Europe of restricting data transfers to countries whose *governments* might misuse it.

But that was about to change.

America marked the first anniversary of the September 11 attacks with candlelight vigils and memorial ceremonies. Near Washington, construction crews raced to finish rebuilding the Pentagon. In New York former Mayor Rudolph Giuliani and a host of other officials joined in reading every victim's name at Ground Zero.

In Europe, meanwhile, the attack on U.S. antiterrorism policy was well underway. A working party of data protection officials was putting the finishing touches on a report that slammed the United States for gathering travel reservation data without "adequate" safeguards. The report acknowledged that "sovereign States do have discretion over the information that they can require from persons wishing to gain entry to their country."[6] But, it went on, U.S. sovereignty could not trump European data-protection standards. The U.S. proposal to collect travel data, the privacy officials declared, was inadequate because the data "could be used for routine purposes related to immigration [and] customs as well as more generally for US national security and may at least be shared amongst all US federal agencies."[7]

The European commission member responsible for the internal market, Frits Bolkestein, was even more blunt: "It is the sovereign right of the United States to determine the conditions under which people may enter its territory. But it is Europe's sovereign right to insist that personal data concerning its citizens enjoy adequate safeguards when transferred to other countries."[8]

At the time, a privacy assault on DHS's travel reservation program seemed like good politics on both sides of the Atlantic. While Congress had authorized access to travel reservations for overseas flights, it had not authorized DHS to review domestic flight data, and support for domestic access was eroding. As we'll see in Chapter 8, the ACLU and other privacy groups had targeted the domestic program for defeat, and they were close to winning. DHS was embroiled in claims that JetBlue and other airlines had violated privacy standards when testing the domestic program. Bolkestein welcomed the flap.

"I may be just about the only person who felt reassured after reading about how JetBlue surrendered passenger records to a firm working for the government," Bolkestein declared, because "I am confident that publicity for cases of this kind and the understandable outrage that they provoke will help to ensure that reasonable counsels in Washington prevail as regards the limits that must be set on the security-enhancing uses of passenger data."[9]

Bolkestein was accurately reading the mood in Washington. Congressional unease about the domestic travel data program grew rapidly in 2003. Sen. Ron Wyden (D-OR) took the lead in raising questions, and by the fall of 2003, he had successfully inserted language into the DHS appropriations bill imposing harsh new restrictions on implementation of any domestic travel data program.

Under siege on the Hill and facing hard lobbying from a financially strapped air industry, DHS had no stomach for a fight with Brussels. It buckled, agreeing to European demands and setting limits on how it would handle travel reservation data. In return the European Commission declared DHS's revamped program "adequate."

The agreement, negotiated during 2003 and early 2004, was meant to put the travel data debate on ice. It didn't. Reservation data was still a point of contention when I arrived almost two years later. Many Europeans politicians felt that they hadn't extracted enough concessions from DHS; they wanted a rematch. At the same time, the more Secretary Chertoff and I studied the deal, the less we liked it.

Chertoff was a former prosecutor. He'd sent a lot of people to jail after trials in which the defendants claimed that the prosecutor and police had violated the defendant's civil liberties and privacy. Every good prosecutor has developed a thick skin for such claims. And I'd been general counsel of the National Security Agency. I, too, had gotten used to separating responsible privacy claims from irresponsible ones.

What's more, both Chertoff and I had personal experience with the wall between law enforcement and intelligence. We were appalled at the idea that foreign governments would reimpose such a catastrophic policy on the United States within a few years of 9/11.

But that's what the agreement did. Pursuing its own notion of what privacy requires, the EU had insisted that that the Customs and Border Protection agency (CBP), and only that agency, would have access to reservation data. The FBI, the CIA, NSA, and the National Counter Terrorism Center, even other parts of DHS—all were on the wrong side of the new European-built wall.

My staff counted nearly a dozen limits that the agreement imposed on sharing of potentially valuable counterterrorism information with these agencies; they made practical interagency use of the data nearly impossible. In addition to this critical objection, there were three or four other practical problems with the deal that we feared could get Americans killed.

Some data was off-limits entirely, for example. European law treats certain kinds of information as "sensitive." This category includes information relating to union membership, race, ethnicity, sex life, and health status. Now, airlines do not ordinarily ask people whether they belong to trade unions, or what their sex life is like. We didn't see much need for a special rule to cover such data, but the European negotiators had insisted on incorporating a provision from European law that set strict limits on the collection of sensitive information. Actually, they went further than European law, making a special and more restrictive rule that only applied to American authorities, prohibiting any DHS access to "sensitive" data. We didn't mind giving up access to the one routinely gathered bit of "sensitive" data—passengers' meal choices, where a *halal* or kosher meal preference might disclose a passenger's religion. But we were troubled by the absolute ban on collecting sensitive information. A passenger's health status is also considered sensitive information. What if DHS received intelligence that terrorists planned to smuggle explosives onto a plane using a wheelchair or a leg cast? Were we prohibited from finding out which travelers had boarded in casts or wheelchairs?

The agreement also restricted DHS's ability to spot problems early. DHS was prohibited from gathering information more than seventy-two hours prior to a flight; and once it began pulling information, it could do so only four times before the flight took off. This greatly limited DHS's ability to watch for the early stages of a large plot. And it made no sense. How did such an arbitrary rule help privacy?

Finally, the data could be used for only seven days. After that, the information could be stored for limited reviews, but it would all have to be destroyed within three and a half years. These restrictions also made no sense if we wanted to use the data to identify unknown terrorists. Al Qaeda and other terrorist groups had already been in operation for well over twenty years, and some of their plots had taken many years to develop. Since terrorists are less likely to use good tradecraft early in their careers, the destruction requirement could prevent DHS from using their early travel patterns and associates to connect the dots.

I had one more problem with the agreement. I'd spent years in private practice giving data-protection advice to companies, advising them on U.S. and European law, the Safe Harbor, and transfers of personal data across borders. I was already quite familiar with the 1995 directive.

And from everything I knew, the EU's claim that its airlines needed an "adequacy" agreement before they could give us data was claptrap. Diplomatically convenient claptrap, but claptrap all the same.

The airlines had at least five good defenses against liability. For example, the directive allows the processing of data "in the public interest or in the exercise of official authority."[10] This is the provision that allows companies to cooperate when the government asks for information, and there was no footnote in the directive saying that American government requests weren't "official."

The second defense was even better; the directive expressly allows transfers of data even to "inadequate" jurisdictions if "the transfer is necessary for the performance of a contract."[11] That was squarely on point, I thought. An airline ticket is a contract, and the airline could not perform the contract if it didn't comply with U.S. law, including our requirement to deliver reservation data.

A third strong defense was provided by the directive's language allowing transfers of data that are "necessary or legally required on important public interest grounds."[12] DHS's legal requirement was meant to keep terrorists off planes, and that surely qualified as an "important public interest."

That gave rise to the fourth good defense. We figured that keeping terrorists off planes would be good for the other travelers on those planes, and the directive also exempts transfers that are "necessary in order to protect the vital interests" of the person providing the data.[13]

Finally, a fifth defense was independent of all the others. The directive allows transfers of personal data to an "inadequate" jurisdiction when the data concerns someone who "has given his consent unambiguously to the proposed transfer."[14] So if push came to shove, the airlines could simply tell customers that their information was required by the U.S. government and get their consent. Most of them would give it willingly; those who did not could take their vacations elsewhere.

Those were a lot of defenses. And even if they all failed, the worst that could happen to an airline was that it might lose a case and face a fine. Since it could also be fined for not complying with U.S. law, the airline would be faced with two inconsistent orders from two different governments.

That's not good, but it wasn't necessarily a reason for the United States to back down. The Europeans wouldn't want to put their airlines in that pickle either. Yet somehow DHS had been persuaded to rebuild the wall just to avoid the *possibility* that some day an airline would face such a choice.

It sounded like a bad deal to me.

So even with a bright sun streaming over the national mall and through the windows of the Arlington high-rise, tension began to build as soon we turned to the agreement. We were discussing a provision that was particularly offensive from an American perspective. European emotions had run so high on the privacy issue that European negotiators refused to rely on U.S. promises to implement the agreement. Instead, the agreement required the United States to stand for inspection once a year. A joint review would be conducted each year so that the European Union could satisfy itself that the United States really was doing what it had promised.

The first such review had just occurred in the fall of 2005. The European Commission sent a questionnaire that DHS had to answer. DHS's Privacy Office conducted an independent investigation and issued a 45-page report card on DHS's compliance with the undertakings.[15] DHS then opened its doors to a delegation of European officials insisting that they had to inspect the department's facilities; it spent a long day answering the delegation's pointed questions.

At last, the Europeans had issued their own lengthy report giving DHS that reluctant "B."[16] They complained about how long our compliance took, and they had several suggestions about ambiguities that DHS should clear up and improvements that DHS should adopt. They seemed to be settling in for years of audits, of auditors' reports demanding remedial actions, and of follow-up audits to make sure we carried out the demands. It looked as though the United States would never be off probation.

As Faull rehearsed these complaints, I had finally had enough.

"You know," I broke in, "you shouldn't push your luck. If I'd been here last year, DHS never would have signed that agreement."

The room went silent. This wasn't in the script.

But Faull did not back off. On he went, dwelling on our minor failings and demanding assurances that seemed to go beyond what the agreement required. The longer he talked, the deeper my conviction grew.

This was a bad deal. We needed to get out.

But why spend time on this issue now? I wondered. I don't like the deal, but it's done. It still has years to run. The Europeans should put it in the win column, I thought, and move on.

The Europeans, it turned out, couldn't let it go because they didn't see it as a win. Indeed, the European Commission's negotiator had been reassigned (some said fired) because the European side thought that the final deal was too easy on the United States. The whole arrangement was still under fire in Brussels. It had become tied up in Brussels's institutional politics. Traditionally, the EU has been run by the European Commission, Europe's executive branch. In fact, for years there was no legislative branch at all. The institution was not taken seriously until the late 1990s, when a revolt in Parliament forced the resignation of an entire commission.

Now the European Parliament was flexing its muscles, and the airline reservation conflict was tailor-made for legislative grandstanding. The European Parliament had played no part in the negotiations, so the parliament found it easy to say that the commission could have gotten a better deal. That view was shared by a committee of the European Union's data protection commissioners—the continent's top privacy bureaucrats. They too were sure that the commission could have extracted more concessions from the United States.

Hoping to make good on its complaints, the European Parliament had challenged the agreement in the European Court of Justice. It claimed that DHS's program did not meet the privacy standards set by the European Convention on Human Rights. It also made a second, more technical, objection: The EU's agreement with the United States was beyond the commission's authority.[17]

The second argument grew from the EU's gradual, and often contested, assertion of ever-greater authority over member states. The European Union was, first and foremost, a customs and economic union. When it built on that "first pillar," it had broad authority to set the terms of private commercial activity across the continent. But if it wanted to set rules affecting diplomacy, national security, or law enforcement its authority rested on a different and weaker pillar; it could only act in these areas with the unanimous consent of the member states. The deal with the United States was about law enforcement, Parliament argued, not economics; the arrangement was built on the wrong pillar and so must be held unlawful.

If the best deals are the ones where everyone ends up unhappy, the negotiators of this one had done a superb job. DHS's leadership abhorred it; we couldn't wait for it to expire.

And most of Brussels held the same view.

Both sides thought they could do better if they tore up the agreement and started again from scratch. If the European Court of Justice ruled against the deal, we were going to get our wish.

We couldn't both be right, of course. One of us had miscalculated. Badly.

6 | To the Brink

On May 30, 2006, we got what we had hoped for. And so did the European Parliament.

The European court struck down the agreement.[1] But only on the jurisdictional ground. The European Court of Justice was reluctant to decide just how much human rights law Europe could impose on the United States. Instead of finding U.S. law "inadequate," it ruled that the commission had fatally mixed up the commercial and the criminal enforcement pillars.[2]

The agreement was dead. But the court agreed to keep it on life support a little longer. Europe, after all, didn't want to kill the agreement right away. It wanted a renegotiation. Unless the court granted a grace period, there would be no time for DHS and the commission to put the arrangement on a new and proper basis. Accommodating the European negotiating interest, the court delayed the effective date of its decision for four months. The adequacy finding would expire on September 30.

On that date, if we did not have a new agreement, the "adequacy" determination would come to an end. Airlines flying to the United States would have no special protection from European data-protection law. But they would still have to comply with U.S. law requiring them to submit reservation data on all their passengers.

For the airlines, September 30 marked the beginning of Armageddon. Without a new agreement, they would face conflicting legal obligations. The European Union's data-protection law would require them to withhold reservation data from the "inadequate" United States. At the same time, U.S. law would require them to hand it over.

If worse came to worst, the airlines that observed U.S. law could be prosecuted criminally and fined by European privacy bureaucrats. And those that refused to comply with U.S. law would be fined by DHS and could lose their landing privileges. Chaos would ensue. Some airlines might cancel flights. Those that flew would fly in fear.

Or so the Europeans thought. Me, not so much. I had confidence in the airlines' defenses to a privacy claim. And I was eager to put my theory to the test.

Oddly, then, the court's decision was welcomed on both sides of the Atlantic. The European Parliament was celebrating, as were European privacy bureaucrats. They had not won a human rights condemnation of the United States, but they were sure that a new negotiation would bring the United States to heel. This time they'd insist on a tougher line. This time they would get the privacy protections they wanted by threatening to throw all transatlantic travel into disarray.

DHS was just as pleased. We, too, thought the old arrangement was unacceptable. And, like the European Parliament and the privacy bureaucrats, we were confident that we could get a better deal the second time around.

Faull called as soon as the court's decision was formally announced.

—I don't think this is a surprise, he began, but I wanted you to hear it from me. The European Court of Justice has invalidated the PNR agreement.

It wasn't a surprise. I was delighted. But this was no time to say so.

—I remember quite well your remarks at the dialogue last year, Faull continued. I understand that you don't like the agreement. And of course we appreciate that the agreement was scheduled to be renewed next year.

What was going on here? I wondered. Jonathan Faull seemed surprisingly muted. He couldn't possibly agree that the deal should be tossed out.

—Under the court's decision, Faull added, we have only four months to find a substitute agreement and to avoid a crisis in transatlantic travel. That is not enough time to complete the careful review and negotiation that I know you'll want.

Ah, I thought, now I see where he's going. Very clever.

—There's an easy way to make this work, he went on. The problem is purely a matter of EU procedure. If the EU approves the agreement under our third pillar procedure, we can solve the problem. So I'd like to get your agreement to simply adopt the same agreement but put it on a different pillar. It will still expire in 2007, and I know you will want to renegotiate it. We will do that, in an orderly way, starting very soon. But we should fix this awkwardness without trying to negotiate with our backs against a four-month deadline. We don't want chaos on September 30.

I took a breath. Faull was being cautious, keeping emotion out of the call. I would do the same. But this proposal was utterly unacceptable. The European court had given us our best chance to remake the agreement, or kill it, and I had no interest in postponing the opportunity.

—Thanks, Jonathan, I said. I understand your thinking. It's like that scene from *Indiana Jones*, where Jones tries to quickly put a bag of sand in place of an idol. Do it fast enough, and perhaps no one will notice the change. But if I remember right, that scene ended with Jones running for his life and a giant boulder rolling after him.

—So I don't want to encourage you to think we'll take the Indiana Jones option. If we don't, though, I promise that we'll do all we can to avoid chaos four months from now.

—I understand, said Faull. Just so you know, I will be seeking a mandate from the European Council authorizing me to negotiate for renewal of the agreement as it now stands. And I hope you will obtain authority to do the same.

—Completely understood, I said, which is what you say in international negotiations when the other side says something you have no intention of agreeing to.

It was an odd conversation, I thought, after we hung up. Faull knew how strongly I felt about the evil the agreement was working;

and he must be under pressure to make progress on the privacy agenda of the European Parliament. Yet there had been no fireworks, no posturing. We had barely sparred.

Why not? The answer was in Faull's mention of his negotiating mandate. The fact was that neither of us had permission to stake out a position. The first task for each of us was to bring our own side into alignment. Only then could we engage each other.

Many negotiations in the private sector skip this step entirely. When negotiating the sale of a house, both the buyer and the seller know what price they want. At the negotiating table, buyer and seller exchange offers; they can decide quickly whether to accept or reject the other's offer. Even in the private sector, however, negotiations may be more complex. If the seller offers to re-shingle the roof rather than reduce the price, the couple buying a house may have to negotiate between themselves before deciding whether to insist on a price reduction or to settle for the new roof.

Government negotiations are closer to the second scenario, except that the buyer has to contend not just with a spouse, but with a mother-in-law, two uncles, and the guy next door who wandered in to borrow a hedge trimmer and has strong views on shingles. Arriving at a single U.S. position for international talks is in itself a major negotiation.

"I always knew when the United States had clear negotiating goals," one British diplomat told a State Department friend of mine in a moment of candor. "Then, they'd just send a negotiator. As soon as they sent an interagency team, I knew they couldn't agree on a final position. The team was there to make sure the lead negotiator didn't go beyond his authority."

Most of the time, he might have added, the United States sent a team.

So did the European Union. The EU has heavily laden processes for getting authority to negotiate anything, particularly with the United States. Any negotiations require a formal mandate from the ambassadors representing twenty-seven nations, all of whom have their own special interests and relationships with the United States. In the best of times, the commission would have had difficulty bringing all twenty-seven to a single position.

But in this case, there were more than twenty-seven agendas to reconcile. The parliament was clamoring for a greater role—and a tougher line. So were the privacy bureaucrats. And because the next negotiations would be based on third pillar authorities, the Brussels institutions that stand atop the third pillar would expect primacy. Those institutions—the European Council and the European presidency (held by a different nation every six months)—have little role in commercial negotiations but would expect a large one now.

As he tried to find consensus, Faull's advantage, a powerful one in any government debate, was inertia. That was his best argument for the quick deal he'd proposed—simply taking the old agreement and putting it on a new jurisdictional pillar. Restoring the status quo would disappoint the parliament and the data-protection bureaucracy, which hoped to squeeze more concessions out of the United States. But they didn't understand the risk they were running, Faull must have thought. Reopening the agreement meant reopening everything, not just the issues the parliament wanted to raise. That, he knew, would play into DHS's hands.

My remarks the year before had made clear that a complete renegotiation was precisely what we wanted. Al Qaeda was looking for radicalized Western Europeans who needed no visas across the Atlantic to attack the United States; passenger name records and advance passenger information were the earliest line of defense that DHS had against these travelers. Why should DHS agree to destroy that data quickly, or to look at it in a tiny window that opened only seventy-two hours before the flight? Why should it put information out of bounds that might reveal plots involving leg casts or wheelchairs or false pregnancies? Why should we let privacy advocates or European negotiators determine in advance what information was useful to DHS and what was not?

I knew where DHS stood. The agreement would have to be rethought and renegotiated from the ground up. All that remained was to get the uncles and cousins and mothers-in-law that made up the interagency process to agree.

That would be my toughest challenge. The costs of the PNR agreement (in time, money and limitations) fell entirely on DHS. They didn't inconvenience any other agency. But the cost of reopening the deal would certainly be felt by other agencies. The State Department had an interest in smooth relations with Europe. It didn't need another dispute if it could avoid one.

DHS had allies, of a sort. Defense and the intelligence community wanted a more effective border defense system, and better information about travelers. They too believed in information sharing. But like the other agencies, they had little stake in particular DHS programs.

As I sketched the roster of supporters and adversaries that I'd face in the interagency debates, the Justice Department was the wild card. It should have been with us. After all, during the first passenger name record negotiations under Tom Ridge, the Justice Department had fought to keep DHS from making concessions on things like information sharing. Justice had been right, I thought, and our entire negotiating strategy would be aimed at taking back that concession. What's more, the Brussels approach was a threat to Justice too. The EU was using the privacy issue as a wedge to create new tensions in the law-enforcement relationship between the United States and Europe. Instead of relying on exchanges with the United States, Brussels wanted to build its own European institutions, such as Europol and Eurojust. So it was strengthening law enforcement exchanges within Europe at the same time that it was raising barriers to sharing of information across the Atlantic.

As I saw it, Justice and the FBI were in the same boat as DHS. The European approach—using the data-protection issue to slowly throttle investigative information exchanges with the United States—was irresponsible. It was going to get Americans—and Europeans—killed. Justice and the FBI should be as eager as DHS to confront

Brussels and back the EU away from this tactic. Wasn't that why Justice had tried to keep DHS from agreeing to the PNR arrangement in the first place?

Now that I was ready to admit that Justice had been right all along, I hoped the two agencies could make common cause to undo the worst aspects of the PNR arrangement.

It was not to be. Justice was still smarting from what it had lost when DHS was created. Until DHS came along, the uncontested representative of U.S. law enforcement abroad had always been the Department of Justice. The FBI was the biggest single federal law-enforcement agency. There might be more law enforcement officials elsewhere in the federal government, but they were specialized and dispersed. Now, though, DHS had pulled most of those law enforcers into one department. DHS's border and investigative duties matched well the responsibilities of interior ministers in other countries. They saw DHS as a natural partner. None of that was good for Justice. And Justice's pique at having to share the table with a second law-enforcement agency was making it hard for us to work together.

I thought that in the end Justice would be foolish not to stand with us. This wasn't just a renewal of the old deal. It would be the first explicit law-enforcement arrangement to set these kinds of data restrictions. For the first time, we'd be taking rules that were written for Safeway and Allstate and agreeing that they could apply to the FBI and Customs and Border Patrol. Once that happened, there'd be more and more demands from Europe to expand the principle—to make us run our criminal and antiterrorism investigations in accord with European standards and sensibilities.

My first job was to come up with a negotiating position—and a strategy—and then to sell it to the rest of the government. The negotiating position fell naturally from the many problems I'd found in my first review of the deal—the wall; the strict ten-day limit on using the data; an annual review that felt like an annual renegotiation; and an arbitrary and dangerous ban on ever using "sensitive data." Our position, I thought, was simple: any new deal would have to cure all of these problems before it would be acceptable. To this list, I added another negotiating goal. I thought any new agreement would need a much tougher reciprocity clause.

At bottom a reciprocity clause means that the rules are the same for both sides of an agreement. I did not believe that European data protection law really demanded as much from law-enforcement agencies as the Europeans had claimed. There had never been a European investigation finding fault with Russian or Chinese or Syrian investigative agencies' use of information obtained from European companies. Was that because their law enforcement agencies had a better privacy record than U.S. agencies? Indeed, there had been practically no efforts to set data-protection standards for *European* law-enforcement agencies.

I suspected that the harsh rules in the 2004 arrangement had been made up by Europeans especially for Americans—that they wouldn't dream of applying the same rules to their own police agencies. But that suspicion undercut the whole rationale of the agreement, which was supposedly to force the United States to live up to high European standards for handling European data. If European privacy standards weren't as high as claimed, we should be able to reduce our own to match the European reality. A tough reciprocity requirement would provide long-term strategic flexibility for DHS; at any time, we could modify our undertakings if it turned out that Europe wasn't following the same rules.

This was an ambitious negotiating agenda, particularly since the Europeans were hoping to get new concessions—not to give them. To overcome their resistance, we needed a strategy. The strategy I came up with was simple but risky: Either the agreement would be completely overhauled or we would let it expire on September 30. I knew the pressure that the European Commission was under to get a better deal than in 2004. We could only combat that pressure if the United States was willing to let the agreement fail entirely.

The last time a deal on travel data had been negotiated, the risk of chaos in the skies over the Atlantic had been used to bludgeon DHS into a quick settlement. This time around, buoyed by my own sense that the threat of chaos was overwrought, I was willing to let the September 30 deadline pass without an agreement.

If we went to the brink, I believed, the Europeans would cave. And if we went beyond, well, we'd find out who was right—the European prophets of doom or the DHS leaders who thought the threat was mostly manufactured.

To take that stance, the United States had to be willing to live with the consequences—expiration of the September 30 deadline without an agreement that protected the airlines. But were we?

I needed to persuade the rest of the government that the airlines didn't need an adequacy determination to avoid privacy sanctions in Europe.

I was sure they didn't. I knew that the 1995 directive offered many defenses for the airlines—data sharing is permitted for public safety or law enforcement, for protection of the interests of the passengers who provide the information, and for compliance with the laws that govern air travel. And, even without those defenses, airlines could fully insulate themselves from liability by obtaining the consent of their passengers for the data transfer to the United States.

The strategy didn't rely entirely on law. It was also grounded in *realpolitik*. The European Commission sets data-protection rules, but it does not enforce them. So if any airline were going to be fined for complying with U.S. law and providing travel data, the decision would have to be made by the country where it operated. Each country would have to decide whether to punish local airlines flying out of local airports. And any country that threatened to punish local carriers for following U.S. law would put those carriers at risk of DHS penalties—fines, delays and the loss of their rights to fly to the United States.

European solidarity went only so far, I thought. If French privacy bureaucrats made it impossible to fly to the United States from Charles de Gaulle airport, well, Schiphol, Heathrow, and Frankfurt would be only too happy to pick up the slack. When September 30 came around and no deal was done, who would want to be the first country to punish its airlines and its airports?

Europe, I figured, was bluffing.

If I was right, it would be no big deal to let the agreement expire. We should be happy to see the entire arrangement die, and the risk that it would hurt the airlines was small. So why not dramatize our confidence? We could take a tough line in the talks, insisting that the undertakings be completely overhauled and all their problems cured. At the same time, we should begin visibly and noisily planning for the end of the arrangement on September 30.

At the National Security Council (NSC), we ran into a buzz saw. The State Department had no interest in another confrontation with Europe—especially not at a time when U.S.-Europe relations were tender from the rancor over Iraq. DHS had signed this agreement two years earlier, State said, and if DHS was willing to live with it then DHS should be willing to live with it now. The Justice Department, which had counseled DHS not to negotiate a passenger names records agreement in 2004, now wanted to leave the agreement in place. DOJ insisted that DHS must renew it without change. It blamed DHS and the passenger names flap for increasing European restrictions on law enforcement data sharing. We should do nothing that might increase transatlantic tension over law enforcement.

Even more troubling, the National Security Council staff made no effort to disguise its determination to keep DHS from pursuing a hard-nosed strategy. The NSC was supposed to be an honest broker, shaping and narrowing disputes among cabinet departments so that only the most difficult and heartfelt conflicts got to the president for decision. But the NSC knew little about DHS, and what little it knew it didn't much like. The Homeland Security Council, created after 9/11, was viewed by many in NSC as an unnecessary subtraction from NSC's authority; and DHS in its infancy was thought incapable of handling hard diplomatic tasks.

NSC had many irons in the fire with Europe. Letting DHS blow up the existing agreement to get better terms sounded risky to the NSC staff. They doubted that DHS was up to the job. Better not let the new guys rock the boat. This attitude showed up in every NSC memorandum, every summary of conclusions from NSC meetings, and even in the invitation list. DHS had to fight just to get NSC to invite Defense and the intelligence community when the NSC met to discuss travel reservation data.

DHS stood alone. But we were determined not to reinstate the old agreement. Secretary Chertoff and I simply would not accept a made-in-Europe version of the wall. The interagency participants and the NSC staff bitterly opposed the DHS strategy, but DHS had two advantages.

First, DHS was the agency whose interests were truly at stake. The others had strong passing interests in the dispute, but only DHS had direct operational responsibility for keeping terrorists out of the country. If DHS believed that a better PNR agreement was necessary to accomplish that end, it was very hard for other agencies to persuasively argue for a different view.

Second, the lines of communication from the bottom of DHS to the top were clear, short and quick. When new issues arose, Chertoff could be briefed and give decisions in hours. This was critical to the interagency debate, because many of the other participants might take weeks to get cabinet-level backup for their positions. Time and again, DHS officials were able to scotch opposition at the NSC by saying, "We've talked to our secretary. That's his view. If you disagree, you'd better bring your secretary to the table to close the deal."

But NSC and the rest of the interagency group had weapons of their own, most especially the power of delay. NSC could refuse to approve DHS's most ambitious and hard-nosed proposals. In a bureaucracy, the power to delay a proposal is often the power to kill it. The agencies that wanted DHS to quietly renew the PNR arrangement might not be able to force us to agree, but they could achieve the same end simply by delaying any decision that would allow us to negotiate an alternative.

So, in the weeks following the decision of the European Court of Justice, an eerie quiet settled over the Atlantic. Both sides were trying to agree on how they would approach the negotiations. The commission was seeking a mandate simply to renew the old agreement. This took time, but the commission seemed confident that time was on its side. The closer we got to September 30, the commission seemed to think, the greater the pressure on DHS to accept a simple renewal.

At the same time, DHS was pressing for authority from the National Security Council to put forward an ambitious rewrite of the PNR arrangement. DHS also wanted authority to go directly to individual member states to begin planning for the expiration of the September 30 deadline. Reluctant to approve these tough tactics, the NSC was slow-rolling the DHS request. It had made the same calculation as the commission, and it seemed to want the same thing. The closer we got to the deadline, the more likely it would be that DHS would have to roll over the existing deal.

I could see the opposition strategies starting to unfold—both in Brussels and inside the interagency process. Both of our adversaries were playing a delaying game. They thought that the approach of the September 30 deadline would force DHS to make concessions. They thought that the deadline helped them, because they couldn't imagine letting the agreement actually expire. They were sure we'd have to get more flexible as September 30 neared.

But the strategy I'd devised for DHS saw the deadline as DHS's friend. I thought that the best thing that could happen to us was for September 30 to come and go. That would expose the Europeans' bluff.

And in the interagency process, DHS's unity would allow it to stand firm as September 30 approached. I was gambling that the September 30 deadline would turn out to be a bigger problem for the Europeans and the interagency players than for DHS. So the key for now was to keep them thinking that delay was their idea, not ours.

With everyone playing for time, June passed without action. Faull told everyone that he was seeking a mandate to renew the agreement without change. Before the EU enters into formal international negotiations, the twenty-seven member states authorize those negotiations and set out the EU's objectives in a negotiating "mandate." This process means that the EU's negotiators are often kept on a very short leash—unable to make concessions or deals that materially vary from the mandate they have been given. The story was often told (I suspect it is apocryphal, though indicative of a larger truth) that an agricultural negotiator had to return to the European Council for a new mandate in order to remove a comma from a trade agreement.

Finally, in July, Brussels reached consensus, giving Faull the mandate he had sought. It was the *Indiana Jones* option—renewal of the old agreement on a new jurisdictional foundation. Faull called to let me know, and to tell me that, as a technical matter, it would be necessary for the United States and the EU to "denounce" the old agreement, since it had been overturned by the court. He wanted to make sure we weren't upset when that request was sent over.

I wasn't upset. I was overjoyed.

I agreed with enthusiasm to join Brussels in denouncing the old agreement. But I made no formal proposal for replacing it. That would have required interagency consensus, and consensus was slow in coming. Instead, I waited for the European Commission to put forward a draft. Once we saw the European draft, I would have to persuade a reluctant National Security Council to authorize DHS's proposal for a complete rewrite. That would be a hard slog, and I was in no hurry to start.

Brussels finally put forward its draft in mid-July. Had it really served up the *Indiana Jones* option, simply repeating the old agreement without change, my strategy might have been in trouble. There was plenty of interagency support for Faull's proposal that we simply renew the 2004 arrangement. But in the end, Brussels had not been able to achieve consensus on a straight renewal. Instead, perhaps driven by its privacy bureaucrats, it put on the table a draft that went well beyond the 2004 agreement. The new draft tried to turn all the U.S. undertakings into a formal and binding international agreement, rather than a loose *quid pro quo*. Worse, it allowed the privacy bureaucrats of the member states authority to investigate DHS and to take enforcement action if they concluded that DHS was not living up to those obligations.

Brussels had overplayed its hand. No one in the interagency process was willing to argue that DHS should accept a worse deal than it got in 2004. The Brussels draft was not a basis for serious discussion. I had unanimous support for rejecting it out of hand. And in that moment, Brussels lost its best chance to force renewal of the 2004 deal.

It was now late July. Two months were gone from the four-month negotiating window that the European Court of Justice had allotted. And August vacation is nearly sacred in Europe. No serious negotiations could be expected then. Pointing out that combining August in Europe with the Labor Day holiday in the United States would leave only three weeks for substantive negotiations, DHS insisted that planning for a possible September 30 crisis should begin.

It was only prudent to do some quiet contingency planning, we told the interagency, and it agreed that we could approach individual member states and ask them what plans they had for avoiding a crisis on October 1.

This, too, fit our strategy. It allowed DHS to bypass Brussels and begin dealing with individual European countries. No matter how quiet the conversations, we knew they would get back to Brussels almost immediately. And that would make the Europeans realize that DHS might not be bluffing, that expiration of the deadline raised no undue fears in Washington. Best of all, we soon learned that several governments were indeed planning steps to avoid lawsuits or disruption of flights if the agreement expired on September 30.

This discovery bolstered DHS's interagency argument that chaos was unlikely on September 30, even if no agreement was reached. The airlines and the member states, I argued, were already working on ways to defuse the crisis and forestall chaos.

In August, the real world broke in. British authorities uncovered a plot to kill innocent transatlantic passengers on a nearly unprecedented scale. British Muslims with ties to al Qaeda planned to smuggle liquid explosives disguised as sports drinks onto as many as ten transatlantic flights. The idea was to blow all of them up the same day. Thousands would have died.

Thanks to British surveillance, the authorities knew that preparations for an attack were well along. They bugged the plotters' apartments and listened, appalled, as some of the men videotaped their final testaments. Unsure exactly when the plan would go into effect, on August 10, 2006, the British moved in, arresting twenty-five people. At the same time, UK and U.S. authorities imposed restrictions on liquids in carry-on baggage.

The incident, which could have caused a death toll that rivaled 9/11, deepened DHS's determination to reshape the 2004 arrangement. If the liquids plot were a test, the 2004 procedures had failed it. We tried to use the plotters' reservation data to track their plans, but only one part of DHS—Customs and Border Protection—had access to that information, and it was hard to share the data with other agencies. Worse, when we turned to the plotters' reservation data to get advance warning of the attack, we ran into the provision that made it hard to get information about travel reservations more than seventy-two hours before the flight. At a time when we needed as much advance warning as possible about the plot, we were instead struggling with an arbitrary EU limit on how quickly we could get reservation data. That made no sense.

Even the liquids plot did not disturb the rhythm of the negotiations, or the vacation schedule in Brussels. Soon August, too, had slipped away, and still no negotiations had been held. September 30 loomed.

DHS and the European Commission still believed that time was on their side. Not so the interagency. The National Security Council was getting visibly anxious. The first negotiations were scheduled for early September, and the United States had to have a position.

DHS was unwilling to consider the *Indiana Jones* option—the same deal on a new footing. We wanted a complete revamping of the

2004 arrangement. Other agencies feared that such a demand would put an end to the talks. But DHS's firmness was beginning to bring the others around. They had no answer to our objection that the 2004 deal was too constraining, particularly after the August plot. They agreed that some renegotiation was needed but they took refuge in delay and procedural objections. Why not wait until the old deal expired by its terms, in 2007? There wasn't time, they said, for a wholesale renegotiation. Couldn't we keep the old deal for a few more months?

I wouldn't budge. I knew that rolling over the deal would give it greater power. It would be even harder to kill after it had been signed twice. And besides, the deadline would work in DHS's favor, I still believed. Why give that up?

DHS was constrained by interagency consensus in the formal negotiations, but it could not prevent Michael Chertoff from speaking his mind in public. In a late August *Washington Post* op-ed, Secretary Chertoff made the case for revision of the agreement in blunt terms, saying that European privacy concerns had limited the ability of counterterrorism officials to do their jobs.[3]

The op-ed made my job as negotiator easier. The NSC could hardly order me not to say in the negotiations what Chertoff had already said in the newspapers. It agreed that I could spend the first negotiating sessions explaining our objections to the 2004 deal and proposing that the deal be reworked. But I could not say that the deal would end on September 30.

There was no consensus in Washington for letting the deal die then. If I couldn't persuade the Europeans to rewrite the agreement by that date, most of the interagency members hoped they could force DHS to roll over the old deal, at least for a while and perhaps for another year.

At last even Labor Day had passed. Everyone was back at work, and we had to meet the Europeans. The interagency remained divided. Even so, I was determined not to compromise DHS's goals. As the lead negotiator, I was determined to make the best of my limited instructions.

With Faull sitting across the table, I blasted the 2004 arrangements. That agreement, I said, was "unacceptable to DHS," a formulation that left open the possibility that other agencies might find it acceptable. I insisted that it would have to be renegotiated, and I laid out the many objections that DHS had identified.

Faull was a formidable negotiator, but he had been given an impossible mandate. He was supposed to get us not only to restore the old agreement, but to accept the privacy bureaucrats' proposals, which would make the deal even harder on DHS. He must have known that he'd never get a deal on those terms. So he acknowledged that DHS's concerns were worth discussing, and he promised to do so. But not now.

We don't have time to negotiate a new agreement in three weeks, he declared, and I don't have a mandate to do anything other than renew this deal.

Hoping to break DHS's resistance at the start, Faull had gone straight to the issue that divided Washington. It was almost as if he were reading our interagency memos—or getting briefed by the U.S. agencies that opposed us.

If we are going to have productive talks, one thing must be understood, Faull told me. The only way to handle these talks is to proceed on the understanding that, while we are discussing the issues that DHS has raised, it must be common ground that we are going to roll over the 2004 agreement on September 30. That is the only basis on which I have a mandate to talk to you. If that's not understood, I might as well pack up and go home.

It was an ultimatum.

Whether we were going to take the *Indiana Jones* option was the crucial issue, and Faull wanted to force a concession right away. The EU's slow pace in scheduling talks now made sense; the Europeans thought that leaving only a few weeks for agreement would force us to postpone substantive negotiations and take the rollover.

Faull was smart enough simply to make his statement and move on. He wasn't asking for explicit assent from the United States, he was putting the EU position on the table. But this would be his position from now on. If the talks went on after his ultimatum, it would be the basis for all further discussion.

For me, the ultimatum posed a tricky problem. I knew that DHS was united in rejecting the 2004 deal and in wanting an immediate revision. Indeed, DHS was willing to let the old agreement expire without renewal, since we thought that the risk of crisis was low. But there was no interagency consensus for the DHS position. The State Department, the Justice Department, and the NSC—all agreed with Faull; they too wanted us to take a rollover. I had no authority to insist that the deal expire without renewal.

But Faull had overreached without realizing it. By stating the understanding so explicitly, he created an opportunity that I would not have had on my own. I had no mandate to threaten the collapse of the deal on September 30, but I certainly could reject Faull's explicit ultimatum.

I waited. After more back and forth, Faull again declared that talks could only go forward on the assumption that the agreement would be renewed by September 30. Choosing my words carefully, I interrupted.

"I'm afraid that these talks can't go forward on the basis you've stated," I said. "I simply cannot promise you that we will renew this agreement at all."

In the dead silence that followed, I wondered whether I had gone too far.

No, I thought, that was a technically accurate statement of the interagency debate. As long as DHS held firm, no one could promise that the agreement would be renewed. Of course, no one could promise that it wouldn't. The issue was still being debated inside the U.S. government.

But in the negotiations with the Europeans, this formulation suddenly put the shoe on the other foot. By categorically rejecting Faull's assertion that the talks could only go forward with a rollover as the goal, we left Faull with the same harsh choice he had tried to force on us. He either had to abandon his earlier ultimatum or walk away from the talks.

Faull called a break.

He had to consult with his delegation. Faull could not have been surprised at my position; he'd heard much the same informally before. But the other European representatives were shocked. Viewed from Brussels, the 2004 deal looked like a capitulation to the United States. Its privacy protections were far too weak, the Europeans thought; the deal had been criticized by the European Parliament, the press, and the privacy bureaucrats—by all right-thinking people, really.

The European negotiators had begun the session expecting to win a new and tougher deal. Now the United States seemed willing to let the deal die entirely—and in just three weeks. Worse, they now had to decide, over a coffee break, whether to fly home empty-handed or to start discussing ways to weaken an agreement their constituents had already spent years condemning as too weak.

The break stretched on and on. Finally Faull and his delegation returned. They would keep talking. Brussels had abandoned its ultimatum.

A new note of urgency suddenly filled the room. If we were truly going to rework the 2004 agreement in three weeks, we would have to begin immediately. Perhaps for the first time, the European negotiators understood just how much was at stake for them in these talks.

To soften us up, the Europeans realized, they had to restore our fear of the September 30 deadline. If the United States really was willing to let the deal die on September 30, then Europe had no leverage.

Faull began to stress the risks for both sides if there was no agreement on September 30. Just a threat of data-protection litigation could cause chaos if no agreement had been reached, he said. Airlines might withhold data from DHS. They might refuse to fly across the Atlantic at all. Hoping to add to this leverage, one or two of the European negotiators hinted that they might open a new front. They noted that Canada could not share PNR data with the United States unless the United States was deemed "adequate" under EU law, a status that would expire on September 30. Did we want to lose access to Canadian data as well, the most anti-American members of the delegation asked.

The tactic was Europe's best hope, but it didn't change the dynamic of the talks. I explained that the airlines should be able to avoid liability and I expressed doubt that Canada would take actions counter to its own interest. I deeply resented the European effort to hold Canadian data-sharing hostage, but as a practical matter the data supplied by Canada was so hobbled by restrictions that it had only limited value. I was willing to roll the dice if those were the only stakes.

The tide of the talks had turned. From now on, the negotiations would be focused not on how the agreement could be made more favorable to European privacy campaigners but on how to address DHS's security concerns. The only question was how much ground Brussels would give up.

Faull declared that he found some of the U.S. concerns to be reasonable, but that he did not have any authority to renegotiate the 2004 deal. I can't possibly get a new mandate in the next few weeks, he explained. He added that he thought some of our concerns were based on too strict an interpretation of the 2004 arrangement.

—You're reading it so strictly that it is hurting your security more than necessary, he said.

It is not usually good negotiating tactics to emphasize your weakness and inability to cut a deal. But in choosing this formulation, Faull seemed also to be hinting at a solution. Could we leave the agreement from 2004 in place while reinterpreting it to avoid the consequences to which DHS objected? We could see that this fallback position had appeal from the European point of view. It would keep the commission within its mandate, if barely. And "interpreting" the 2004 agreement set natural limits on the concessions that Brussels could be asked to make. Interpretation might allow the negotiations to stretch the terms of the agreement; it would not allow the negotiators to rewrite them.

Perhaps to Faull's surprise, I was also willing to explore the idea. That was because I believed the 2004 agreement could in fact be rewritten under the guise of interpretation. The arrangement included a clause that allowed DHS to adapt to changes in U.S. law. If amendments to U.S. law affected any of DHS's undertakings, then the amendments would trump DHS's promises, as long as DHS gave notice to Brussels. I thought that this clause might open the door to major changes, as long as I could tie the revisions to a change in U.S. law enacted after the 2004 agreement.

And there had been such a change. A bill implementing the recommendations of the 9/11 Commission had been signed into law in December of 2004, less than six months after the agreement. The legislation wasn't very specific. It didn't address travel reservation data; but it had the usual post-9/11 provisions requiring more information sharing. The act created a federal "information sharing environment" to facilitate the exchange of all terrorism information among federal, state, and local agencies. Because this measure was intended to respond to the 9/11 Commission's criticism of the "wall," we thought, it could be the basis for undoing the new wall constructed by the 2004 agreement for sharing of travel data.

In fact, read broadly, it could be the basis for repudiating large swaths of the 2004 agreement that affected information sharing. That, plus a generous view of what constituted "interpretation," meant that I could squeeze most of the changes that DHS wanted into Faull's formula, allowing him to stay at least technically within his current mandate. The 2004 agreement could be rolled over, in accordance with the commission's instructions, but with a sweeping set of changes based on the new U.S. law.

I was happy with the first negotiating session. It had forced the talks onto our terrain; I had been able to pooh-pooh the September 30 "deadline" without misrepresenting the state of interagency deliberations; and the way had been paved for a potential compromise—the interpretive letter. I couldn't have planned on any of that, but our hard fights in the interagency process had left me prepared to pursue each of these opportunities when they arose.

But we had no victories yet. Time was short, and the Europeans had not agreed to any concessions. They couldn't. I had not actually asked for any. Indeed, we had no authority to put forward a proposal of our own. The interagency was still deadlocked. With only three weeks left, though, it was time to force the issue. Faull and I agreed to meet again in a week—at which time I would offer U.S. proposals for an interpretive letter and for what would be done on September 30 if agreement had not been reached.

Now came the hard part. We would have to fight off the other federal agencies that still wanted DHS simply to renew the 2004 agreement despite its troubling privacy restrictions. But DHS's interagency position was improving. First, DHS's judgment had been vindicated. We had successfully called Brussels's bluff. Its negotiators had stayed at the table after DHS refused to treat a rollover as the only possible outcome. The agencies that predicted a breakdown in the talks if DHS took a tough line had been proven wrong. And their efforts to minimize DHS's objections to the 2004 deal had been undercut when Faull acknowledged that our concerns had weight. Interagency debate was now moving to a battleground that favored DHS.

But compromise is the soul of interagency discussion. The process is designed to force agencies to make more and more compromises as disputes move up the ladder from assistant to deputy to secretary. If we walked into the interagency process and put our bottom line on the table, we'd soon find that we had in fact put it on the block, that serious security measures would be knocked down just to satisfy demands for compromise from State, Justice, and the NSC. To keep that from happening, we decided to ask again for what we really wanted—either the 2004 agreement should be rewritten from scratch or it should be scrapped. DHS put forward a rewritten draft of the agreement, reducing the whole thing to broad principles; the resulting document emphasized that passengers could consent to U.S. security measures, and it dropped the strict regulation of DHS's data practices.

Interagency opposition to this proposal was heavy, and—oddly—it was led by the Justice Department. We thought that Justice would want privacy limits on law enforcement to be carefully circumscribed and reciprocal. As it turned out, Justice did feel that way about privacy limits on its own law-enforcement practices, but it saw no reason to apply the same principle where DHS's practices were concerned. As the interagency debate raged, Justice replayed earlier arguments: The EU would walk away if we put forward our proposal, and a failure of the talks would spoil the atmosphere for what Justice thought of as "real" law-enforcement data exchange—the trading of information in criminal investigations. To avoid even the possibility of a chill in that area, Justice wanted us to stop defending our own interests.

Our proposal had forced the interagency debate to focus on whether to put forward a complete rewrite of the 2004 agreement. For DHS, this was good news. We recognized that a sweeping reconsideration of the passenger names records arrangement would be hard to achieve. But our interagency opponents were concentrating all their fire on that part of our agenda. And that had the effect of making the rest of DHS's position less controversial.

There were two other pieces to DHS's interagency proposal. The first was an "interpretation" letter that would largely tear down the EU-imposed data-sharing wall and interpret away DHS's other problems with the agreement. It was a sweeping document that we believed could solve nearly all of our immediate concerns about the 2004 deal. Of course it went well beyond what most lawyers would call interpretation; parts of it were in truth a revocation of the original arrangement. But if the EU was willing to accept those provisions and to call them interpretations rather than amendments, why should we disagree? Calling them interpretations would give Europe a victory on paper while giving DHS a victory on substance. And if the alternative was giving up the 2004 agreement entirely, I thought, a paper victory might look good to Brussels. It was aggressive, but I thought it might look good to the interagency when compared to DHS's other, more sweeping proposals.

Our final proposal was certainly harder for the interagency to swallow. I wanted to put complete abandonment of the 2004 agreement on the table. That was the best response to the European claim that there wasn't enough time to revise the entire agreement in just two weeks. There might not be time to rewrite it, but there was plenty of time to kill it. So we asked for authority to propose a joint statement that the parties could issue if we didn't reach agreement by September 30. I liked this proposal because it dressed up a hard-nosed negotiating position as simple prudence. There were only two weeks left, after all, so it only made sense to plan for the possibility that the talks would fail. But the very fact of planning for failure emphasized again how unconcerned we were about the September 30 deadline.

As drafted by DHS, the joint statement was uncompromising. DHS proposed to say that the two sides had not reached agreement but they were committed to keep talking and the EU would not take any action that would harm airlines or the flow of data during this period. Conspicuously, DHS did not commit to keep its undertakings in effect. We would make no promises about what we'd do come September 30. After much discussion, however, NSC brokered a compromise. DHS agreed to promise that it would give Europeans all of the privacy rights that Americans had under U.S. law—other than the right to sue the U.S. government (a right the executive branch could not confer in any event). We were happy to make this promise, first because we had already begun to apply U.S. law to all passenger name records and second because the formulation dramatized our view that U.S. privacy law was already at least as good as EU law and that the two should be treated as equivalent.

That was a small price to pay for approval of the rest of the document, which would dramatize how lightly we took September 30. Putting it forward would show for the first time that the U.S. government was united in that stance. Important as it was, approval of the document came surprisingly easy. With the other agencies focusing all their fire on DHS's completely rewritten version of the 2004 agreement, I finally agreed to drop that proposal in favor of the "interpretive" letter and the joint statement.

But at the last minute the interpretation letter ran into a completely new set of Justice Department objections. Justice did not want to say that the 9/11 implementation law required the sharing of airline reservation data within the U.S. government. It argued that the new law was more or less meaningless, imposing no serious sharing obligations on U.S. agencies.

Since the interpretation letter was widely viewed as the best way to reach agreement and avoid a blow-up, Justice seemed to have switched sides. After insisting for months on compromise at any cost, now Justice was holding up the best hope for achieving a compromise.

Finally, after long discussions, we figured out what the problem was. The FBI apparently had many agreements with foreign agencies that required it to keep the data to itself and not share it with other U.S. agencies. Such clauses are disconcertingly common in international agreements—especially if the agreements are not reviewed by other agencies. The clauses are common because both sides are happy to adopt them. The foreign agency providing the data wants to know that its distribution will be limited; and the receiving agency (often the FBI) is happy to be given a legal monopoly on important data.

If the United States declared that the 9/11 implementation law required reconsideration of such restrictions, we realized, the FBI and Justice might have to reconsider their own restrictions on sharing data with other agencies. And Justice did not want to do that. These were the same prosecutors who had fought like tigers to tear down the wall that restricted their access to intelligence agencies' information; but now, with the shoe on the other foot, they were fighting almost as hard to keep other agencies from seeing the data they were getting from foreign partners.

I was disgusted. After suggesting that DHS should sacrifice its interests almost without limit just to keep the negotiations from blowing up, now Justice was prepared to put the entire deal at risk, and in the worst possible cause—preserving the FBI's authority to keep terrorism data behind walls. The irony ran deep. DHS was fighting tooth and nail to win the right to share terrorism data with Justice, to break down the wall; and Justice was fighting just as hard to keep us from succeeding—for fear that it might then have to share more data with us.

It was the worst sort of bureaucratic politics, but Justice was determined. It played its trump card, saying, "We're the Justice Department. We're in charge of interpreting the laws of the United States, and we reject your interpretation of the 9/11 law." It looked as though the entire strategy would founder on the rock of Justice's self-interest.

But for once NSC took DHS's side. It badly wanted a compromise with Europe, and the interpretation letter was its best hope. NSC pressed for a solution. Finally, in a series of tense weekend phone calls, DHS proposed one. Instead of saying that the 2004 agreement's limits on information sharing were "inconsistent" with the statute, could we say that the limits, if read restrictively, would "impede" operation of the statute? The 2004 deal allowed us to modify our obligations if the obligations "impeded" compliance with U.S. law. I felt ashamed of this compromise, because it would give Justice and the FBI an excuse to keep their own barriers to information sharing in place. But it broke the deadlock over the letter. We had what we needed for the next negotiating session—a unified U.S. negotiating position on the substance of the deal, even if we still hadn't quite agreed on what would happen if we had no agreement on September 30.

That was looking more and more likely. The interagency squabbling had eaten up a lot of time. Now there was just a week left before September 30.

But the collapse of interagency resistance left the EU with no options. It was quite clear now that the United States was determined to rewrite the 2004 deal. And, it looked willing as well to let the old deal expire without regret.

With just days to go before September 30, the Europeans dropped their effort to postpone negotiations until the next year. But old assumptions die hard. The EU negotiators still seemed to believe that it was the United States that needed a deal or a rollover by September 30, and they seemed surprisingly unhurried as the days ticked away.

This was fine with me. My biggest worry all along was that the NSC would intervene at the last moment to force DHS to keep the 2004 deal in place if we missed the deadline. But the closer we got to the deadline without NSC forcing the issue, the less likely that became. I was sure that inertia and delay were on DHS's side. If we did nothing, and NSC did nothing, the deadline would pass. If I was right, that event would prove that the deadline was no big deal, and DHS's leverage would increase. If I was wrong, well, all hell would break loose.

I was starting to get a feel for just how bad it could be. Industry had been following the talks through intermediaries, but it had assumed, along with the EU and much of the interagency, that a rollover was inevitable and that DHS would have to cave in eventually. So the airlines had not pressed the two sides to reach substantive agreement. But when the U.S. proposed a joint statement to be issued if no agreement was reached, everyone suddenly realized that failure really was an option. The "adequacy" determination that the industry was relying on might simply evaporate on October 1 with nothing to take its place. The airlines would be flying naked. They didn't want that. They began pressuring DHS to accept a deal, any deal. But they were too late. Our course was set. The slow-moving interagency process had labored and brought forth the two documents. They could not be changed now; they would have to be the basis of further negotiations.

Talks proceeded all through the last week, as Saturday, September 30 loomed. The interpretive letter was proving to be the key to a deal. As I hoped, it allowed EU negotiators to stay technically within their mandate to renew the 2004 agreement while giving DHS time to argue for all the substantive changes it wanted. But many of the substantive changes were hard for Brussels to swallow. Finally on

Friday we put our best offer on the table. Only then did the EU realize that we weren't bluffing. They had evidently hoped against hope that with less than a day to go, we'd be forced to compromise further.

This wasn't in Europe's script. It could not accept DHS's last offer without further consultations in Brussels.

So, they asked, would we agree to leave the 2004 deal in place while negotiations continued? I was firmly opposed, of course. I wanted everyone to see that the threat of chaos and liability all around was mostly hype. But the issue was going to be decided well above me. That was good news. Chertoff was firm in wanting to break free from the European data-protection shackles, and he understood the value of ending the threat of transatlantic chaos. What's more, with the interagency issues elevated well above the usual players, the entire process was growing smoother. At the Deputy and Secretary level, both State and Justice were more supportive of DHS. At that level, the interagency reached agreement on a final step to demonstrate U.S. resolve.

Chertoff contacted his counterpart in Brussels, Franco Frattini. Commissioner Frattini was a charmer. As far as I know, he never really wore his topcoat over his shoulders like a cape, yet somehow that's the impression he left. Always smiling and full of energy, he had the dash of a young Marcello Mastroianni. He had made his career not in Brussels but in Italy, as a right-of-center politician and interior minister. He represented the European Commission's views with enthusiasm, but when push came to shove, he was on the side of law enforcement. His practical experience as a law enforcement minister allowed him to reach across the Atlantic and find common cause with Chertoff whenever tensions rose.

Encouraged by his conversations with Frattini, Secretary Chertoff decided to dramatize how close the parties were. He initialed the last DHS offer and sent it to Frattini. And he issued a public statement revealing that the ball was in the EU's court. The commission had only to initial the same document by the end of the day to avoid any further delay.

If it did not, though, the 2004 undertakings were dead. DHS made clear that it would unilaterally implement the changes it had proposed in the interpretive letter as promptly as possible. And we also declared that on October 1, "planes will continue to fly uninterrupted and our national security will not be impeded. Importantly, the proposal ensures the appropriate security information will be exchanged and counterterrorism information collected by the department will be shared, as necessary with other federal counterterrorism agencies."[4]

The wall was going to end, agreement or no agreement.

The crunch had truly arrived. All Saturday, airline representatives burned up the phone lines, trying to reach the negotiators. One association called me to insist that the United States had to get a deal; some airlines were already making plans to put their planes on the ground at midnight, the association claimed. Only a deal, or perhaps an agreement to roll the arrangement over for a time, would forestall chaos.

But we were determined not to bend. The threat of chaos was the weapon that Brussels had used in 2004 to extract dangerous concessions on security from the United States. No more. The statement we issued on Saturday quite deliberately made no mention of continuing to abide by the undertakings. DHS was willing to acknowledge informally that changing its procedures would take a bit of time, but the undertakings would be at an end—dead—at midnight.

Once the EU's negotiators had left for the airport, there was nothing to do but wait. The other negotiators and I were on tenterhooks all Saturday night and Sunday morning. Had we miscalculated? Would the European airlines stop flying or stop providing data? Would DHS have to begin imposing fines to force the airlines to cooperate? Would the EU lean on Canada to end its cooperation on passenger name records with the United States?

If the gamble failed, and the threat of chaos turned out not to be a bluff, my strategy would be discredited, and DHS's control of the talks would be at risk. Those who believed that DHS was not competent to manage a high-stakes negotiation successfully would roll out their I-told-you-so's. And resistance to the EU's information restrictions would begin to crumble.

By Sunday afternoon, though, it was over.

Not one airline had canceled a single flight. Not one had withheld passenger name records. The UK had even issued an order requiring its airlines to continue supplying them to the United States. And on Monday, Canada quietly let the United States know that it would continue to share data despite the end of the EU adequacy determination.

In Brussels, too, Sunday was a strategic turning point. But not a good one from the EU's point of view. The airlines had been pressing DHS to reach a deal right through Saturday. But when that didn't work, they shifted their tactics. Now they were pressing the EU to take the deal that Chertoff had sent to Frattini on Saturday. The airlines didn't care who gave ground, or what compromises had to be made. Every day without a deal was a day of risk, the airlines believed. And since the United States had made clear that it wasn't moving, the airlines now wanted movement from the European Union.

Even as its leverage was collapsing, though, the EU could not take the deal that was on the table. By Wednesday, sources in Brussels were complaining that Chertoff had scuppered the deal by introducing new last-minute demands, and EU negotiators sent back a marked-up draft of the U.S. proposal that made dozens of changes. Indeed, the draft tried to pull back concessions the EU negotiators had already signaled they would accept.

I was puzzled. This kind of negotiating tactic was almost willfully self-defeating. It was like the first EU text, which Brussels had claimed would simply roll over the 2004 agreement but which in fact made it worse. That aggressive proposal had united the U.S. government behind DHS for the first time.

Now the EU's Wednesday draft had the same effect. With the planes still flying and the data still flowing, DHS's interagency stock had risen, and the EU's Wednesday draft was so unacceptable that

DHS's tough line came to seem like the only appropriate response. There was no more talk in the interagency of showing good faith by agreeing to leave the wall in place voluntarily.

Why did the EU take this tack, I wondered, not once but several times? Faull was too good a negotiator not to realize the harm done by such maximalist positions. The source of the problem, I thought, had to be the EU's own internal politics.

Negotiating with the United States was in the European Commission's blood. For some of the EU's founders, the whole point of uniting Europe was to act as a counterweight to the United States. In trade talks with the United States, Brussels had made real headway by taking a tough line. Parts of the commission viewed their job as finding ways to confront the United States. Unless Faull had extraordinary authority, these elements would always press for the toughest possible line. And it was simple group dynamics that negotiating positions would harden if there was not a single clear decision maker. Proponents of aggressive measures could always say, "Well, why not try it? They can always say no." But the result of that approach was to produce drafts that lacked credibility in Washington and undermined the assumption that Brussels and Washington shared the same antiterrorism goals. And it ratified our view that only the toughest tactics would yield an acceptable outcome when dealing with Brussels.

Once again unified by the EU's overplaying of its hand, the interagency now backed DHS in its determination simply to stare down the maximalists on the European side. DHS was given broad authority to reject practically all of the European positions. As the airlines continued to pressure Brussels, a videoconference negotiating session was set for the end of the day on Thursday, with the hope that a deal could be reached and recommended to a permanent representatives' meeting on Friday.

The timing was bad from the start for the EU. The U.S. negotiators were beginning the talks at 11 a.m. Washington time. For the commission, that meant starting at 5 p.m. in Brussels. And as the United States rejected change after change proposed by Brussels, the time difference grew more important. Impasse after impasse forced delays and consultations on the European side. The phones would be muted but the video showed the European team's body language. It was not pretty. Bitter arguments were clearly breaking out whenever the talks paused. But in the end, each argument was followed by a European retreat.

It became clear that the commission itself had a deadline. It had to have an agreed document to recommend the next morning to the permanent representatives. We were in the catbird seat. If they wanted a document by the following morning, they would either have to persuade us to accept their change, at best a lengthy process, or recede. Moving systematically through dozens of proposed changes took many hours, so that the last issues were not finally addressed until eight or nine at night in Washington—two or three in the morning in Europe. At last we had not just the calendar on our side, but the clock as well.

That did not mean that DHS had everything its own way. This was still a negotiation among equals, and there were some issues where DHS did not press for unequivocal victory. It's never a good idea to press a tactical advantage so hard that the other side feels trounced. That only sets up a grudge match for the next set of talks.

DHS gave ground on information sharing, mainly to defuse a few of the most explosive fantasies being peddled about U.S. practices. To reassure the EU that other agencies would not have free rein to rifle travel records at will, DHS agreed not to grant "unconditional" and "direct" electronic access to other agencies. This formulation would, of course, allow other agencies to log into the database, as long as their access was conditioned by the requirement that they obey the rules that governed access. Perhaps most important, DHS agreed to share data only on a case-by-case basis. We could live with this because "cases" were defined very broadly. They did not have to be classic criminal investigations but could include all the common-sense circumstances in which DHS needed another agency's expertise or assistance to address an actual concern.

And DHS retreated at least for a time on the question of how long it could retain passenger name records. The three-and-a-half-year limit on record retention was a sore point for DHS; we believed that travel data was likely to have value for many years. But Faull stressed that there was no need to address the issue now. The retention period could be revisited in the next negotiation; no data would have to be destroyed before then. Much as DHS wanted to expand the retention period, Faull's point made sense. We agreed that the issue could be postponed.

These compromises sealed the deal as dawn broke outside the windows in Europe. With no time for sleep, Faull carried the marked-up documents to the member states' permanent ambassadors and got their approval that day.

The last round of negotiations was tough for the Europeans, but not as tough as their next task. They had to explain the deal to the parliament members and the privacy bureaucrats who had pressed to reopen the negotiations.

"European data protection authorities are choking on their baguettes after seeing the detail of the data-sharing agreement the EU signed with the U.S. on Friday," a reporter for *The Register* in Britain summed up colorfully. "European data protection authorities said they were 'amazed' when they saw the letter yesterday because it watered down the new agreement so that it was even weaker than the last."[5]

It was true. The European privacy bureaucrats—and the European Parliament— had gambled and lost.

"Unfortunately, the outcome of the court hearing was such that we basically sidelined ourselves," said Sophie in't Veld, a parliament member who opposed the U.S. deal, in an appearance before the UK House of Lords.[6]

But it was worse than that. The European Parliament had not been on the sidelines. By going to court and getting the first deal knocked out, it was the parliament that made it possible for DHS to remove the most onerous privacy terms from the arrangement.

What's more, letting the September 30 deadline expire had done permanent damage to Europe's position in future talks. The fear of chaos that was the EU's most valuable bargaining chip had been devalued by two weeks of calm between the expiration of the first agreement and adoption of the second.

Recognizing the facts of life, parliamentary and data-protection agency complaints about the second agreement and the interpretive letter sputtered on for a time and then died away.

The lesson was not lost on either side. Each now knew that the bark of the data-protection ideologues was worse than their bite. It seemed likely that the next negotiations would end much as the last negotiations did—with the EU in gradual retreat.

Within a few months, of course, we were back at the negotiating table. As Faull had pointed out, the 2004 agreement had to be replaced in 2007. The drama surrounding September 30, 2006, was followed almost immediately by another round of negotiations, this time about whether to renew the agreement. DHS again took a tough line, suggesting that the agreement simply be allowed to expire in July 2007.

"It has outlived its usefulness," I insisted. But the interpretive letter had taken much of the fire from our opposition. It gave DHS the flexibility it needed in most cases. If the concessions Europe had made in the letter could be incorporated into the next agreement, and the three-and-a-half-year retention period could be greatly extended, there was no practical reason to kill the arrangement entirely.

So, in a long anticlimax, that's how the second round of negotiations in 2007 played out. Because DHS was willing to live without an agreement, the EU had to make further concessions just to hang on to an agreement of some sort. The principal issue was how long data could be kept. The old agreement had insisted that data would be kept only three-and-a-half years and that the data collected under the agreement would be destroyed on that schedule no matter what. Both provisions had to go, in DHS's view.

This time around, the negotiations quickly moved to a higher level. By now, the European Council's presidency had rotated to Germany. That was good news for us. In April 2007, Secretary Chertoff made a quick, one-day, trip to Berlin to meet with the head of the German Ministry of the Interior. The German interior minister, Wolfgang Schaeuble, was as forthright an ally as we had found in Europe. (He has since become finance minister in Germany's center-right coalition government.) The victim of an attempted assassination himself, Schaeuble was confined to a wheelchair. A practical man with a sharp mind, he had a cheery affinity for Chertoff.

They met in September 2006, when Schaeuble first came to see Chertoff in the United States. Germany had recently concluded the "Pruem Agreement," allowing European countries to share information about criminal records. We'd briefed Chertoff on the agreement. Schaeuble was impressed with Chertoff's grasp of the agreement, and before the conversation was over, he half-jokingly invited the United States to join the agreement. He must have been surprised when Chertoff, who'd been briefed on the possibility, immediately took him up on the offer. Within two years, though, the deal had been done, and a friendship had been cemented.

With Schaeuble and Frattini leading Europe's team, we hammered out a deal with far less drama than in the first talks.

The two sides agreed that data would be kept for fifteen years instead of three and a half. But to cushion the public reaction, we agreed that the data would spend only seven years in an active database and the next eight in an inactive database. All of the data was put on this schedule, including anything gathered under the old agreement with its three-and-a-half-year schedule. Faull had been right to urge that we postpone that question.

On the crucial question of information sharing, Chertoff again stood firm. He was not going to rebuild information-sharing walls after the failures of 9/11. In the end, the Europeans agreed that DHS could use and share data based on any case that it was investigating or examining. This allowed DHS to identify routes of concern and to share travel data if the routes were the objects of DHS scrutiny. So long as the concern and the examination arose in good faith, data could be shared easily, assuming good security protections were in place.

As the talks proceeded, the text grew simpler. Many of the detailed and prescriptive security and procedural rules from the 2004 agreement were simply dropped. We began to think that we would have an uneventful second negotiation.

Unfortunately, not everyone in Brussels was reading from the same script. In 2007, the Cricket World Cup was held for the first time in the Caribbean. The Caribbean Community (CARICOM) nations worried that terrorism might mar the games, which attract visitors from India, Pakistan, and other South Asian countries. They asked the United States for help in screening travelers to the Caribbean. The United States helped CARICOM set up a system to collect and process advance passenger information. Data sent to the Caribbean nations was collected by the CARICOM nations and shared with DHS, which alerted the countries to risky travelers bound for their airports. A number of dangerous travelers were identified and refused entry or arrested as the games drew near.

The screening was a success for the United States and the CARICOM nations. But as the deadline for a third agreement on passenger name records drew near, a European representative decided to put the CARICOM arrangement in play. We learned about it when we got an agitated report from one of the top officials in a Caribbean nation that the EU was "essentially blackmailing CARICOM." The EU told CARICOM's trade negotiators in Brussels that it would withdraw all development funding for the region, if the United States did not follow "international standards." If the EU followed through on this threat, the official declared, the economy of the region would essentially be destroyed.

At the next negotiating session with the EU, I lost my temper. This was beyond the pale—an attempt to bully weaker nations into denying us information about dangerous travelers on our doorstep. After a brief attempt to justify the action, the EU beat a quick retreat, blaming the incident on unauthorized action by a British member of the European Commission staff. The threat to CARICOM was withdrawn. The EU's effort to find additional leverage in the talks, if that is what it was, had provoked so much outrage in Washington that it backfired.

But we weren't satisfied. Counting the Canadian gambit from the earlier talks, this was the second time that the EU had tried to organize an international information boycott of DHS. In reaction, we insisted that the new agreement make clear that such efforts would not be repeated. As long as the agreement was in effect, we insisted that the EU not interfere with third-country transfers of passenger name records to the United States. Jonathan Faull reluctantly agreed.

For the same reason, we pressed successfully to strengthen the reciprocity provision. We wanted an assurance that Europe could not insist on one rule for the United States while allowing its own terrorism authorities to follow less demanding rules at home. If the EU did not apply to its own members the rules in the new agreement, then the rules would not apply to the United States either.

With these changes, the agreement was signed in July 2007. We were finally through. After three negotiations in four years, neither side was interested in a rematch. The Americans were satisfied with the changes, and the Europeans had no appetite for further negotiations on a subject where their leverage had turned out to be so limited.

In fact, the Europeans were about to execute a remarkable pivot, from confrontation to imitation. After three years of complaining about the U.S. travel data system, the commission suddenly proposed that Europe adopt one of its own. More remarkably, the system resembled the U.S. system in almost every detail—except that it provided fewer protections for personal data.

The U.S. negotiators reviewed the proposal for European PNR systems with amazement. "Thank God we insisted on a reciprocity clause," said one. "By the time they're done making the rules for themselves, they'll relieve us of half the obligations in the new agreement."

What had happened? It would be tempting to chalk the about-face to a kind of institutionalized blind spot that makes American systems look inadequate to the EU just because they're American, while European systems look adequate just because they're European. The truth is a little more complicated.

The ironic effect of the conflict over PNR was that it forced us to justify our system. And we did. While the debate was ongoing, France and Denmark enacted laws authorizing the collection of PNR. The UK and the Netherlands launched pilot PNR projects. A committee of the UK House of Lords, deeply skeptical at first, declared in the end, "We are persuaded that PNR data, when used in conjunction with data from other sources, can significantly assist in the identification of terrorists, whether before a planned attack or after such an attack."[7]

Persistence and a full-throated defense of our program had won the day. Even so, DHS had been lucky. There was still a large body of opinion in Europe that wanted to thwart—or at least hobble—most of the U.S. data programs initiated in the wake of 9/11. To understand what could have happened if DHS had been less determined, it is only necessary to look at the U.S. and European handling of the SWIFT affair.

The Society for Worldwide Interbank Financial Telecommunication (SWIFT) is one of the great rivers of financial data that flow around the world each day. It carries international bank transfer messages for thousands of banks in two hundred countries.

Some of those transfers have helped fund terrorism. Terrorist groups must raise money to pay for their outrages. Then they must move the funds to their operational units. To do so, the terrorists must either physically carry cash or use modern financial institutions. A host of electronic networks and links among banks make the international transfer of funds easy. Al Qaeda often took advantage of these networks to move its funds. The alternative, sending cash by courier, runs the risk of interdiction, since carrying large, undeclared amounts in cash is illegal in many countries.

After 9/11, the United States Department of Treasury decided to ramp up its efforts to prevent terrorist groups from using modern financial networks. Banks were already under an obligation to "know their customer" and to report suspicious transactions. But often, Treasury was aware of information about suspicious persons or activities that it could not share widely with the banks. It therefore had to gain access to a large amount of data and then sift that data, using its own classified search terms and algorithms.

Treasury was doing the financial equivalent of what DHS did on the border. Far and away the vast majority of financial transactions—like the vast majority of travelers—held no interest for the government. They were simply part of the vast ebb and flow of money from institution to institution for legitimate purposes. Hidden in that river of transactions were a tiny few that bore the hallmarks of terrorism—a known al Qaeda financier, a suspected middleman, an institution that made a business of supporting suspect groups. Using modern information technology, it was relatively easy to pluck those transactions from the stream for more detailed review. But just as DHS did not rely on the airlines to decide which passengers should be scrutinized, Treasury could not rely entirely on the banks. The names and other facts that triggered scrutiny were sensitive; Treasury could not simply hand the list to SWIFT and ask it to conduct a search.

Treasury had full legal authority to simply order SWIFT to hand over its data. SWIFT kept a full set of records for its transactions in two locations, Belgium and the United States, and records kept on U.S. soil are routinely subpoenaed in criminal investigations. But even after 9/11, SWIFT was extraordinarily reluctant to disclose the transactions it carried. SWIFT could have resisted in court, forcing Treasury through public litigation that would have greatly diminished the value of access to the data. If terrorists and their financiers knew that interbank transfers were being monitored, they would switch to other methods.

To avoid litigation, Treasury and SWIFT negotiated an agreement that seemed to give each party what it wanted. SWIFT would carry its transaction records to Treasury, where they would be run through a "black box" that applied Treasury's patterns, names, and other algorithms. Neither side would have access to the other's sensitive data. At the end of the process, Treasury would be given only transaction data that had triggered one of its tripwires.

It worked. Treasury later credited the program with allowing it to track and capture the mastermind behind the Bali bombings that killed two hundred people. The program was also said to have allowed Treasury to identify and convict a Brooklyn man who had laundered $200,000 for al Qaeda.

Alas, the program was soon to lose much of its value. In June 2006, the *New York Times* evidently decided that the program must be scandalous; over the vehement objections of the Treasury, it published a lengthy expose′ about it.[8] The public editor of the *New York Times* would later conclude that the paper had been wrong to compromise the secret program, declaring "I haven't found any evidence in the intervening months that the surveillance program was illegal."[9] But by then it was too late. The *New York Times* had managed to create a storm over the program in Europe.

Because SWIFT was a Belgian company, Treasury's access to its records was quickly wrapped into the same storyline as PNR. Americans, the European media claimed, were overreaching to extract private European data from compliant companies without proper safeguards. Investigations were begun in more than a dozen countries. The Belgian data-protection authority seized the initiative. By September, it had issued a report declaring without citing much evidence that SWIFT was in violation of Belgian data-protection law.[10] By November, the entire working party of European privacy bureaucrats had joined in support of the Belgium ruling.[11]

This was, to say the least, an aggressive reading of European law. The data that had been subpoenaed was located in the United States. And SWIFT had done everything it could to minimize intrusions into the privacy of transactions that did not trigger suspicion.

What exactly had SWIFT done wrong?

In essence, the Belgian data-protection authority concluded, the United States Treasury had not lived up to European standards of conduct, and SWIFT had failed to force the Americans to adhere to those standards: "From the beginning, SWIFT should have been aware that the fundamental principles of European law were to be observed, apart from the enforcement of the American law, such as the principle of proportionality, the limited retention period, the principle of transparency, the requirement for independent control and an adequate protection level."[12]

No company had ever been found in violation of European law because it failed to bring a sovereign government to heel, but for European privacy advocates, that was just the beginning. SWIFT soon faced actual civil investigations in Germany and Canada, as well as Belgium, plus complaints in more than thirty countries. On top of all that, SWIFT executives were being criminally investigated and threatened with jail time. All for the crime of obeying U.S. law, in the United States, to assist in pursuit of an enemy that had killed more Americans on U.S. soil than anyone in a hundred years.

The legal theory being used against the company was dubious at best: Even the notion that the U.S. program somehow violated European law was doubtful. DHS's Privacy Office would later publish its findings that European programs to collect and analyze hotel registration were far more intrusive and less carefully constructed than Treasury's program; but they had never been questioned by the privacy bureaucrats who claimed to be so outraged by the U.S. program.

All that hardly mattered in the frenzy of objection to an American program that everyone knew, even without evidence, must be an abuse of power. For SWIFT, having legal defenses that ought to prevail was cold comfort; it could not afford even victory if the price was this public beating. SWIFT is a cooperative owned by banks in many nations; and most of the owners were none too pleased to learn about SWIFT's cooperation in breaching the secrecy of their transactions. They no doubt made this displeasure felt through their representatives on the SWIFT board. SWIFT began looking for an exit.

Desperate, Treasury opened talks with the European Commission, and within six months, in mid-2007, the two sides struck a deal that we found familiar. Treasury offered the Europeans unilateral representations, setting out the protections it was prepared to implement. And the commission relied on those representations to declare Treasury's protections "adequate," setting at rest the preposterous claim that SWIFT was somehow liable for violations of data protection law. Treasury's undertakings followed the PNR model, too; the department agreed that it would search only for terrorism data, that it would delete data that was not relevant to this search, and that most data would be deleted in five years. In another mark of European distrust, the Treasury's compliance with its promises would be audited by an "eminent European person"—who would have to be given a U.S. security clearance so as to be able to investigate even classified activities.

Separately, SWIFT agreed to apply European law to data stored in its U.S. offices, and the U.S. government agreed to enforce European law under a "safe harbor" agreement with the EU. In case there were a few terrorist financiers who had missed the *New York Times* article and the European flap, SWIFT also agreed to provide notice of the program.

By the end of the Bush administration, a kind of peace had been restored. SWIFT was protected from liability, and the furor had died down. Subpoenas were being served and honored. The Belgian data-protection authority issued a report admitting that, after a more detailed examination, what SWIFT was doing was consistent with European law. The "eminent European person" also concluded that Treasury was keeping its word.

But it was the peace of a patient on life support. The secrecy of the program had been breached fatally. SWIFT's American CEO, who had defended the program as necessary to combat terrorism, retired in 2007. He was replaced by a Spaniard. Shortly thereafter, SWIFT announced that it would restructure its data systems to store data on European transactions only in Switzerland.

European privacy bureaucrats crowed that they had crippled the American program, at least as far as European terror finance was concerned: "the creation of a new operation centre in Switzerland . . . means personal data in intra-European transactions will no longer be processed in the US."[13] The Belgian data-protection authority also cited the new Swiss center favorably when it announced in early 2008 that SWIFT actually hadn't broken Belgian law. Coincidence? Nope. SWIFT admitted that pressure from the privacy bureaucrats was one of the reasons it adopted the new architecture: "Distributed architecture will improve resilience, add capacity, control long-term average message costs, *and alleviate European data protection concerns.*"[14] In short, it's pretty clear that SWIFT was forced to withhold European terrorist financing information from Treasury by European government officials.

The lessons here are disturbing, to say the least. It now appears, in the wake of the UBS tax evasion scandals, that renowned Swiss bank secrecy laws will be modified to allow the pursuit of tax cheats. Yet a substantial number of European officials seem to think that those same secrecy laws should remain inviolate when the subject of scrutiny is terrorist financing. There's no justification for this distinction.

Having made a mess of an effective U.S. terrorism program without substantially serving privacy, some in Brussels tried to minimize the damage. The European Commission negotiated an agreement to give the United States access to intra-European bank transfer data even after the Swiss operations center is set up—but only if Treasury continued to live up to European standards.

Remarkably, even this was too much for the privacy campaigners of Europe. In the first exercise of new authorities granted to it by the Lisbon Treaty, the European Parliament rejected the agreement, essentially creating a European safe haven for terrorist finance.

What lessons can we draw from these stories? Certainly the implications for U.S.-EU relations are not good. DHS's passenger screening system was deployed at the direction of a Democratic Congress and in reliance upon a series of Supreme Court rulings; in effect, both parties and all three branches of the federal government participated in the decision. The EU could have acknowledged that, while American law policy did not comport with its own preferences, the United States nevertheless was entitled as a sovereign to choose differently. It could have let the United States follow its own path in fighting terrorism.

It did not.

Instead, Brussels claimed the right to sit in judgment on American data privacy practices. Worse, it assumed that its natural role was to thwart any new American initiative, either permanently or at least until it had been persuaded to imitate the program in Europe.

Perhaps most troubling for anyone who believes in multilateralism and international law, the tactics adopted by the European Union cannot easily be defended. The European Union never explained why its domestic commercial data-protection directive should override the spirit and text of the longstanding multilateral Chicago Convention, which clearly says that airlines must give the countries where they land personal data about the travelers they carry. Ignoring this convention and putting the airlines at risk of penalties for obeying U.S. law was a breach of settled principles of international law and comity. Nor did Europe ever justify its assumption that no criminal data-protection law could be adequate unless it was nearly identical to European law. In fact, the European Union never defined "adequacy" in the law-enforcement context, leaving the concept a moveable feast that can be modified on the basis of political, rather than legal, judgments. Finally, and most troubling for large multinational enterprises, the European Union seemed almost enthusiastic about threatening private companies with sanctions as a way of attacking U.S. government practices.

Putting private actors in a position of having to violate the laws of one sovereign in order to heed the laws of another is dubious practice under international law. But far from being reluctant to do so, the European Union seems to have concluded after the PNR episode that the tactic should be applied to new fields. It encouraged a criminal data protection investigation of SWIFT, saying in essence that, before complying with U.S. law, SWIFT had to ensure that the U.S. government met European standards. Since no private company, particularly after receiving a subpoena, has the leverage to demand such assurances from investigators, such an analysis dooms the company to simply deciding which law to violate.

Why would Europe sacrifice its traditional commitment to multilateralism and international law for the purpose of thwarting terrorism investigations in other countries? There are many possible explanations, but in fact the fights over SWIFT and PNR seem more and more to be of a piece with fifty years of Brussels policy making. The first instinct in Brussels, it seems, is always to oppose U.S. initiatives, perhaps directly, perhaps obliquely, and then to call for negotiations. There's an institutional reason for such a stance. Forcing the United States into negotiations demonstrates Brussels's relevance; at the same time it pulls authority away from the member states and toward the commission and its negotiators.

This dynamic is not just an artifact of Europe's dislike for President George W. Bush. President Obama got a taste of the same thing within months of taking office. After years of clamoring for the United States to close Guantánamo, how did Brussels react when President Obama proposed to do just that, and got a few European countries to agree to take a handful of the prisoners?

With a kind of genteel horror the EU asked, "How could the United States do such a thing without first getting permission from Brussels?" The European Commission insisted on interposing itself between the United States and the European countries that were willing to take a few prisoners. It then took months of negotiations to get Brussels to agree that, yes, the member states really could help out the new administration by accepting detainees. Only then could the United States and the member states negotiate actual transfers of prisoners.

The Brussels instinct to say "*non*" to American initiatives, at least until they have been milked for a contribution to European solidarity, is a force for global conservatism. If Europe's first inclination is always to slow the Americans down, question their motives, and make them pay for any changes in policy, there will be no quick responses to the challenge of accelerating technologies. This international conservatism is among the most powerful forces favoring a kind of exponential status quo.

It was a force we'd have to face again as we implemented the next step in our strategy for responding to the challenge of commercial jet technology.

7 Al Qaeda's Frequent Traveler Program

In the days before Christmas 2001, the attacks of September 11 were still an open wound. But international flights were slowly returning to normal. Americans were going home from Europe for the holidays; Europeans were taking their holidays in Florida's warmth.

Now was the time for a second strike, al Qaeda's leaders thought. Americans must know that military success in Afghanistan was irrelevant—it could not protect them at home. The first attack inside the United States had succeeded beyond expectations. Another would be devastating.

But the U.S. response had been tougher and more effective than al Qaeda expected. Its agents and sympathizers inside the United States had mostly been rounded up or expelled, often on immigration charges.

To launch a new attack, al Qaeda would have to send terrorists into the United States. But that path was perilous. American border officials were on high alert; customs and immigration controls had been tightened.

Visa applicants from Muslim countries faced tough new scrutiny. U.S. visa processing had returned in many ways to the 1950s. All applicants had to complete a form filled with personal questions. All applicants were interviewed by consular officials at a U.S. embassy or consulate. And in a new measure, all were fingerprinted to confirm their identities. Before allowing visa travelers in, the United States learned a lot about them—their family status, prior travel to the United States, present employment, the purpose and length of their planned trip to the United States, where they planned to stay, and who was paying for their trip.

The original focus of the questions may have been whether the travelers would overstay their visas and take illegal jobs in the United States, but the process was quickly revised to search for terrorist ties. If any doubts were raised on that score, the applicants simply didn't get a visa. And without a visa, the airlines wouldn't even let citizens of those countries get on a flight bound for the United States.

That was al Qaeda's problem as it looked for a way to launch a second strike on the United States. It had no trained terrorists left inside the country and it couldn't send a new team in, at least not from Saudi Arabia or Yemen or Egypt.

It sounded like a riddle. How do you attack the United States without entering the United States?

But al Qaeda had the answer. It had a plan.

And a man to carry it out.

Boarding Flight 63 from Paris to Miami, Richard Reid did not exactly blend in. He was huge—six-feet-four and over 200 pounds—and the son of an English mother and a Jamaican father. In other circumstances, he might have made the other passengers a bit uneasy. He was, after all, a hardened street criminal who'd spent time in England's notorious Feltham Prison. But in the jittery months after 9/11 what mattered most was that he bore no resemblance to the Arab hijackers.

In fact, though, Reid had converted to a radical brand of Islam in Feltham. Al Qaeda was eager to use a Western convert on a suicide mission. He would get less scrutiny, and a successful suicide mission by a British subject would show the West that it was rotting from within.

But the real beauty of sending Reid on the mission was his passport. All the visa controls imposed by the State Department were irrelevant to Reid. As a British subject, he was part of the Visa Waiver Program. Citizens of developed countries were permitted to travel to the United States without a visa and to stay for up to ninety days. Launched in the 1980s as a flood of commercial jet travelers overwhelmed U.S. border controls, the VWP was widely praised by business groups and travelers. It allowed easy, spur-of-the-moment trips to the United States, and it allowed Americans to make similar trips to Europe, Australia, Japan, and other popular destinations.

After 9/11, it was also the answer to al Qaeda's prayers. VWP travelers could get on planes without any screening by U.S. authorities. They could fly from Europe into American airspace without any scrutiny until the plane landed. And if the plane never landed—if they blew it up while it was near or over the United States, U.S. authorities would be helpless. All its border controls would be for naught.

That was al Qaeda's plan. It could evade all of America's new visa and border measures and still bring death to American skies.

Reid took a row to himself. He refused food and drink, even though it was a ten-hour flight. But he didn't draw much suspicion until hours into the flight. Then one of the attendants smelled smoke. Walking the aisles, she saw Reid hunched over in his seat.

"I thought, he's smoking," she told *Time* magazine. "It got me mad. I was talking to him, saying, 'Excuse me,' but he just ignored me. I leaned in and said, 'What are you doing?'"[1]

Then she saw.

"He's got the shoe off, between his legs. All I see is the wiring and the match. The match was lit," she says.[2]

I'm going to die, she thought.

She might have been right. According to the FBI, that one shoe held enough plastic explosive to blow a hole in the side of the plane.

She called for help. Another attendant grabbed Reid from behind, and he sunk his teeth into her hand.

"I couldn't get my hand out of his mouth" the second attendant told *Time*. "I thought he was going to rip my hand apart it hurt so bad."[3]

Passengers rallied to the attendants' aid. They helped pour water over Reid and his match. (It was a flight from Paris, so they used Evian.) Crew members used everything on hand to truss up the massive terrorist—plastic cuffs, headphone cords, and a seatbelt extension. A doctor on the flight injected Valium.

Reid still tried to break free; he bared his teeth at the crew when they spoke to him.

But passengers and crew had done their job well. When the plane finally landed, he was so thoroughly hogtied that the FBI had to cut Reid out of the improvised restraints. After a trial and conviction for terrorism, he was sentenced to life in prison.

Al Qaeda had been thwarted once by an alert air crew. Five years later, no one boarded a plane without sending one's shoes through the x-ray machine. But the real hole in American defenses hadn't been patched. The VWP was still going strong.

So al Qaeda—which doesn't easily let go once it gets an idea in its collective head—decided to try the same thing again, but on a bigger scale.

Al Qaeda planned several simultaneous suicide attacks on transatlantic flights from Great Britain to the United States. It couldn't use shoes this time, so the terrorists would smuggle common household chemicals onto the planes, then mix them together into an explosive concoction.

Later tests by the Transportation Security Administration found that the liquids were more than enough to blow holes in each of the planes, bringing them all down over the Atlantic Ocean or the United States.

And how were the plotters going to evade U.S. security controls? The same way Richard Reid did. They planned to use British passports to get on the planes, and then destroy the plane and its passengers before American authorities ever laid eyes on them. At least eight British citizens of Pakistani descent were part of the conspiracy. Every one was eligible for visa waiver treatment. Visa waiver had become al Qaeda's favorite travel program.

Once again, overlapping security measures managed to compensate for the lack of controls on visa-waiver travelers. This time it was good law enforcement and intelligence. The British discovered the plot while it was still in the planning stages. They monitored the plotters before swooping in to arrest them.

We had dodged a bullet again. But we couldn't count on luck to keep us safe forever.

So why didn't we just get rid of the visa waiver program? That was the question that some in Congress kept asking. Senator Dianne Feinstein and Senator Jon Kyl were particularly dubious about the VWP, and they regularly complained about the program's flaws.

But the reasons for adopting the program hadn't gone away. All in all, travel to the United States helps the economy and may even reduce anti-Americanism. Tourism and business travel are crucial in a country like ours that runs trade and payments deficits each year. Each year more than four million travelers come here from the UK and more than three million from Japan. In all, nearly twenty million visitors arrive in the United States under the VWP. Whole business models had been built on the ever-increasing pace of international travel. Were we willing to bankrupt those companies?

And what would we do at the embassies that were suddenly asked to process visas for millions of European and other travelers? Lines would run around the block. State Department officials would have to be drafted for consular duty in these countries, and the pressure to process the applications quickly would make rigorous scrutiny almost impossible.

What's more, international pressure to undo the change would mount quickly. At the time, twenty-seven countries were part of the U.S. visa waiver program, including all the most important American allies in the Cold War—nations like the United Kingdom, France, Japan, Germany, Australia, Italy, and New Zealand. Every one of these governments listened to their businesses and their travelers. They, too, expected the exponential rise in jet travel to go on forever. And they would not tolerate an American policy that interrupted that trend. They would insist that the program be reinstated. If it was not, they would retaliate, withdrawing visa-free treatment from U.S. travelers and forcing Americans to stand in lines around the block for visas to enter their countries.

If all that came to pass, Senator Dianne Feinstein's high-tech constituents would not thank her. Right now, they can catch a flight to Europe or Japan on less than a day's notice, and so can the customers or investors that visit them. Travel barriers that ran both ways would crimp their international ties.

No one wanted less travel. No one wanted a return to the 1950s. The forces of exponential conservatism still wanted jet travel to double and double again every decade. These were the forces that had created the VWP. And they were building again, making the case for expansion of the program.

We couldn't just stand in their path and shout, "Halt."

But the world had changed while the VWP had not. If it was meant to be an exclusive club for American allies, then it was out of date. It was like a museum exhibit of American allies from the Cold War era. When the United States decided to attack Saddam Hussein, the old alliance was ripped apart. Countries like France and Germany more or less switched sides, working with traditional U.S. adversaries such as Russia and China to thwart the U.S. plan. In contrast, the United States received backing from Eastern Europe. Poland, the Baltic states, Hungary, the Czech Republic, Slovakia, Ukraine, Romania, and Bulgaria all sent troops to fight in Iraq alongside the Americans. Asked why his little country had sent a force to Iraq, the Latvian ambassador's reply was poignant: "Because you asked."

We didn't have allies like that in Western Europe. But as far as VWP was concerned, Eastern Europe was still behind the rope line waiting to be let in. Indeed, some of the hardest conversations we regularly had with Jonathan Faull and others at the European Commission were about the VWP. Faull routinely pressed for inclusion of the new EU members from Eastern Europe in the program and, to be frank, his case was convincing.

Actually, it was more convincing for Eastern Europe than for Western Europe. Sure, travelers from these relatively rich countries were a lot less likely to become illegal immigrant laborers than travelers from poor countries. But after 9/11, the biggest danger posed by foreign visitors wasn't that they'd take dishwashing jobs away from New Yorkers.

If you're worried about Islamic terrorists traveling without visas, the last countries that should belong to the visa waiver program are those with large and disaffected Islamic populations. That's true of most of Western Europe. In contrast, Eastern Europe still hadn't needed to import much labor from abroad. If we were making generalizations about "safe" countries, in short, we'd have let Eastern Europe into the visa waiver program before France, the United Kingdom, Germany, or the Netherlands.

The new alignment hadn't gone unnoticed elsewhere. Ethnic politics reinforced a sense of obligation to our most committed allies as Polish, Lithuanian, and Latvian communities across the country campaigned to bring their homelands (and their relatives) into the program.

Shortly after the Iraq War ended, Senator Rick Santorum, a deep-dyed conservative Republican from Pennsylvania, introduced a bill to give VWP status to Poland. His Democratic cosponsor, Senator Barbara Mikulski of Maryland, pointedly asked why France had VWP status while Poland did not. That was troubling. If even security-minded legislators like Senator Santorum wanted to expand the VWP, our security concerns about the program weren't getting through.

Then, in 2006, Senator Santorum got his bill attached to the massive immigration reform bill being shepherded through the Senate. It was a classic legislative move. The senator knew the Bush administration would have to swallow the change in order to keep its priority legislation on track. DHS might squawk, but it would be ignored.

The test didn't come that year, it turned out. Immigration reform failed, and Senator Santorum was not reelected.

But as far as I was concerned, trouble was surely coming. Senators Kyl and Feinstein might rail against the VWP, but as memories of 9/11 faded it was likely to be expanded, not cut back. If we didn't do something, the security hole would get bigger soon.

Luckily, we'd already begun thinking about alternatives. In 2005, at the urging of the State Department, we'd agreed to lay out a "road map" to VWP status for a new group of countries, mostly in Eastern Europe. But that effort was doomed from the start. We didn't want to expand the program as it stood and the way the law was written, we probably couldn't have done it even if we'd wanted to.

But we had to do something. In November of 2005, a storm broke in Europe over an allegation that the CIA was moving detainees from one secret prison to another in parts of Eastern Europe. European institutions, backed by Western European politicians, excoriated the Easterners for aiding this controversial tactic. It was clear that the split over the war had not been forgiven in Brussels. Countries like Poland would be made to pay and pay again for deviating from the Franco-German line on Iraq.

I stopped by Secretary Chertoff's office. We had several things to talk about. When we were done with our main business, I dropped in another idea. "You know, our best friends in Europe are getting the worst deal under VWP," I said. "I'd like to spend some time thinking of ways to get them in—and improve security at the same time." He was walking around his desk at the time. He stopped in midstride and turned with a glint in his eye. He pointed a thin finger at me and with a smile that was almost mischievous said simply, "Let's do that." That was all the policy guidance I needed.

The deputy secretary at the time was named Michael Jackson. A tall gray-haired workaholic from Texas, Jackson was also a gifted government official. He had worked his way up from the bottom of the bureaucracy to become deputy secretary at two different departments—Transportation and Homeland Security. His easy Texas twang and aging athlete's spare tire hid a canny political mind.

He, too, could see the trap about to spring. He called me and my deputy, Paul Rosenzweig, into his office not long after my conversation with the secretary. "The road map," he said, "is a road to nowhere. I feel like we're just stringing these folks along." He asked the policy office to develop a series of options for completely rethinking the VWP program. The secretary's three-word guidance was going to become a full-fledged DHS initiative.

But this was not a problem we could fix under the law as it stood. Written to keep illegal dishwashers out of the United States, the law set a host of requirements for VWP status that had nothing to do with security. If consular officials in a country turned down more than 3 percent of the visa applications that they received, the result was fatal for the country's VWP candidacy. The theory was this: consular officials usually turn down applicants because they fear the applicants really intend to immigrate to the United States illegally. So countries with a high visa refusal rate are countries that may send us too many illegal immigrants.

That may be true. You could argue about what the exact cutoff should be, and you could object that countries were being graded on consular officers' perceptions and not actual conduct. But those arguments weren't our concern. The big problem was that the law focused mainly on immigration risk. It failed to do anything about security risk.

Congress had sprinkled a bit of security over the program after 9/11, saying that no country could stay in the VWP unless it adopted secure electronic passports with biometric identifiers. But resistance even to this modest requirement was fierce. The deadline had to be extended by a year, to 2005, and then again to 2006. Even with two extensions, some countries were not able to deploy the new passports on schedule.

It had worked in the end. More than two dozen countries had raised their passport security standards in order to stay in the VWP club. Why not do that on a much larger scale, we asked? If countries would revamp their passports to stay in the club, surely they'd improve security even more to get in the club in the first place. We could re-engineer the VWP to screen for terrorists as well as dishwashers. We could ask VWP candidates to offer reasonable security measures as part of the VWP negotiation. Those measures would set a new security bar for participation in the program. Once the bar was set, the rest of the club members could be held to the same standard.

Outside the department, the world was divided between those who hated the VWP and wanted it closed down immediately and those who wanted it expanded as soon as possible. We had to assemble a coalition of the middle. The expansionists, we figured, couldn't get past the VWP haters without accepting our security measures. And the VWP haters might get no security measures at all if they didn't accept our view that the measures should be tied to expansion. We were a small part of the debate, not strong enough to prevail on our own. But by carefully shifting our weight from one side to the other, we could provide the crucial swing vote that shaped the final outcome. That was my hope, at any rate. But if either the VWP haters or the expansionists gained a decisive advantage in Congress or the administration, the leverage we were using to set new security standards would be gone; we'd fall off one side of the tightrope or the other. We would need luck, determination, and leadership.

Working quickly, my office pulled together the elements of a traveler security program. At the top of the list was information. We could not continue to let travelers hop on planes in Europe without giving DHS enough information to decide whether they ought to be allowed into the country. We had to know who was coming. Our only sources of traveler information right now were provided by the airlines, and the European Commission was still trying to cut off that data flow. Well, they couldn't have it both ways. If they wanted to be part of the VWP, they would need to agree to better data sharing. We finally settled on three measures that would give us the kind of information we could get from a visa program—without the hassles and endless queues created by the visa system.

First, we'd set up a website to collect information directly from the traveler. That would let us control the kind of information we were gathering, rather than depending on what the airline reservation clerk decided to write down. It would also allow us to identify a suspect traveler in time to tell him that he couldn't come to the United States—thus keeping him off the plane and making it harder for al Qaeda to carry out transatlantic plane bombings.

As a bonus, it would even make the traveler's life easier, since the website could be a substitute for the aggravating forms he'd otherwise have to fill out with a borrowed pencil on the arm of his seat while the plane was landing. We even had a name for the system (one we borrowed from our Australian friends, who already had a similar program up and running). It would be the ETA, or Electronic Travel Authorization.

Implementing the ETA wouldn't actually require anything from our VWP partners, other than restraint and understanding. But knowing who was coming was just part of the job. We also needed to know who *shouldn't* come. And for that, we needed information from the traveler's home country. We needed to know which of their citizens they considered a terrorism risk. And we needed a way to find out whether someone coming to the United States had committed crimes at home.

These items seemed almost embarrassingly obvious. But the State Department had been trying for years to get other countries to share lists of terrorists with us, and their successes could be counted on the fingers of a single hand. When drivers are stopped by highway patrolmen in this country, their criminal records can be quickly obtained from other states—and from Canada. But when a traveler was stopped at the border, not a single VWP country had agreed to tell the United States whether he had a criminal record.

Imagine: Even if a border agent is suspicious of a man who says the young boy traveling with him is his nephew, he would never know the man was a convicted sexual predator at home. DHS had no idea whether the traveler it was inspecting had been convicted at home of smuggling drugs or of committing terrorist attacks. That had to be fixed.

Finally, as always, screening for risky travelers would fail if terrorists could switch identities at will. So we would need a second generation of protections against passport fraud—both better security for the passports and better reporting of lost and stolen passports. To deal with the threat to transatlantic flights, we added provisions to strengthen airport security, air marshal cooperation, and other safeguards we cared a little less about. We knew enough about negotiation not to ask only for the things we had to have.

In exchange for these security measures, we proposed to relax the strict 3 percent refusal criterion in the law—essentially taking a bit of risk on the immigration front to get a lot of new protection on the terrorism front. Without that relaxation, none of the Eastern Europeans would qualify for VWP. In 2005, Poland had a visa refusal rate above 25 percent, while Latvia's was nearly 22 percent. The rates were coming down fast in many countries, but getting below 10 percent would be an accomplishment; 3 percent was, for most of our allies, but a distant dream.

We knew what we wanted. But we didn't know whether we could get it. Like any tightrope act, this proposal would be at risk right to the end. If it hadn't been fully executed by the end of the administration, it could be delayed or the security measures could be watered down.

That shouldn't be so hard, we thought. After all, the president had been sworn in for a second term just that year. The administration had more than three years to run.

But in those years we had a lot to do. First, we needed to make sure the Eastern Europeans were as eager as we thought—and as willing to take security seriously as we hoped. Then we had to get our security measures through the same National Security Council and interagency process that was fighting us on PNR. Then we had to get Congress to adopt the same balanced proposal we were advancing in the interagency. And once Congress acted, if it did, we'd have to negotiate something like two dozen international agreements at the same time we were launching an unprecedented Web-based travel authorization application capable of handling millions of transactions a year.

Suddenly, three years didn't look like much time at all.

Petr Kolar, the Czech Republic's ambassador to the United States, is a bookish man with the mild and friendly air of a college professor. Kolar had barely finished school when the Communists fell. His timing was good. Untainted by service in the old regime, he moved easily from academia to stints in the Czech foreign ministry. He became a confidant of the Czech prime minister, who sent him to Washington. That turned out to be a wise move.

The Czechs are a proud people who spent most of the twentieth century under one autocratic boot or another. Austro-Hungarian emperors, Nazi *gauleiters*, and Soviet apparatchiks all took turns ruling the Czechs.

None found the job particularly comfortable.

Even today, the Czechs are prone to insisting at inconvenient times that their allies actually live up to their high-minded diplomatic pronouncements. That's understandable; twice in the twentieth century the West gave strenuous verbal support to Czech democrats and then stood idly by while first the Nazis and then the Soviets crushed them.

For Kolar, the Czech Republic's absence from the visa waiver program was a last vestige of the Iron Curtain. It had to go. He pulled together the rest of Eastern Europe in the hope that they could achieve the goal more quickly as a group.

Kolar developed a close relationship with Paul Rosenzweig, my deputy. Kolar kept prodding for action, but he seemed to understand that the world had changed on 9/11, and that security concerns about the program could not be dismissed. Rosenzweig trusted him. So, once we had our wish list of security measures, Rosenzweig urged that we ask Kolar for a confidential assessment: Would the Eastern Europeans be able to accept these measures as the price for VWP?

They met one afternoon at the Starbucks on New Mexico Avenue, near the department's headquarters. With him, Rosenzweig brought our wish list of security requirements.

Kolar took the draft list away with him. A few days later he called Rosenzweig to tell him that by and large the security requests were feasible; no promises, but they could form the basis for substantive discussion. We knew that we were in shouting distance of a successful negotiation.

But we knew that our hardest international talks didn't take place overseas. Once again, the toughest negotiations would be inside the government.

We knew there would be no difficulty persuading the National Security Council or the other cabinet departments that the visa waiver program should be expanded. President Bush felt a deep connection to the newly independent Eastern European states that had backed his campaign against Saddam Hussein when older allies turned against him. The National Security Council would be on board.

The State Department, too, wanted to stop requiring visas in these states, both because they saw how it hurt our reputation and for a more practical reason. All those visa-processing consular officers took up valuable embassy office space and distracted ambassadorial attention from more interesting diplomatic issues. The Department of Defense would also be glad to do something for their brothers in arms.

Justice, too, would favor easing VWP standards. The department was used to supervising the immigration agencies, which had been part of its domain until 2003, and it was usually willing to sacrifice immigration interests to improve prosecutorial and law enforcement relations. Indeed, there were press reports that Justice and State had already slipped up to Capitol Hill to offer clandestine support to the Santorum bill—cutting DHS out of the process because they knew we'd never support a VWP expansion that did not improve security.

Everyone, in short, would be pleased to expand the VWP. That was the problem. At the level of bureaucratic interest, all the other players would be willing just to surrender to the exponential logic of international travel. But our job was to guarantee that the border failures of 9/11 wouldn't be repeated. We were alone in wanting to tie expansion to the new security measures.

That would be the battleground.

We had two advantages in the battle. The first was a short chain of command and superb top cover. Chertoff and Jackson were the smartest leadership duo in the cabinet. We briefed them, and they at once saw the logic of the principal security measures. We knew they'd back us up all the way.

The second was the rest of the team. Rosenzweig was committed to winning the fight against terrorism. Stout, balding, and ebullient, he wore the bow ties favored by men who are proud of their quirks and independence. He was loyal, smart, and one of our fastest writers, a crucial skill in interagency fights where words are weapons.

He was too high-ranking to kick off the interagency scrum. For that I chose a young and talented lawyer who had already served at the Justice Department as well as in private practice. Nathan Sales was a thin, intense lawyer whose cowboy boots were a clue to his spirit. He was a fighter with a sharp mind. If he couldn't fight terrorists, I figured, he would gladly settle for fighting the National Security Council staff.

Sales drafted our proposal. Chertoff and Jackson blessed it. We took it to the interagency.

Unlike our PNR proposal, this initiative met with cautious interest rather than determined resistance. DHS had for so long simply said "no" to VWP expansion that the other players were delighted to hear us say, "Yes, but ..." And, like good negotiators, they first wanted to pocket our "yes;" there'd be time enough later to water down our "but."

And that's how it went. As we negotiated over the precise nature of the legislation, time and again the National Security Council staff or the Justice Department would suggest that maybe we didn't need to include all the security measures. That could be left to Congress, they suggested. Or perhaps the security measures could just be "factors" for the administration to keep in mind while expanding the program. Anything but a clear, straightforward statement that the security measures were as crucial as the expansion. We had to fight for the security half of the package at every turn.

This was the highest of high-wire acts. Like a man on a tightrope, we had to keep the proposal balanced as we moved forward. Over and over again, from Sales to Chertoff, the DHS representatives insisted that we could not support expansion of the VWP without closing its security holes. I'd like to think that we were persuasive, but we also owed a lot to Senators Feinstein and Kyl. In the current climate, we said, this bipartisan pair would kill any proposal for expanding VWP unless we could show a net gain for security. Many senators, particularly the Homeland Security committee leaders, Senator Susan M.

Collins and Senator Joseph Lieberman, were skeptical about expansion but open to persuasion. Only if DHS could make a heartfelt security case for expansion would we be able to persuade the Homeland Security committee's leadership. And we wouldn't be persuasive if the interagency compromised away the security features of the plan.

Dan Fried, a wily lifer in the Foreign Service who had risen to become assistant secretary of state for Europe, was the first to realize that the game had changed. State had tried pushing a reluctant DHS into adopting individual "road maps" to VWP status for candidate countries; when that failed it had tried getting the same result from Congress without telling DHS. Nothing had worked.

Fried had served on the NSC and spent years in Poland, eventually rising to become U.S. ambassador there. He knew the region, he knew the issue, and he knew the Hill was deeply split between hardliners and expansionists. DHS's proposal to link expansion and security measures offered the first new idea after years of deadlock. Still, it was a hard idea to swallow—not least because of where it came from.

From the moment of its creation, DHS had been State's adversary. At the outset, State barely prevented Congress from transferring its consular service to the new department lock, stock, and barrel. And we were constantly complicating State's diplomacy, either demanding more of foreign nations on the security front or sending their most prominent citizens to hard-nosed secondary inspections at the border. Worse, DHS was still building its international capability, from nothing. The department's reputation for international follow-through was not good. Even if we were sincere, Fried wondered, could we deliver?

In the end, Fried decided to take a chance on the DHS proposal. Perhaps he figured that State could always step in if we stumbled. In any event, he agreed to the essence of the idea—legislation that would both set new security standards and relax the 3 percent refusal standard that stood in Eastern Europe's way.

Once State was on board, the way was clear, though both Justice and NSC kept trying to water down the security measures.

The president seized on a November 2006 trip to Estonia to announce that he was sending Congress a new approach to VWP expansion.

We were now launched on a very public high-wire act. The other end of the wire was far away. We needed legislation, followed by dozens of agreements, not to mention a new computer system. And we'd burned a year of the president's second term—a third of the time we had—just getting the interagency on board.

Actually, it was worse than that. During that year, the American people had gone to the polls. After four years when Republicans controlled both houses of Congress as well as the presidency, they'd had enough, electing Democratic majorities to both the Senate and the House. Now, campaigning for the Democratic presidential nomination also shifted into high gear. The outgoing President Bush had a whiff of lame duck about him. Anything on his legislative agenda was likely to get a cold shoulder and a slow walk.

This was going to be a squeaker.

VWP reform would require legislation. We knew that. But members of the executive branch are always wary of Congress. Football coach Woody Hayes, it is said, used to defend his conservative ground game with the aphorism, "There are three things that can happen when you throw a pass, and two of them are bad."

That's how we felt about going to Congress. If we asked for legislation, a lot of things could happen, and most of them were bad. We could lose, of course, but almost worse would be to get a win that upset the balance between security and expansion.

We had no choice, however, and no time. Early in January 2007, Rosenzweig and Sales went to the Hill to brief the Senate staff. We had legislative language and a rough consensus from the interagency on what should be in the bill. The early reaction was as good as we could hope. Senators Feinstein and Kyl were opposed, as expected, but the crucial Homeland Security leaders—Senators Lieberman and Collins—were open to the idea.

Then we got lucky. The new leadership of Congress announced that it was going to adopt legislation implementing the recommendations of the 9/11 Commission.

This was an odd thing to be doing in 2007. The commission had delivered its report in the middle of 2004. It had pressed for rapid and bipartisan implementation of its recommendations, and that's what it got. By December of that year, Congress had passed and the President had signed a law to implement the commission's recommendations. But the new House leadership wanted to dramatize its view that the first law was inadequate. A second bill implementing the 9/11 Commission recommendations was duly introduced with the coveted title of "House Resolution No. 1," signaling that it was a top priority in the new Congress.

Even better, the bill would go through the Homeland Security committees that we had already briefed on VWP reform. Maybe, we thought, we could hitch a ride on this powerful locomotive.

Our proposal was attracting bipartisan support. In the House, Rahm Emanuel had long favored expansion of the program. His district had a huge Polish-American population. As part of the new leadership he could provide crucial help. In the Senate, the cause was championed by Senator George Voinovich, a member of the Homeland Security committee.

There was just one problem with adding VWP reform to a bill implementing the 9/11 Commission's recommendations. The commission hadn't actually made any recommendations about the VWP. It hadn't even asked for the information sharing and other security measures we were adding to the program. But, we reasoned, it did express strong views about terrorist travel. So it wasn't too much of a stretch to suggest that maybe VWP reform ought to be part of the new legislation. Representative Emanuel, Senator Voinovich, and the Homeland Security committee's leaders agreed. Perhaps they thought it would give substance to a bill that was otherwise largely symbolic. Or perhaps they wanted to make sure that President Bush had a reason to sign the bill rather than vetoing it. Whatever the reason, all of a sudden we found ourselves holding a ticket on the first legislative train out of the station.

Until then, we had been wary of the groups that were campaigning on the Hill for VWP expansion. We feared that they would cheerfully push for expansion without security. But once the administration's position took legislative form, it was their best hope. If anything showed the wisdom of our fight to include security measures as part of the President's package, this did. To be our allies, the expansionists had to offer at least some support for the security provisions. And they did. Energized and convinced at last that the United States was serious, Kolar and the other Eastern Europeans began mustering support from sympathetic ethnic constituencies. They made common cause with other VWP applicants (most notably the South Koreans) to expand their base, a tactical move that helped us win the support of Hawaii's tourist-conscious delegation.

It wasn't quite enough. Not everyone thought our security measures were sufficient. Senator Lieberman liked the ETA, but he didn't want VWP expanded until ETA applied to every VWP traveler. Senator Feinstein wasn't giving up either. She could see that the reforms would improve VWP security, but she wasn't satisfied that it did enough to prevent illegal immigration. That was a hot button issue in 2007. If she took to the floor to attack reform as a new avenue for illegal immigration, she might knock out the provision.

It was time to make a deal. To ease Senator Feinstein's concerns, we agreed to new conditions on expansion. No new countries would come in, we agreed, until the secretary certified that all the security measures were in operation—including the ETA. That would further reduce the time we had to get everything done, but it was good for security. If we left the hardest part of implementation to the new administration, they'd be lobbied endlessly to stall or drop the ETA. Unfortunately, when Congress drafted the provision, it inadvertently used language requiring that all our security measures had to be in place by October of 2008. Congress had cut three months from our already tight schedule.

We had a tougher time with Senator Feinstein and the immigration provisions. We didn't think that illegal immigration from Eastern Europe was that big a risk. Most Eastern Europeans could already work legally in places like the United Kingdom; how many would turn down legal work in Britain to live an underground life in the United States? But the committee was wary of the immigration issue, and of giving the executive too much discretion. Rather than dropping the 3 percent visa refusal requirement in exchange for security improvements, the committee decided that the 3 percent requirement could be waived—but only up to a maximum of 10 percent.

This was a tough blow. It meant that one of our strongest allies would be left out of the first round of expansion. Poland had gotten the reform movement rolling, and it was one of our best allies. But the refusal rate for Poles was still too high; they could not get under 10 percent before the end of President Bush's term.

The legislative train was moving; we had to take the deal if we wanted to stay on board. The tight timetable had claimed its first casualty.

And Senator Feinstein wasn't done. She had long believed that the United States should fingerprint everyone who leaves the country. If we tracked everyone who came in and everyone who left using their prints, she thought, then by process of subtraction, we'd also have the prints of people who came in but didn't leave when they were supposed to. Armed with that information, she thought, we could track them down and deport them. She insisted that we implement fingerprint exit monitoring, at least in airports, before we were allowed to expand VWP.

This was a deal killer. We weren't opposed to exit measures on principle, but identifying people on their way *out* of the country didn't have much to do with security. It was a bookkeeping measure. And it was based on a misunderstanding. First, we already had a paper-based system for recording departures. It could be better, of course, but it identified better than 90 percent of all departures. What's more, even if DHS had a dazzlingly accurate list of everyone who overstayed their visas, it didn't have anything like the resources to track down and deport all of them. We had to set priorities. Terrorist risks and criminals were our top priorities, and we were already tracking them down using the paper system. On top of everything, the Feinstein system would be staggeringly slow and expensive to implement. We could never do it in the time remaining.

We said no. The senator insisted.

We were stuck.

Then, at the last moment, I got a call from the Homeland Security committee. Could we live with alternative language? The new language, drafted by a creative travel industry lobbyist, said that we would have to implement an exit system in airports by the middle of 2009; if we didn't, we couldn't expand the program. As I parsed it, that meant we could expand VWP until mid-2009, but the curtain would come down on additional expansion if we didn't implement air exit. That wasn't good, especially for countries like Poland that missed the first cut; and it would create a real headache for the next president, whose Homeland Security secretary would have to work overtime to get the air exit program in place by mid-2009. But in the near term, it would allow us to bring in most of Eastern Europe and set a new security standard.

Well, hell, I thought. We only had eighteen months left to get this job done. This was no time to be worrying about the next president's problems.

I took the offer.

So did the senator.

There would be no floor fight.

Despite Woody Hayes's dictum, we had put the ball in the air, and it had come down all right, battered but still recognizable. VWP reform became law in August 2007. It had gone from proposal to enactment in just eight months—a miraculously rapid legislative voyage. But we had no time to celebrate. We had only seventeen months left, and in that time we had to draft multiple standard security agreements, shunt the text through the interagency process, then bring home eight separate but simultaneous negotiations over the texts. It was a tall order.

But that wasn't all.

We also had to get the electronic approval system up and running before any country could be admitted. Designing, developing, field testing, deploying and operating a new computer program in seventeen months is well-nigh impossible. Especially for the government, which has to follow strict procurement procedures and must issue proposed and final regulations before it can actually put a program like this into effect.

Governments have a history of failure where big new computer systems are concerned. We all knew that. The managers may stay on schedule for months, then one day announce the discovery of flaws that will take months and millions to cure. Customs and Border Protection was the responsible agency, and it was better than most of the other DHS agencies at implementing programs, but that was no guarantee. I once compared the agency to a trophy wife—the implementation might be as good as you hoped, but the cost was likely to be far more than you could ever have imagined.

This time, we couldn't have any surprises. I put Kathy Kraninger in charge of overseeing the program. Kraninger is a blond wisp of a woman. She looks like the first strong breeze might waft her away. But she had brought order to the DHS credentialing programs with a combination of expertise, steely charm, and persistence that agency executives could not resist. She made an odd contrast to the burly men who dominated CBP, but she worked well with Paul Morris, the experienced program manager who oversaw the team of programmers and technicians who would build the ETA.

Morris and Kraninger had begun planning the system in the late spring of 2007, as our legislative hopes began to rise. Now with the passage of the 9/11 bill, they kicked the team into gear.

Soon, the programmers had a schedule showing that the system would be up and running by October 2008, but few of us were comforted. There were dozens of contingencies built into that schedule. If any problems arose, any at all, we were going to disappoint a lot of people very publicly: our allies and friends overseas, Secretary Chertoff, our colleagues at State and the NSC, and, most of all, the president.

Managing big government IT projects is hard, in part because the usual rules for fast government action don't apply. Usually, being able to get quick decisions from the top is an advantage, and top-level monitoring of progress is a good way to smooth the project's path. Not so with computer projects, where most of the problems come from contingencies that don't yield to the kind of help high officials can offer. Once launched, the program can't usually be speeded up by throwing more resources at it—putting nine women on the job, as they say, won't produce a baby in a month. All the top officials can do is count the contingencies and wake up in the middle of the night worrying about whether the technical managers can overcome them.

Actually, it's worse than that, because one of the keys to making progress on government computer programs is: Don't change the instructions you gave the programmers at the start. Unfortunately, the top decision makers in government are used to, well, making decisions. The more they learn about the project the more they want to decide its details. They don't like to hear that their good idea was overruled by design decisions reached four months earlier when a batch of low-ranking techs set the specs.

So when the National Security deputy adviser told me he wanted regular briefings on the progress the ETA was making, my job was a little tricky. I needed to reassure him without inviting the kind of help that turned into change orders.

I kept the briefings short.

I'd show up in his office, show him the timeline, and say, "We're still on track."

And we were. I just hoped he wouldn't ask how many contingencies were still open.

Then he wouldn't sleep any better than Kraninger or me.

While the programmers toiled in pressure-cooker anonymity, we were trying to deliver the international agreements on which we'd based our entire strategy. With somewhere between eight and ten candidate countries and several agreements to be reached with each, just keeping track of the paper and the schedules would be a challenge.

My most experienced assistant secretary, Rich Barth, took point on the task. When I first met Barth in the early 1990s, both of us had other jobs. I was at the National Security Agency and he was a staffer at the NSC. I'd stayed in touch with him when he went off to be a senior executive at Motorola. Instead of the usual legal or liberal arts background, Barth brought a chemist's discipline to his work: problems were there to be solved, not admired. We'd lured him to DHS to manage the policy development process. For the delicate task of delivering all the deals in cooperation with the international office, Barth recruited Marc Frey, a young staffer who bore an uncanny resemblance to Clark Kent, minus the glasses.

Their task was complicated by the interagency process. As usual, negotiations with State and Justice were more difficult than with our foreign counterparts. To avoid squabbles over text, we first put forward a high-level memorandum of understanding on all of the security measures we wanted; it would be followed by a detailed set of agreements that would take longer to clear the interagency process.

To minimize conflicts and speed negotiations, we wanted all of the agreements to be as similar as possible. So Barth's team set out to nail down a standard-setting partner. Once again the Czechs were willing to lead the way. But the calendar was slipping away. Not until February 2008 did we get both the interagency and the Czechs to agree on a memorandum of understanding that could be a model agreement for the other countries.

We had eight months left.

And a lot still to do. After we signed the memorandum of understanding with the Czechs, we'd have to agree on the same principles with eight or nine more countries, and then negotiate the detailed agreements with all of them before October. With enough determination on both sides, though, we still reckoned that we could get it done.

We reckoned without Brussels.

As DHS's plan for a secure VWP unfolded, the European Commission had spent the winter quietly simmering. This was not the way it wanted events to unfold. The commission had told the Eastern European states to stand back and let it take the lead. It would use the combined might of European solidarity to force the United States to expand VWP—without any new security measures. That was its raison d'être, after all, and its business model. The first play in the Brussels playbook was, "Confront the United States with a United Europe; extract concessions that no one European country can obtain on its own."

Despite years of trying, that approach had gone nowhere. DHS had quietly turned aside the commission's demand for talks, saying that U.S. law required a separate evaluation of each country.

Worse, from the Brussels point of view, the Eastern Europeans seemed to be doing better on their own than the commission had been able to do on their behalf. Instead of invoking privacy to slow the U.S. initiative, they had readily agreed that sharing information about travelers would improve security on both sides of the Atlantic.

Now, with the signing of the Czech memorandum, visa-free travel was at last on the horizon. And it was met with something close to full-blown rage in Brussels.

For daring to take the initiative on VWP, the Czechs were pilloried. The commission's leaks to the press portrayed them as bad Europeans who were splitting the EU and delivering their citizens' personal data to the Americans. The commission publicly threatened to take the Czechs to court to punish them for their deviation, and the European Union summoned them to a meeting with the entire council for a tongue-lashing and a possible European repudiation of the memorandum of understanding.

The Czechs gave as good as they got. Asked to justify the decision to follow its national interests rather than the commission's wishes, Czech Interior Minister Ivan Langer could not have been more blunt.

"I am a free man, and not a slave of the commission," Langer told the press after one bruising confrontation in Brussels.[4] At DHS, someone suggested having Langer's words printed up on T-shirts for the next U.S.-EU negotiating session on passenger name records.

Despite the leaks criticizing the Czechs for compromising European privacy, it was clear that the dispute ran deeper than that. Brussels and the new members had already lost patience with each other when DHS showed up with its proposal. A European Commission official once complained to me over wine that, "The Eastern Europeans are different. They're not like the other new member states. They just don't seem grateful that we let them in."

That wasn't inaccurate. After years under the Soviet boot, the Eastern Europeans treasured their sovereignty. In Western Europe, nationalism had been tainted by World War II. The surrender of sovereignty to Brussels could be cast as the key to avoiding a repeat of that conflict. In the East, nationalism was a secret flame that flickered behind the iron curtain until it could at last revive when the walls fell. Surrendering sovereignty to another distant capital had no great appeal for these newly freed nations.

From our perspective the European Commission's gambit was a disaster. We could not negotiate productively with the European Commission on these topics. European countries had widely varying practices where passports and airport security and information sharing were concerned. We couldn't ignore those differences, or U.S. law.

But there was more. The EU's unremitting campaign of privacy objections to U.S. policy on travel data had left a scar. DHS had no confidence that the commission would agree to cooperative arrangements or exchanges of information, even when U.S. lives were at stake. Quite the contrary. The leaks coming out of Brussels seemed to promise yet another effort to keep the United States from knowing more about the travelers who showed up at its borders.

DHS had learned its lesson from the PNR talks. We had productive, collegial relationships with the European interior ministers, who had the same interest in fighting terrorism as DHS. The commission did not. It had sown its combative approach to PNR, now it would reap ours to VWP.

Still, we were running out of time, and the whirlwind in Brussels was threatening to pull apart the entire strategy. The commission was trying to blow up the whole deal, or take over the talks, claiming that the Czechs had no authority to enter into the agreements we were seeking. It was getting backing from the countries at the core of the Union—France, Germany, Italy, and Benelux. The Czechs in turn were getting support from the East, even from countries that wouldn't be eligible this time around.

It was ugly. When the Czechs were summoned to Brussels the stakes were high. The commission wanted to take over the talks; and even if that gambit ultimately failed, the rancor could stall negotiations long enough to kill all hope of a deal.

Then Brussels overplayed its hand.

Determined to use the privacy weapon to punish the Czechs, it began suggesting that they had no authority to sign an agreement on sharing criminal information with the United States. Only Brussels could allow an agreement on that topic, commission staff argued.

This was a strike at the heart of our security strategy. To focus our enforcement on the riskiest travelers, we needed better access to foreign criminal records. Turning that agreement over to the commission would kill progress on a critical security issue. But the agreement was not something we made up for the Czechs. It was a carbon copy of the agreement that Secretary Chertoff had worked out with Wolfgang Schaeuble, Germany's interior minister. The deal had cemented their friendship with substance, and it was dear to both men's hearts. When we told our German counterparts that Brussels was playing the privacy card and questioning their landmark deal, they were visibly displeased.

That was the turning point. Not long after, the EU met in Brussels to decide whether to discipline the Czechs or let them go their own way. According to second hand reports, at the showdown meeting the German representative broke ranks with the commission. Without German support, the European Union could not muster a consensus to bring Eastern Europe to heel.

We offered an olive branch as well, agreeing to talk to the European Union on two topics—a small issue where it clearly had jurisdiction and, in a triumph of hope over experience, the sharing of EU enforcement data. The European Union did have some data on visa and refugee applications; finding ways to share information to reduce fraud would be good for both of us, we thought.

By the middle of March, when it was clear that the EU's power play had failed, it accepted our offer and then more or less dropped from sight. Despite several efforts on DHS's part, no progress was made on the issues ceded to the EU. Since none of them were central to our security concerns, the lack of progress was disappointing but would not stall reform. The only concrete result of the consultations was that we agreed to change the name of the system from ETA (which evoked the initials of a Basque terror group) to Electronic System of Travel Authorization, or ESTA.

We were back on track.

Except that now we only had seven months left.

And while we had been focused on the memorandum of understanding and the drama in Brussels, the interagency process was grinding toward gridlock over the detailed agreements.

With Brussels back on the sidelines, the candidate countries had quickly signed on to the memoranda of understanding. Now we needed to complete the detailed agreements that would define more particularly what information would be shared, in what manner and by whom. DHS wanted those protocols complete before the expansion took place. Only by negotiating detailed protocols could we avoid lingering disagreements and get enforceable commitments.

But now the Justice Department was balking. DHS had come up with the proposal for criminal data sharing because we needed the data for evaluating travelers. Justice was glad to share data with other countries. But it wanted to keep DHS from doing the same.

Its argument was a convoluted take on the principle of reciprocity—the notion that we shouldn't ask other countries to do things for us that we wouldn't do for them. Justice claimed that under U.S. law, border inspections aren't always treated as law enforcement operations for purposes of disclosing criminal convictions. So Justice wouldn't always be able to give criminal conviction data to foreign border inspectors. For the sake of reciprocity, Justice argued, DHS border inspectors should be forbidden from getting criminal information from the authorities in other countries. This was laughable. Our allies weren't insisting on importing U.S. law into every aspect of the deal. All they wanted was a rough reciprocity that would give them information they actually needed.

I wondered again if some of Justice's fault finding and obstruction had a deeper cause. Until DHS came along, foreign interior ministers had only one counterpart in the United States—the Justice Department. But in some ways, DHS's role was closer to that of an interior minister than Justice's. As DHS expanded its contacts abroad, even when it used its contacts to help Justice, the Justice Department's international staff couldn't help but feel crowded. Perhaps its insistence that DHS was doing everything wrong was a natural reaction to the fear of losing turf. Certainly, cutting DHS out of criminal data exchanges would put Justice back at the center of the international law enforcement; we suspected that was a more potent motivator than some abstract notion of reciprocity.

Whatever the reason, Justice continued to insist that the criminal data-sharing agreement couldn't be executed as we'd written it. We tried arguing that Justice was wrong about U.S. law. It made no sense to read the law as denying criminal records to border officials, even for early screening decisions. But Justice insisted that its position was driven not just by law but also by concern for privacy and civil liberties. Prosecutors could use the data freely, of course; the FBI could use the data, too; hell, highway cops in every corner of the country could see the data every time they stopped someone with a broken taillight. But letting DHS use the data to screen travelers as they crossed the border—well, that raised serious privacy concerns. This was evidently a wall the prosecutors could live with.

The summer was nearly over. Rich Barth pressed me to yield. Justice must have thought that the ticking clock would bring us around—or that the buzzer would sound and we'd lose the deal entirely. The countries we were negotiating with had to see text right away. We were weeks from the deadline. Negotiations couldn't begin until we told our partners what we wanted. And we couldn't do that without an interagency agreement.

I was willing to take this one to the mat, though. Trying to isolate Justice, I called Dan Fried at the State Department. "Isn't this the deal you proposed three years ago?" he said to me. "You've done what you promised. There's no reason to change the rules now." We were still deadlocked, but Justice was the lone holdout.

Finally, the NSC took fright. It had always been more interested in VWP expansion than in the security improvements. Time was up. If the deadlock continued, NSC feared, expansion would be at risk.

The NSC staff set a deadline for DHS; if we didn't reach agreement with Justice right away, they would come down on Justice's side. In fact, they threatened to push VWP expansion through without the criminal information sharing protocols.

Close as we were to the finish, the tightrope walk was not over. We still might get visa expansion without adequate security.

But DHS still had one last advantage—short lines of communication. I walked down to Chertoff's office and briefed him on the NSC's threat. He understood the stakes. He refused to buckle. Under the new VWP law, he said, new nations could not be admitted to the program unless he personally certified that visa expansion would not jeopardize American security interests.

"There are a couple of people who can instruct me to make that certification," he told me, "but none of them are staffers at the National Security Council. And none of them are likely to think that the criminal data agreement should be dropped."

Told of the secretary's position, NSC blinked. They instead pushed Justice into a compromise. It was August by then, almost too late. But we had a free hand at last.

It was up to Barth and his team to deliver.

August slipped into September. The heat was on. We needed everything signed and sealed by mid-October. We broke our staff into teams so we could negotiate with several countries at the same time. One by one, our counterparts began signaling that we were close to a deal. But there were problems everywhere. Every country has different criminal procedures; different privacy rules; different requirements for approving international agreements. Some of the obstacles were substantive, some were procedural, but any of them could prevent us from signing the countries up by October.

In the end, two countries missed the deadline. Tiny Malta had trouble keeping up the pace—and had not been a negotiating priority. And Greece had booted its chances months earlier. It had failed to take the security provisions seriously, perhaps hoping that European solidarity would make a security agreement unnecessary.

The rest made it. Barely. On October 17, 2008, in a Rose Garden ceremony, President Bush announced the expansion of the Visa Waiver Program. He announced that effective November 17, citizens of Estonia, Latvia, Lithuania, the Czech Republic, Slovakia, Hungary, and South Korea would be allowed to travel to the United States without a visa. Malta was added a few weeks later. The Greek ambassador attended, glowering amid the smiles. It was the one sour note on a sweet day.

All we needed was a computer system.

One month later, on November 17, we turned on ESTA in test mode. Czech Deputy Prime Minister Alexandr Vondra and Interior Minister Ivan "Not-a-Slave-of-the-Commission" Langer flew on the first flight from Prague to New York. Barth and Kolar were proudly there to greet them as they got off the plane. A few days later, at a celebration marking Latvian Independence Day, the Latvian ambassador proudly announced that the violinist who was performing had arrived, visa-free under the new program, from Riga.

It looked as though we had made it to the end of the tightrope. Except for ESTA. In test mode, it could process a few dozen new

VWP travelers from Eastern Europe each day. Come January 2009, when the system went live it would have to apply to everyone traveling under the VWP program—twenty million of them a year.

And so, from November to January we waited with bated breath. Every day Kraninger would bring in the statistics on ESTA's performance. Every day we saw improvement. And glitches—problems in translation, problems in operation, and problems in decision making.

Day by day, CBP fixed the glitches and expanded the system. We started taking advanced ESTA applications from the other VWP countries that would be covered by the system in January. Meanwhile we ran stress tests on the system to assess its stability. All seemed to be ready.

Finally on January 12, we turned the switch and ESTA went live for everyone coming to the United States without a visa—more than 400,000 arrivals each week.

It worked. For the first time since the 1980s, American border officials knew who was coming to the United States in time to say "no" or to flag some travelers for closer scrutiny.

We were done.

Four working days later, President Bush was out of office, and so was I.

We could not have cut it finer.

8 Privacy Victims in the Air

If you've got to fly during the holidays, Christmas Day is as good as it gets. For a brief moment, the crowds drop off. Airports are almost peaceful. And if you start the day early in Europe, you can be in the United States in time for Christmas dinner.

Nearly three hundred passengers were taking advantage of that brief respite on December 25, 2009. Northwest flight 253 from Amsterdam to Detroit had been uneventful. No one thought anything about the young Nigerian complaining of a stomach bug; he had spent twenty minutes in the toilet and then covered himself with a blanket when he returned to his window seat in the middle of the plane.

The flight was well into its descent when Umar Abdulmutallab burst into smoke and flames. As the flames climbed the wall of the plane, and a brave Dutch passenger struggled with the man at the center of the fire, the passengers must have felt an unsettling sense of déjà vu. For the 2009 attack bore an eerie resemblance to another Christmas season attack eight years earlier.

It was another transatlantic flight, another al Qaeda terrorist from outside the Middle East, and another near miss. Once again, the solo terrorist had trouble triggering the explosive—in his underwear this time instead of his shoe. Once again, he didn't get a second chance, as passengers and crew subdued him and extinguished the flames.

Counting the "liquids plot" of August 2006, this was al Qaeda's third post-9/11 attempt to bring down transatlantic jets. The fixation on destroying transatlantic flights is reminiscent of an earlier fixation on the World Trade Center. It's safe to assume that they'll keep trying until they succeed.

We'd known that for years. We'd revamped our entire Visa Waiver Program just to make it harder for European al Qaeda members to launch transatlantic attacks. Yet we hadn't managed to keep an al Qaeda operative and explosives off flight 253.

Why not?

As I write, detailed reviews of the incident are under way. But the basic facts are not in dispute, and they raise serious questions about our air security strategy.

Abdulmutallab began his journey in Ghana, flying first to Lagos and then to Amsterdam before transferring to flight 253. He had 80 grams (about three ounces) of plastic explosive sewn into his underwear and carried a syringe full of acid to use as a detonator. He passed through airport screening three times, attracting no special attention at any of the airports.

Abdulmutallab had only carry-on luggage for a purported two-week trip, and he'd paid cash for his round-trip ticket. None of that was deeply suspicious by itself. Cash purchases aren't as rare in Africa as they are in Europe or North America. And for anyone who's waited—and waited—for luggage at the end of a long flight, a traveler who can carry on the luggage he needs for a two-week stay is cause more for envy than for suspicion.

But there was plenty of reason to be suspicious of Abdulmutallab, and the information was already in the hands of the U.S. and UK governments.

Umar Abdulmutallab began his journey to Islamic terrorism where so many did. In Europe. While attending University College London, Abdulmutallab established communications with several dangerous Islamic radicals who were under surveillance by MI5, the UK domestic intelligence service. But MI5 evidently lacked the evidence and manpower to follow up. In the absence of a reason to believe that Abdulmutallab was an immediate threat, MI5 never put him under surveillance. Worse yet, MI5 decided that privacy and politics required the agency to withhold information about Abdulmutallab from American agencies. As one British official told London's *Sunday Times*, "You can imagine the public fuss if they passed the Americans everything they had on all those who simply hold radical views."[1]

Indeed you can. This attitude permeated European thinking. It was the reason we had revised the VWP program to insist on greater information sharing about suspected terrorists from our counterparts in Europe. Unfortunately, even the British, with whom we had a relatively close counterterrorism relationship, had not agreed to a broad sharing of information about Islamic radicals—even foreign radicals—operating within their borders. In 2008, lacking any information from the British that might have spurred a deeper inquiry on terrorism grounds, the United States Embassy in London issued a two-year visa to the young man, whose wealthy father guaranteed that he would pose little immigration risk.

But it wasn't just our European allies who let us down. Our own government made plenty of errors as well. Abdulmutallab went on to study in Dubai and then Yemen, where he made the transition from radicalism to terrorism. He cut ties to his father, saying that he had found the true Islam and that, "You should just forget about me, I'm never coming back."[2] Alarmed, the father contacted the United States Embassy in Nigeria just five weeks before the attack, warning officials of his son's extreme views and presence in Yemen. In the end, he was interviewed by both consular officials and CIA officers, who prepared reports on the conversation but did not revoke Abdulmutallab's visa—perhaps because of an error in spelling his name.

They did enter Abdulmutallab's name into a lookout system in case he sought a visa in the future. Information on the Nigerian was also added to a 550,000-name classified database on terrorism suspects. But the information was not deemed sufficient to add Abdulmutallab to the formal Terrorist Screening Data Base, with its 400,000 names—let alone to the much smaller and more selective lists used to screen air passengers, the 4,000-name no-fly list or the 16,000-name list of "selectees" who are always screened with care before being allowed on a plane. One reason for this decision was a failure to connect Abdulmutallab to a separate stream of intelligence suggesting that al Qaeda's Yemeni arm was planning attacks, perhaps involving a Nigerian operative.

Despite all these failures, our border security system seems to have worked. The Transportation Security Agency (TSA), which screens air passengers, had no clue that Abdulmutallab was a risky traveler, and so it did nothing special as he boarded flight 253. In contrast, Customs and Border Protection (CBP), the agency responsible for screening travelers at the border, had access to both the 400,000-name Terrorist Screening Data Base and the State Department's consular databases. It also very likely had information about Abdulmutallab's lack of baggage and his cash ticket purchase, both of which should have been included in his travel reservation data. According to press reports, this information had already led CBP to flag Abdulmutallab for secondary screening when the flight landed in Detroit. There, border agents could have inspected his passport and asked about his travel to Yemen and his father's concerns. It seems likely that, as a result of that screening, Abdulmutallab would have been turned away at the border. The information-centered screening process that we had built at the border, in short, seems to have worked as we hoped.

But a system that only works after a transatlantic flight has landed doesn't do much good if al Qaeda is trying to blow up the plane before it lands. Protecting the flight, as opposed to the border, is supposed to be TSA's job. If CBP can construct a workable screening system that uses all of the government's data, why didn't TSA have such a system eight years after 9/11?

The short answer is that TSA tried to build such a system and was rebuffed by a well-organized privacy campaign. In fact, during the years since 9/11, privacy lobbyists managed to stall a host of new air security measures. In particular, they forced TSA to postpone and largely neuter the kind of data-based screening system that has worked so well at the border.

They had help from history. Keeping weapons off planes was our central strategy for years—since the days of the Cuban hijackings in the 1960s. But it was obvious for years that that strategy was played out. Weapons kept getting smaller and their hiding places kept getting more imaginative and harder, or more embarrassing, to find. (The 80 grams of explosive that Abdulmutallab was carrying weighed a bit more than a hot dog, and a bit less than bra inserts that can change a B cup to a C.)

The focus on weapons had to change (about which more later), but at present searching for weapons is the system we have, and it needs improvement badly. As everyone now knows, we actually do have better ways to find small weapons hidden in embarrassing places. The millimeter-wave and backscatter machines that look beneath clothing are far preferable to a "pat-down" that probes everywhere that three ounces of explosives could be hidden. And, creepy as the scanners are, the privacy issues can be handled by making sure the images can't be stored or copied and the image screeners are nowhere near the people being screened.

TSA had been using these machines as an alternative to pat-downs in "secondary" screening for about a year. But most travelers don't trigger secondary scrutiny. Abdulmutallab didn't. If keeping weapons off the plane is our main line of defense—and it is—we need to screen everyone for the weapons Abdulmutallab was carrying.

So why don't we? After the attack, everyone was clamoring for the scanners, and the privacy groups seemed quite responsible on the subject. As Marc Rotenberg, head of the Electronic Privacy Information Center (EPIC), told the *New York Times*, his group "had not objected to the use of the devices, as long as they were designed not to store and record images."[3]

For an organization committed to staving off 1984, EPIC seems remarkably adept at dropping things down the memory hole. Just three months before claiming that it didn't want to prohibit whole body imaging, EPIC and nearly two dozen other privacy groups sent a letter to Congress saying that whole body imaging ought to be, well, prohibited.[4]

In fact, the groups said, DHS's Chief Privacy Officer had violated the law when she *failed* to prohibit TSA's new policy on whole body imaging. If the law had been followed, the groups said, "the new policy would not have been implemented in the first place."[5] Such screening, they declared, "is exactly the type of action that the Chief Privacy Officer should be preventing in satisfaction of her statutory obligations."[6]

For the privacy groups, it was just another day at the office. The coalition that signed the letter was by now a well-oiled machine. It had stalled many new security measures since 9/11. And as far as whole-body imaging was concerned, the privacy machine was on the brink of another success.

In June, a bipartisan majority of the House of Representatives had voted to prohibit TSA from using the machines for primary screening. With a three-to-one margin of victory, it was nearly inevitable that the restriction would have found its way into an appropriations bill or some other must-pass piece of legislation. If not for the inconvenient timing of the Christmas attack, another new security technology would have been taken off the table.

This wasn't a victory just for the left-leaning groups that have traditionally scoffed at a war on terrorism. The privacy coalition that nearly killed imaging also included the American Association of Small Property Owners and the Gun Owners of America, and they persuaded large numbers of conservatives to vote against the security interests of air travelers. The alliance reflects a kind of political circularity, in which the far left and the far right discover that they have more in common with each other than with the center.

But in a deeply divided Congress, where each side counts on its most vociferous supporters to turn out the vote, one way to achieve bipartisan action is to propose legislation that appeals to the fringe of each party. The ban on whole-body imaging was just such a proposal. Republicans and Democrats alike could claim a victory for their base. Republicans and Democrats alike were protected against partisan second-guessing in the event of an attack because the measure had support in both parties.

It is a magic combination that has worked for the privacy coalition for years, despite the fact that most Americans are far more concerned about effective security than privacy.

In fact, nothing illustrates the clout of the left-right privacy machine than a second failing demonstrated on Christmas Day, 2009. That is TSA's inability to use screening information that is routinely used by all the other security agencies in government.

The United States has pretty good information on four hundred thousand terrorism suspects, but fewer than twenty thousand of them are on the lists that TSA uses to screen air travelers. That means that 95 percent of the identified terrorist suspects can get on a plane bound for the United States without receiving any more scrutiny than a grandmother from Dubuque.

CBP knows about these four hundred thousand suspects. The FBI and CIA know about them. So does the State Department. But not TSA. For TSA, if you aren't on the no-fly or selectee lists, you're just regular folks.

Why? Because that's the way the privacy campaigners want it. It's the intended result of their remarkably successful effort first to stall and then to roll back the security reforms undertaken after 9/11.

There's a well-establish civil libertarian mythology about the nation's response to 9/11. In the myth, a frightened U.S. government throws civil liberties out the window within weeks of the attacks, launching a seven-year attack on our privacy that a new administration is only now slowly (too slowly, say the advocates) beginning to moderate.

In real life, privacy groups mobilized within weeks of 9/11, and they won victory after victory, right from the start. First, within a month of the attacks, they forced the Justice Department to negotiate the USA PATRIOT Act line by line with Chairman Leahy of the Judiciary committee—a process often ignored when the act is presented as a *fait accompli* imposed on a panicky Congress by the executive branch.

Then within eighteen months of the attacks, the privacy campaigners killed the TIPS program, designed to encourage citizens to report suspicious behavior, as well as Admiral Poindexter's Total Information Awareness program.

After that, they went looking for bigger game. What they found was TSA, a gift that would keep on giving for half a decade.

DHS was brand-new in 2003. One of its priorities was to do exactly what the talking heads have been demanding in the wake of the Christmas Day attack. It wanted to transform TSA's screening system from one that looked mainly for weapons to one that looked for terrorists as well. The tool for doing that would be a second generation of the Computer Assisted Passenger Prescreening System, or CAPPS II. CAPPS II would process passengers' travel reservations to identify possible terror suspects much earlier and screen them more carefully—both before they got to the checkpoint and while they were there.

Until 2003, because it lacked access to travel reservation data, TSA had relied on the airlines to do the screening. It sent over a list of names, and the airlines checked to see if anyone with that name had made a reservation. If the person was on the no-fly list, the airline refused to give him a boarding pass. If he was on a selectee list, his boarding pass was marked so that screeners could single him out for additional screening.

That system was deeply unsatisfactory for many reasons, particularly as information sharing took hold, and a consolidated list of terrorism suspects was assembled from the many separate databases that existed before 9/11. Once these names had been assembled, the list was long and sensitive. No one wanted to trust unknown airline personnel with the crown jewels of U.S. counterterrorism intelligence, so giving them the entire list was out of the question.

Plus, the airlines weren't that good at figuring out when they had a name that matched. They'd flag Abdulmutallab for screening if that was the name they received from the government. But not Abdul Mutallab. Or Abdulmuttallab. If even the U.S. government can't manage to match a misspelled Abdulmutallab to the real thing, it's asking too much to expect the airlines to do better. So, to make sure that planes were not brought down by a typo, the government tried to supply all the likely variants and misspellings and aliases for every suspect's name.

But that created a new problem. Millions of Americans have names that resemble those on the list. Of course they have different addresses and birth dates, so a halfway decent computer system would not flag those people for scrutiny. The problem was that the many in the perennially bankrupt airline industry didn't have a halfway decent computer system, and they weren't eager to spend money upgrading their systems just to do the government's screening job for it.

So in 2003, DHS proposed to take over the processing of the list. The idea was straightforward. TSA would collect reservation data from the airlines and run its terror suspect lists against the reservations. The reservation data would help resolve ambiguities where two people had similar names. It would also provide new security capabilities, allowing TSA to identify connections between suspects that were on its list and previously unknown passengers who shared addresses or phone numbers with the suspects and who might be conspiring with them.

In short, it would create the one tool that could have stopped the attacks of 9/11. It would give security officials quick and easy access to domestic travel reservations. If they'd had that in August of 2001, officials could have first located the two known al Qaeda operatives and then spotted most of the others through links in their reservation information.

With that background, the new system must have seemed like a no-brainer to the leadership of DHS. But, fresh from their victories over TIPS and TIA, the privacy coalition had other ideas.

"This system threatens to create a permanent blacklisted underclass of Americans who cannot travel freely," an ACLU counsel told the Associated Press in February 2003.[7] Another declared that CAPPS II would "give the government an opening to create the kind of Big Brother program that Americans rejected so resoundingly in the Pentagon," a swipe at Admiral Poindexter.[8]

By June 2003, the organization had filed suit to block the program. By August, a left-right privacy coalition was lobbying against it. And by September, just two years after 9/11, the privacy groups had won. Congressional appropriators stopped the program dead in its tracks, prohibiting implementation of any such program until the General Accountability Office (GAO) certified that ten strict conditions had been met.

DHS spent the next five years trying to meet those requirements. Finally, in late 2008, DHS announced that it was launching Secure Flight, a pale imitation of the original program that gave TSA access to no traveler information other than name, gender, and birth date.

Even then, GAO demonstrated that it had learned the facts of life in Washington—you can't go wrong overestimating the clout of the privacy lobby. Knowing that it would never be criticized for refusing to certify compliance, GAO declared that TSA had met only nine out of ten requirements and let the appropriators deem that sufficient to begin Secure Flight. To its credit, the Obama administration did not treat that as an excuse to delay the program; it continued to roll out Secure Flight in 2009.

But if you've wondered why, eight years after 9/11, we're still looking for weapons and not for terrorists, now you know. Privacy advocates turned the use of even ordinary data like travel reservations into the policy equivalent of a toxic waste site. No one wanted to go anywhere near it, and those who did rarely survived the experience.

Remarkably, that wasn't all. The episode turned out to be far worse for security and far better for the privacy campaigners than even they could have hoped. Because as long as Secure Flight was stalled, we were all stuck with the old system of sending lists to airlines and living with whatever their creaking computer systems dished up. Most of the airlines couldn't tell Senator Stevens's wife, Catherine, from the singer formerly known as Cat Stevens, a reported apologist for the fatwa against Salman Rushdie.

As the lists grew and Secure Flight languished, you might have thought that the privacy groups and the airlines would start to take some heat. After all, their opposition was the reason that so many people were being hassled for no good reason. But they didn't feel any heat at all. Quite the reverse. In an unexpected bonus, the blame fell entirely on the agency that had tried to fix the problem years earlier.

That must have been deeply satisfying. The privacy machine had created a vicious cycle. As long as Secure Flight was stalled, administering even a small no-fly and selectee list was painfully difficult—and a massive inconvenience for travelers whose names resembled those on the no-fly and selectee lists. Even better, TSA took all the blame, thus discrediting both the idea of screening for possible terrorists and an agency that no traveler was much disposed to love in any event. Every time TSA's reputation took a hit for mismatched names, it became easier for Congress and the privacy groups to argue that the agency couldn't be entrusted to administer a new program.

Better still, from the privacy groups' perspective, the millions of privacy victims created by the mismatched names became an excuse for rolling back other security measures, including the terrorist watch-list. In 2008, when TSA began to get close to meeting the Congressional requirements for Secure Flight, Barry Steinhardt of the ACLU held a news conference to announce that the watch-list had reached one million names (he was wrong, but the coverage was good anyway). "The list is out of control," he said. "There cannot possibly be one million terrorists threatening and poised to attack us. If there were, our cities would be in ruins."[9]

And with a chutzpah rarely equaled in American policy circles, Steinhardt mourned "the tens of millions of Americans [who would now be] caught up in a Kafkaesque web of suspicion."[10]

He should know.

He had spun the web those Americans had been trapped in.

That brings us back to Christmas Day, 2009, and the question of why Abdulmutallab wasn't on a no-fly or selectee list, or for that matter why 95 percent of the terrorist suspects known to the U.S. government are treated like upstanding citizens when they get to the TSA checkpoint.

Imagine for a minute that you were a security official watching the ACLU press conference in 2008. You see that the organization got the number of names on the list wrong, trashed TSA for a problem they'd created themselves, and received fawning coverage for it. Do you really want to stick your head over the parapet and suggest a substantial expansion of lists that the ACLU says are already "out of control" and are victimizing tens of millions of Americans? Nope, in those circumstances, there wasn't much chance that standards for getting on the lists would be eased, or that TSA would soon get operational access to the other 95 percent of the database.

In the end when all is said and done, the investigations of the incident will find errors in how the agencies handled the lists and the screening. But when they do, for once we should skip the football analogies.

The errors weren't "fumbles" or "dropped balls." Instead, the most apt analogy comes from tennis.

Because if ever there were a "forced error" in policy making, this is it.

And as in tennis, full credit should go to the privacy advocates that forced it.

PART THREE

TOMORROW'S TERRORISM

9 Moore's Outlaws

In the years since 9/11, we had done a lot to meet the challenge posed by the exponential growth of international travel. Our border procedures weren't airtight, of course; they never had been. But we weren't flying blind, making decisions at the border on thirty seconds of chat and intuition, either. We'd come a long way, and while we still had further to go, at least everyone understood how important it was to finish the journey.

The challenge posed by computer security was different. There had been no dramatic meltdown. Most people still scoffed at the idea that the exponential growth of information technology revolution could lead to disaster.

Yet for some of us, losses from the information technology revolution are already greater than the gains.

Just ask Howard Crank's widow.

Howard Crank lived a quiet life that revolved around his modest California duplex. He was seventy-three years old, after all, and he'd had both legs amputated above the knee due to diabetes. His wife's health was not good. He was living on his Air Force veteran's pension. But he could afford a computer, and he loved it. It helped him find old Vietnam buddies and research new charities to add to the three dozen he already supported. He might be halfway to housebound, but the new technology was a godsend. Thanks to Moore's Law and the Internet, the whole world was at his doorstep.[1]

The Internet, it appears, is how he discovered that he'd won $715,000 in a Spanish lottery. Money was tight on an Air Force pension, so this was amazing news. Of course, it turned out that there were transfer taxes for him to pay before the winnings could be sent to him. It grew expensive, but his share of the lottery was also growing—to $115 million.

Howard Crank's life savings were $90,000. Bit by bit, he sent it all.

It wasn't enough. He got calls from Spain, explaining the hassles and delays. He mortgaged his home and sent the proceeds. More calls. When he wondered aloud whether he'd ever see the money, the caller asked him to have faith. They prayed together.

A few weeks later, he took out a second loan on the house. He maxed out two credit cards. All the money, perhaps $300,000 in all, went to Spain. Even that was not enough to break his lottery winnings free. He asked his stepdaughter for $40,000. He didn't want to explain why.

She thought that was odd. So when he was hospitalized a few weeks later with a broken thigh, she checked his financial records. She found that Howard Crank had ruined himself and his wife in an apparent Internet hustle. The Spanish scam artists disappeared without a trace. Crank died of a heart attack before he could explain how it happened.

"I think he probably knew it was a fraud at the end," his stepdaughter told me. "But he was hoping against hope. He'd sent them so much money already, and they were so convincing. But by the end he'd lost his zest for life. He was so desperate."[2] Desperate he should have been. He had not just squandered his own assets. A year after his death in early 2010, his widow had lost her home and been forced into bankruptcy by the debts he left behind. "She's had to move in with us. She's starting over again at the age of eighty," her son-in-law told me.[3]

Howard Crank would never have let a con man into the quiet life he and his wife were living. But the Internet that brought the world to his doorstep brought the world's con men as well. Information technology empowered Howard Crank to search the world for old buddies. And it empowered fraudsters to search the world for the handful of people who might be ripe for their scam.

For Howard Crank, the exponential growth in information technology turned out to be a disaster. It was great for a while. He loved what the new technology did for him, and how cheaply it performed its miracles. But in the end, nothing he gained by embracing it was worth what he lost.

Will the rising curve of information technology eventually leave the rest of us where it left Howard Crank? You're probably thinking that Howard Crank, sympathetic as his story may be, just wasn't savvy enough. You would never fall for such a scam. And you will never suffer the harm that he did.

Well, don't be so sure. The science fiction writer William Gibson once declared that, "The future is already here. It's just unevenly distributed."[4] He was thinking of the wonders of new technology, but bad futures are distributed as unevenly as good ones. And Howard Crank may have been in the vanguard of Americans ruined by information technology.

Thanks to information technology, it is now cheap to screen millions of people to find those who were susceptible to the lottery fraud. That same technology will make it cheap to screen the world for people and machines that are susceptible to other forms of fraud as well. You may not fall for the Spanish lottery, but you're probably susceptible to *something*. And even if you aren't, your machines are.

Are you really sure the fraudsters won't find you in the end?

Exponential technologies always seem to serve dessert first. That's why they grow exponentially. Their benefits are immediate and irresistible, so we use them in numbers that double and double again. In the beginning, it seems implausible that they will be misused. Indeed, at the outset, people do use them mostly in good, socially responsible ways. I leave it to the philosophers whether that's because people are basically good or because it takes time for people to figure out how to be bad using new technologies.

Whatever the reason, information technology certainly followed the same path as commercial jets. It took decades between the time the technology was first democratized and the first really frightening misuse.

Until the late 1980s, the risks of misuse were almost entirely theoretical. Computer viruses had been invented by then, but mainly just to show how they would work. It wasn't until the mid-1980s that "wild" computer viruses began to spread from one PC to another via floppy disks. Then, in 1988, a worm caused much of the Internet to grind to a halt. For the academic and defense users who then dominated the Internet, the worm was a shock. But they relaxed when they found that the worm's author, Robert Morris, wasn't a spy or a criminal. He was a student, and he claimed he'd been testing a concept that got out of control.

In retrospect, what's most notable about the malware of that era is its comparative innocence. It caused damage, sure. But it was either academic or nihilistic in purpose; it demonstrated the capabilities and perhaps the ill will of the author. It wasn't really much of a threat, although the worst examples could destroy stored data.

Most attacks were the digital equivalent of the Plains Indians "counting coup" by striking an enemy with a stylized stick and escaping. Like counting coup, the purpose of early hacking was to gain prestige—more by demonstrating prowess rather than by causing harm. And computer security only needed to be good enough to outfox adolescent malcontents, a task both industry and government felt fully capable of handling.

By the mid-1990s, though, the Internet had become a fully democratized place, and money had replaced showing off as a motive for hackers. Spam was the earliest form of profitable Internet crime. And when network administrators started blocking spam by refusing to accept mail from spammers' machines, hackers found they could compromise other people's computers in bulk, then use those machines to send the messages. If the senders of unwanted email were widely distributed, spam couldn't be stopped by quarantining a few suspect computers. Hacking wasn't just fun anymore; it could put money in the hacker's pocket.

Once underground networks of compromised machines had been assembled, it turned out that they could be used for other profitable crimes as well. If all of the captured machines could be induced to send meaningless messages to a single Internet site at the same time, the site would be unable to process them. The site would falter and fail. Legitimate users would be locked out.

Such "distributed" denial of service attacks turned into a new-style protection racket. Gambling sites, for example, simply cannot afford to be unavailable in the days and hours before the Final Four basketball tourney. If a site suffers an effective denial of service attack, there is a good chance that it will pay a reasonable "security" fee just to get back online quickly. That wasn't the only use to which criminals could put herds of zombie machines. The machines could be programmed to visit ad-supported websites and mindlessly click ads, earning illegitimate click-through fees for those sites.

But security professionals at large firms still had confidence in their defenses. Denial of service was a concern, sure, but the risk could usually be managed by retaining an ISP with lots of bandwidth and an ability to filter packets quickly. Distributed spam took away one tool for discouraging spam, but there were plenty of other ways to filter unwanted mail. For most users, spam was at worst a nuisance.

But malware continued to grow more sophisticated, and it could use the Internet to spread rapidly. Several viruses in 2000 and 2001 caught large companies unprepared and forced a shutdown of their networks while the viruses were eradicated. Hackers began to find ways to intrude into important financial and military systems.

This was getting serious.

Even so, most security experts thought the plague could be contained. They blamed systems administrators who didn't patch their systems quickly enough. Most of all they blamed Microsoft. The company had emphasized new features over security, they complained, and in its drive to be first to market it had written sloppy code. Other operating systems were said to be more secure; and many thought that relying on a variety of operating systems was inherently superior to the "monoculture" created by Microsoft.

Stung, Microsoft fought back. Bill Gates himself took on the problem. Gates was famous for his insight into the future of the personal computer. Previous Gates messages had produced profound changes in Microsoft's strategic direction, most famously when he wrenched Microsoft into the Internet age, focusing the entire company on the challenge posed by Netscape—and leading to Microsoft's (temporary) victory in the browser wars.

By January 2002, Gates had a new focus. He announced that security was the key to Microsoft's future. From now on, all of its products would be built with security in their foundation: "When we face a choice between adding features and resolving security issues, we need to choose security. Our products should emphasize security right out of the box, and we must constantly refine and improve that security as threats evolve."[5]

The email was a call to arms. All of Microsoft's employees were expected to bring this new focus to their jobs. In the past, a single-minded focus had enabled Microsoft to beat some of the most talented companies in the world. IBM, Lotus, WordPerfect, Ashton-Tate, Digital Research, Sun, Real, Apple, AOL, and Borland—not to mention much feared and rarely bested Japanese electronics makers like NEC and Toshiba—all had tried to stand between Microsoft and its strategic vision of the future. Microsoft had defeated them all.

Now Microsoft was gearing up for battle again. This time, though, it only had to beat a bunch of punk hackers. That should be a piece of cake. Once it was done, a new age of online security would dawn, with Microsoft's trusted products at the heart of every online transaction.

More than seven years have passed since Microsoft set out to beat a ragged band of hackers. The company has rewritten its operating system more or less from scratch. And its code is indeed far more secure than in 2002.

But it has not won the war. The second Tuesday of each month still brings a boatload of corrections and patches that the company must make to even its newest and most secure operating systems. By 2009, the ragged band of hackers was looking a lot more sleek and prosperous than before, and Microsoft had suffered its first revenue decline in history.

More important than Microsoft's security failures are its successes—and how little difference they have made. Microsoft has indeed tightened up the operating system. But the structure of the PC world has made that almost irrelevant. The point of the PC is the control it gives to the user—who can decide what applications to run—and to the developers, who can create new applications quickly and easily. At the end of the day, Microsoft must empower users and developers. And so that's what its security approach does. Windows Vista, for example, was famous for nagging users to confirm their dangerous decisions to run new code or open new attachments—so famous that Windows 7 has had to cut back on the nagging, despite the security risks. The one thing Microsoft can't do is forbid users to make dangerous decisions. If Microsoft tried that, it would leave its users angry and looking for a new operating system. The same is true for applications; Microsoft can't require developers to write secure code without discouraging them from writing Windows applications. And if it does that, it loses its main advantage in the market—the overwhelming number of applications that run only on Windows.

So, to the extent that Microsoft has succeeded, it has simply displaced the risk. Online security is still getting worse, but it's getting harder to blame the operating system. Instead of exploiting the operating system, more and more attacks exploit holes in applications. Or they induce the user to do something he shouldn't do.

Or both.

One night in January 2009, at about the same time that Howard Crank was sending thousands of dollars to Spain, Beny Rubinstein was getting ready to turn off his computer and go to bed.

Suddenly he got an instant message from Bryan Rutberg, a friend who worked for a technology company. Rutberg's message got right to the point.

"Look, I really need your help."[6] Rutberg had taken a quick trip from Seattle to London, where he'd been robbed. He was broke in a foreign land. His Facebook page said the same thing, carrying an update that said, "Bryan NEEDS HELP URGENTLY!!!" Bryan needed a loan to get home. Could Rubinstein help?

Rubinstein could. He wired $600. That wasn't enough, so he sent another wire transfer—$1,143 in all.

In fact, Rutberg was still in Seattle. His Facebook account had been hacked, and the hacker was messaging Rutberg's friends, asking them all for quick wire transfers.

Rutberg, meanwhile, was locked out of his own account. He tried to stop the impostor by posting a comment on his own page, using his wife's account. Rutberg's comment was quickly deleted, and his wife was "unfriended." He had lost control of his online identity to a brazen scam artist.

A couple of days later, Facebook closed down the account, but Rubinstein's money is long gone. Neither Rubinstein nor Rutberg is a technological naïf. But both were defeated by the mass customization of online fraud. It's not hard to write programs that will look for weak Facebook passwords, or that will send urgent instant messages to the friends listed in compromised accounts. Only when someone responds to the messages do the scammers need to become personally involved. The marks are all prequalified.

Best of all, it's possible for the scammers to get in and get out in hours, then disappear halfway around the world. Local police are helpless; they "are not investigating this case," said a police spokesman. "It is pretty much at a dead end."[7]

As Microsoft has tightened the operating system, hackers increasingly rely on mass social engineering and insecure applications to open a hole in the victim's defenses. Facebook is, of course, free, and the company is famous for not having a revenue model to match its massive user base. So it's not surprising that its site still has security problems. But it's the social engineering that made this scam work. Rutberg's friends may not trust strangers who tell them they've won the Spanish lottery, but they do trust him.

In fact, the combination of "authorized malware" and targeted social engineering is so powerful that, despite Microsoft's efforts, it's now easier than ever to compromise computers, and their networks.

No one can say we weren't warned. The United States government told us all that a computer security crisis was brewing. Twice, in fact, and under two different presidents.

President Clinton cautioned in January 1999 that, "We must be ready—ready if our adversaries try to use computers to disable power grids, banking, communications and transportation networks, police, fire, and health services—or military assets."[8]

A year later President Clinton proposed a series of measures to address the security problem.

Two years later, President George W. Bush created a special adviser on cybersecurity who spent a year developing a computer security strategy.

Neither effort made much headway. The public didn't see the problem. The network attacks that alarmed Washington were classified. Officials couldn't talk about them. Meanwhile, privacy and business interests worked overtime to persuade the public that national security concerns were overwrought. The real risk was government monitoring and government regulation, they insisted.

And, by and large, that was the view that prevailed—twice, and under two presidents. Nothing was done about computer security that anyone in the privacy or business lobbies might object to.

In 2009, a third president promised to make computer security a top priority, and shortly after taking office, the Obama administration also produced a security strategy. Once again, though, the strategy lacked punch. It failed to call for any action that could possibly irritate business or privacy groups. It spoke of cybersecurity only in alarmed generalities, unable to explain why Americans should be concerned enough to suffer even modest inconvenience.

But this time may be different. Thanks to the work of a band of Canadian security researchers, we now have a remarkable—and completely unclassified—insight into just how easily computer hackers can penetrate even carefully secured computer networks.

The young Tibetan girl waited quietly in line at the border. Call her Dechen, though that's not her real name. She had spent two comfortable years studying in Dharamsala, India. Now she was going home. She had made the long trip across Nepal to the border with Tibet. The border crossing made her uneasy, but she told herself the Chinese border guards had no reason to stop her.

Dechen was a follower of the Dalai Lama, and she had spent much of her time in India conducting computer chat sessions with his supporters inside China. But she had been careful. She really had been a student. There was no way the Chinese government could know what else she had done. Or so she hoped.

Dechen stepped forward and presented her identification to the guards. They looked it over with care. Too much care. Something was wrong. Her heart sank. She was under arrest.

She was sent to a detention center. No one would tell her why. Could she have been compromised somehow in Dharamsala? She couldn't understand it.

Finally, after two months in captivity, she was called to the interrogation facilities, where two plainclothes officers immediately began questioning her about her activities on behalf of the Dalai Lama. She denied the charges, clinging to her story.

"I was a student. They cannot know what else I did," she must have told herself.

But over and over, intelligence officers accused her of working for the Dalai Lama's youth group. Over and over, she denied it. She had gone two months without contact with friends or relatives, but if she held firm, they would have to let her go. She stuck to her story.

Finally, the officers lost patience. They pulled out a thick file. The folder held a full transcript of her online chat sessions. It covered years. They'd known everything, recording it as she typed. They told her the names of all her coworkers. All the attempts at security, all the work of the Dalai Lama's youth group, had been defeated.

Dechen was devastated. But the officers were more interested in sending a message.

—Go back to your village, they said, and tell your coworkers that we know who they are. They are not welcome in China anymore. They can expect the same treatment you got, or worse, if they return.[9]

It was over.

The Office of His Holiness the Dalai Lama is partly a religious, partly a diplomatic mission. The Dalai Lama travels widely and seeks audiences with foreign diplomats and officials to demonstrate support for his faith and for Tibetan autonomy. The Chinese government in turn vehemently opposes autonomy for Tibet and does all it can to discourage official meetings with the Dalai Lama.

The Dalai Lama's travel schedule is thus a matter of high state interest, and the planning of his meetings has an element of cat and mouse about it. The Dalai Lama's office finds that the best way to set up those meetings is first to send an email to the officials the Dalai Lama hopes to meet and then follow up quickly with a telephone call.

But around the early part of 2008, something odd began to happen. The Dalai Lama's office would send an email to a diplomat as usual, proposing a meeting. Then it would call to discuss the details, again as usual. But the diplomat's office would be strangely cool. "We've already heard from the Chinese government," the diplomat's staff would say, "and they've strongly discouraged us from having this meeting."

The Dalai Lama and his office had been using the Internet since the 1990s. His network administrators know the risks, and they've been careful about computer security for years. They'd implemented the standard defenses against network attacks. They didn't know what had happened. But the evidence of a serious breach was simply too strong.

They called in a team of Western computer security experts. What the experts found was deeply troubling, and not just for the Dalai Lama.

Some of the Dalai Lama's staff participate in Internet forums. They chat with other, like-minded individuals about the Dalai Lama's goals and activities. Sometimes one of their online acquaintances sends them Word or .pdf documents relevant to those activities.

The experts concluded that hackers had monitored these forums and then forged an email from a forum participant to a member of the Dalai Lama's staff. Attached to the email was a document of mutual interest. When the staff member opened the document, he also activated a piece of malware packed with it. While the staff member was reading the document, the malware installed itself in the background.

The malware was cleverly designed; two-thirds of commercial antivirus software programs would have missed it. (Hackers often subscribe to antivirus software so they can test their malware against it at leisure.) Even if one attachment were stopped, it would be a simple matter to retransmit the message using a different bit of malware; the attackers could keep trying until something got through.

Once installed, the malware would "phone home," uploading information about the victim's computer and files to a control server operated by the hackers. Next, the captured computer would download more malware to install on the staff member's machine. This was often a complete administrative program that would allow the attackers to control the staffer's computer, and in some cases the entire network.

The administrative malware took full advantage of the empowerment made possible by today's technology. It featured a graphic interface with dropdown menus offering even an unsophisticated attacker a wide variety of options.

Want to record every keystroke as the user types so you can steal all his passwords? Check one of the options on the menu.

Want to turn on the user's microphone, turning it into a bug so you can listen to the office conversations? Check another box.

Want video straight from the user's desktop camera? That's just another option on the menu.

In the end, the Dalai Lama's office was living a version of Orwell's *1984*. Telescreens in each room spied on the occupants. But in this version of *1984*, Big Brother didn't even have to pay for this spy equipment. It had been purchased and installed by the victims.

Once the hackers had compromised a single computer on the network, it wasn't hard to compromise more. Every time an infected computer sent a document by email, malware could be attached to the file. The recipient couldn't possibly be suspicious; the email and attachment were exactly what he expected to receive from his colleague. He opened the document. The malware installed itself in the background. The cycle began again. It was an entire network of surveillance, dubbed Ghostnet by the security team.[10]

Ghostnet has lessons for all of us. You may be sure you wouldn't fall for the Spanish lottery, and perhaps not even for a Facebook call for help, but it's hard to find any comfort in this story.

Do you rely on standard commercial antivirus software to scan attachments? Do you open documents sent by people you've met online? How about documents from prospective customers or clients? Or old friends you recently connected with online? Do you open mail and documents sent to you by coworkers?

Of course, you do. So do I. And that means that most of us are no more able to defend ourselves from this attack than the Dalai Lama was.

If there were any doubts about the scope of such attacks, they were eliminated by what the security team did next.

They took another look at the IP address of the hacker's control server, and asked a simple question.

"Do you think hackers who need a graphic interface to steal secrets are really good at locking down their own computers?" I imagine the Canadian team sharing a mischievous smile as they asked.

Perhaps a veil should be drawn over exactly what they did next. Hacking is illegal in most jurisdictions, even if you're hacking someone who has just hacked you. Using methods they decline to specify, the security team was able to verify that whoever attacked the Dalai Lama's network was indeed much better at breaking into other people's computers than at keeping intruders out of their own.

Finding themselves inside the hackers' control servers, the security team naturally had a look around. They watched as reports came in from the Dalai Lama's computers. But that's not all. Reports were coming in from other computers as well. Hundreds of them.

The hackers who compromised the Dalai Lama's network were collecting data from nearly thirteen hundred other computers. Who else had been targeted by the attackers? That wasn't hard to find out. All the security team had to do was to ask who owned the IP addresses of the compromised computers.

What they found was a Who's Who of Asian organizations that ought to be highly concerned about—and pretty good at—computer security: Indian embassies in the United States, Germany, and the United Kingdom; the foreign ministries of Iran, Indonesia, and the Philippines; the prime minister's office in Laos. All were in thrall to the attackers' servers. Computers in sensitive businesses, from the Asia Development Bank to Vietnam's petroleum company, were also sending the attackers their data.

And, even though this set of attacks does not seem to have been aimed at the United States, Ghostnet was collecting reports from computers that belonged to the Associated Press and the auditing firm of Deloitte & Touche. Oh, and NATO too. In early 2010, Google announced that it and many human rights campaigners using Gmail had been targeted with the same attacks.

No one was safe.

The security team split on the question of whether to assign responsibility for Ghostnet to China. Some said it must be the Chinese government. Others were willing to let the facts speak for themselves. The Chinese government denies everything.

But there's not much comfort for us in the denials. The attacks happened, and they worked. If a government wasn't responsible, then this kind of capability is already in the hands of organized crime. Indeed, with its script-spy graphic interface and unsecured control servers, the whole episode underlines a troubling fact. Thanks to exponential empowerment, today's hackers don't even have to be very good. Empowered by democratizing technology, they can still beat our best defenses.

In fact, something similar to Ghostnet is already being used by organized crime. Most businesses depend on bank clearinghouse accounts or electronic fund transfers to pay their bills. They log on to bank sites using passwords; for larger amounts they may also be asked a set of "challenge questions" seeking information only the businesses know. But corporate officials also open email attachments from business contacts, and once attackers have access to the officials' keystrokes, neither the password nor the challenge questions offer any security. Hackers have stolen more than $100 million from U.S. businesses using this technique, the FBI reported in October 2009.[11]

I wasn't in government in 1998 or 2003, when the Clinton and Bush administrations called for new computer security measures. I didn't get the classified briefings that galvanized both presidents. Now I figure I don't have to.

This is scary enough.

But maybe you're not ready to agree. Maybe you're worried that these security alarms are a little too convenient—perhaps just an excuse for the government to spy on Americans and interfere with the economic engine of Silicon Valley. Surely, you think, there are still a few good defenses left.

Well, let's take a look at some of the top reasons that people think computer security risks can be managed successfully.

It's a Microsoft Problem. I know plenty of people who still believe that Microsoft's products are uniquely insecure, and that all we need to do is get Microsoft to clean up its act or take our business elsewhere.

For some, the security of Linux was an article of faith; its source code is open to inspection by anyone, so it is protected from exploit by all those watching eyes. And Apple, which didn't even offer an antivirus program for decades, was protected by, well, by Steve Jobs's sheer animal magnetism.

The last few years have been hard on those illusions. As Apple gained market share, malware authors began writing for its operating system, and they didn't have any trouble finding holes. It turns out that, according to a 2009 talk at the Black Hat security conference, even Apple's keyboards can be hacked to reveal all the user's keystrokes.[12] Apple now recommends that its users run multiple antivirus programs.[13]

And all those eyes on Linux's code? In August of 2009, two Google researchers discovered a bug in the central core of Linux; it would allow an attacker to acquire complete administrative control of any machine to which he had physical access.[14] You might call that a success for open source, except that the bug had been hiding in plain sight for at least eight years.

Why, then, is there so much more malware running on Windows than on Linux? Almost certainly for the same reason that there are more applications of every sort running on Windows than Linux. Like other application developers, malware authors want to reach the largest number of users with one piece of code. And the way to do that is to write your application for Windows.

It's a Password Problem. I used to take a lot of comfort from the fact that I didn't use just passwords for the things I most wanted to keep secure. I used a token. Every thirty seconds it displayed a different security code, known only to me and my home server. Even if a hacker could compromise my machine and record all my keystrokes, he couldn't know what the token was going to say next.

But this is the age of Twitter—and real-time hacking. For at least the last couple of years, criminals have been able to beat these token systems. Now, when the owner of a compromised machine starts typing in his temporary code, the malware phones home immediately. As the owner types, each digit is sent to the hacker, who simply logs in with him.[15]

Really Important Transactions Can Be Confirmed Offline. If you're really worried, you may have locked down your financial accounts, so no money can leave the institution without a call to verify the transaction. In fact, even if you haven't locked everything down, you may get a call. Like the credit card companies, mutual funds and financial institutions have stopped trusting their customers' computers. For risky transactions, they insist on offline, or out-of-band, confirmation.

Out-of-band communication is today's most common fail-safe solution for computer compromises. To restore control of his Facebook account, for example, Bryan Rutberg had to send Facebook a separate, out-of-band message from a separate account.

But using another line of communication won't solve the problem for long. Hackers have already begun to build blocking programs into their malware. The programs prevent users from getting to Web sites that might detect and cure their infections. In the future, these programs may be able to thwart other efforts to cure an attack—diverting emails, for example, or corrupting the user's attempts to log on to hijacked sites.

The banks' offline solution is also at risk. Finding a truly offline method of communication is going to get harder. Businesses and consumers are switching in large numbers to "voice over IP," or VoIP, telephony. They cannot resist the allure of bringing to voice communications the cheap, flexible features of Internet communications. They cannot resist going just a little faster on the bike.

But the switch means that they are also bringing to voice communications all the insecurity that plagues other Internet communications. This raises the prospect of a whole new set of attacks, from "voice spam" and fraudulent telephone calls to the theft of incoming and outgoing phone calls. If an attacker who has compromised your computer's online bank account is also able to appropriate your Internet telephone, then it will be easy for the attacker to answer the phone when the bank calls—and to confirm that you really do want to transfer your life savings to Spain or Nigeria. At that point, it will be cold comfort that switching to VoIP cut your monthly phone bill from $40 to $10 or even to $0.

The Military Has Solved the Problem With Classified Networks. The government used to have its own illusions about security. Maybe our unclassified networks are compromised, Defense Department officials used to say, but the *classified* networks are still bombproof. They can't be compromised by all this malware floating around the Internet. Because they aren't connected to the Internet. There's an "air gap" between the two.

That assumes, of course, that network security decrees are perfectly enforced—and that the most important secrets are only discussed on classified networks—notions that contradict everything we know about human nature.

But never mind, because the air gap illusion, too, has fallen prey to the exponential empowerment of hackers that we've seen in recent years.

The French navy's Rafale Marine jets train out of Villacoublay air base, in the southwest suburbs of Paris. These fighters are state of the art, packed with stealth and electronic warfare capabilities and capable of landing on carriers. But to do that, they first have to take off. And for two days in January, the jets couldn't take off. They'd been grounded by a hacker.[16]

The "Conficker" computer worm had been exploiting vulnerabilities in Windows servers for months. It was the most ambitious computer infection in years. At the time it had infiltrated as many as 15 million machines around the world. One of the ways it spreads is by infecting the USB thumb drives that carry data from one machine to the next. Even classified or isolated networks could be captured if a bad thumb drive was used to transfer data to a machine on a secured network.

That's what grounded the French fighters. Before the navy even knew it was under attack, the worm was coursing through its internal network. Rushing to contain the damage, the navy told its staff not to turn on their machines, and its systems administrators began quarantining parts of the network. Too late for Villacoublay. Its systems were already hosed.

The Rafale fighter downloads its flight plans, a far more efficient process than paper-based systems. But once the contagion had spread to Villacoublay no flight plans could be downloaded. Until an alternative method of delivering the flight plans could be cobbled together, the Rafales were no more useful than scrap iron.

The French press reported the embarrassment in detail. Perhaps as consolation, it was careful to note that things could have been worse—and were, in Great Britain. There, the press said, twenty-four Royal Air Force bases and three-quarters of the Royal Navy Fleet had succumbed to Conficker.

The British and French navies may have been unintended victims of a worm designed for criminal ends. But after Conficker, no one can believe that an air gap is a security fail-safe.

They're Not Looking for Me. The last of the illusions, or at least the last of mine, is that I'm just not that interesting. Other people have more money. Other people have more valuable secrets. Who's going to come looking for me?

That's the last hope of every herd animal. The predators can't eat everyone. If you lie low and blend in, they won't pick you.

Wrong on two counts, I'm afraid. First, take this test. Add up your savings, car value, house equity, and investments. Is the total over $65,000? If so, you've got a lot of company on the globe. Probably 10 percent of the world's 6.8 billion people have assets exceeding that amount—say 700 million in all. Being one in 700 million sounds like pretty good herd-animal odds until you realize that, for every person with more than $65,000, there are nine people with less.

As computers become exponentially cheaper, most of those nine people will be able to get online. Then there will be nine people looking for ways to take money from you. And another nine for your spouse, nine for your neighbor, and nine for each of your business partners. Maybe nine each for every person you know.

So they *can* eat everyone.

There are already Nigerian hip-hop anthems and videos celebrating the rolling-in-money "Yahoozees" who fleece Americans like Howard Crank. The world is already full of scam artists willing to work for less than minimum wage. Most of them know English and have access to the Internet.

The relentless march of empowerment will soon give the Yahoozees of the Third World new tools for finding you. In a way, that's what a Spanish lottery email does. Most of us delete lottery spam. But if one in ten thousand responds, even with great caution, that person has selected himself for fleecing, and the pitch can then be tailored precisely to his failings. So what if that part of the scam is a bit labor intensive? There are nine people with nothing better to do than sit around trying to get into the mark's head.

Remember that real-time password-stealing program? Well, the thieves don't have to go looking for rich people to infect. Instead, they infect everyone, and let the malware find the rich ones. The password-stealing program consumes an infinitesimal part of a modern chip's processing power to run quietly in the background, watching and waiting until its victim logs on to one of about fifteen hundred predetermined financial sites. Anyone logging in to one of those sites, the authors figure, probably has enough money to be worth cleaning out. So when an infected computer sets itself apart from the crowd by logging on to a financial site, the malware alerts its author, who can now focus on taking money from that computer's owner.

Moore's Law has taken a lot of the work out of the hunt. And, thanks to the empowerment of information technology, it will keep making the job exponentially easier, year in and year out.

Until the predators find you, too.

You might think that's the worst of it.

But it's not, quite. It's not just that you could lose your life savings. Your country could lose its next war. And not just the way we're used to losing—where we get tired of being unpopular in some

Third-World country and go home. I mean *losing* losing: attacked at home and forced to give up cherished principles or loyal allies to save ourselves.

Plenty of countries are enthusiastic about using hackers' tools as weapons of war. At the start of a 2008 shooting war between Georgia and Russia over South Ossetia, for example, numerous Georgian websites were swamped by "denial of service" attacks. Security researchers found evidence that the attacks were coordinated and organized by Russian intelligence agencies. The year before, Estonian government agencies and banks were also crippled by denial of service attacks after the Estonian government moved a World War II memorial that had become a symbol of Soviet colonial rule. Estonia's foreign minister charged that the Russian government was behind the attacks. Russia denied the allegation. NATO, and European investigators were unable to refute their denial.

China has also been accused publicly of audacious computer attacks. German Chancellor Angela Merkel discovered that her office computers had been compromised in an attack blamed on the People's Liberation Army. India, France, and Taiwan have also suffered intrusions and attacks attributed to China. The compromise of the Dalai Lama's network was also widely blamed on China, as were a series of serious attacks on Google and other large U.S. companies in 2010. Like Russia, China has consistently denied all charges.

As I said before, in a strategic sense, the denials don't really matter. If the attacks weren't carried out by Russian and Chinese government agencies, that just means that there are more organizations and countries with effective cyberintelligence and cyberwarfare capabilities than we thought. And, in fact, five or ten years from now, there will be. That's because cyberattacks don't require heavy capital investments, the way nuclear weapons or stealth fighter jets do. Any nation willing to put ten of its best computer experts to work on a cyberintelligence program could probably have one in a year or two. (The Conficker worm that brought down British and French military systems could easily have been written by a single well-trained person.) Many cyberattacks are simply a matter of individual effort. Put enough smart people on enough targets, and some of them will get through.

And that's why attacks on computer networks pose such a strategic threat to the United States in particular. We are an important intelligence target for practically every nation on earth. And attacking our networks is nearly risk-free; the list of suspects is about as long as the UN membership roster. In fact, there are incentives for them to help each other break into our networks. ("I've seized control of an email server at USDA, but what I really want is USTR's (Office of the U.S. Trade Representative). Want to trade? I could throw in the Commerce secretary's password to balance the deal.")

If you're a foreign government, breaking into U.S. networks is a twofer. You can start by stealing secrets. But if push comes to shove, you can use your access to destroy the same systems you've been exploiting. Corrupt the backup files, then bring the whole system down. Or start randomly changing data and emails until no one can trust anything in the system.

It wouldn't take much to create chaos. The financial crisis of 2008 became a panic when bankers began to disbelieve each other. No one trusted the other guy's books, so they stopped lending, and the world crashed. Could that same mistrust be created by modifying or destroying a few firms' computer accounting and trading records? We probably don't want to find out.

It's no secret how to fight a war against the United States. Slow us down, then cause us pain at home and wait for antiwar sentiment to grow. Cyberattacks are ideal for that strategy. Everything in the country, from flight plans and phone calls to pipelines and traffic lights, is controlled by networks susceptible to attack. A determined, state-sponsored attacker could bring them all down—and blame it on some hacker liberation front so we wouldn't even know whom to bomb.

The Pentagon has heard fifty years of warnings about not fighting land wars in Asia, where hand-to-hand fighting and sheer numbers can overwhelm an American army's technological edge. But now it turns out we've opened an electronic bridge, not just to Asia but to the rest of the world, and now we're trying to defend ourselves hand to hand against all comers. It's hard to see how that ends well.

So that's the nub of the problem. No law of nature says that the good guys will win in the end, or even that the benefits of a new technology will always outweigh the harm it causes.

The exponential growth of information technology has made the Pentagon far more efficient at fighting wars; it has made our economy far more productive.

So far, it's been very good to us as a nation.

But it was good to Howard Crank, too, for a while.

10 | Big Brother's Revenge

Somehow, this problem too ended up on DHS's plate: We were supposed to figure out what could be done to improve the country's network security.

It was a snake-bitten assignment. Two presidential cybersecurity strategies—one devised by the Clinton administration and one by the Bush Administration—had already run into the ground before DHS was created.

Perhaps those who created DHS hoped that it could succeed where two presidents had failed. In any event, they gave the new department responsibility for civilian cybersecurity. The National Communications System, which ensures the availability of telecommunications in the event of an emergency, was transferred from Defense. The FBI gave up its National Infrastructure Protection Center, which focused on cybersecurity (and promptly recreated the capability under another name so that it could keep fighting for the turf). The Federal Computer Incident Response Center, which handled computer incident response for civilian agencies, came over from the General Services Agency.

These offices fit well with other DHS missions. Two of its big components—the Secret Service and Immigration and Customs Enforcement—have cybercrime units. And DHS was supposed to protect from physical attack the critical infrastructure on which the economy depends.

In carrying out these duties, DHS could get technical help from the National Security Agency, which was in charge of protecting military and classified networks. But the responsibility for civilian cybersecurity obligations left DHS on the hot seat. If we couldn't find a way to head off disaster, no one else in government would.

To be candid, for the first few years of the department's existence, we didn't accomplish much on this front. There were lots of reasons for that. Fixing travel and border security was more urgent. Staff turnover was high and expertise thin in our cybersecurity offices. But the real reason we didn't get far was that the same forces arrayed against change in the travel arena were lined up against change in information technology.

Businesses had staked their futures on continued exponential growth in information technology. They didn't want policy changes that might change the slope of that curve even a little. Privacy groups instinctively opposed anything that would give the government more information about, well, about anything. And even when it was supportive, the international community was so slow to change direction that it posed an obstacle to any policy that was less than twenty years old.

It didn't matter how obviously necessary a security measure was. Resistance to any change was strong. A case in point was the effort to install intrusion monitoring on the federal government's own networks.

To succeed, most cyberattacks must do two things. The hackers first have to get malicious code into the network they've targeted. Then they have to get stolen information out. If we can detect either step, we can thwart the attack. So one way to defend our networks is to do a thorough job of monitoring traffic as it goes in and out.

We've known this for a decade. The Clinton administration's cybersecurity strategy, drafted in 1999 and released in early 2000, called for a network of intrusion detection monitors that could inspect packets going into and out of all federal government networks. President Clinton requested funds for intrusion monitoring in his outgoing budget. But civil libertarians quickly launched a campaign against it.

It was an odd battle for them to choose. The point of the monitoring network was to inspect government communications. Even the most extreme privacy zealot shouldn't be shocked to discover that the government was reading its *own* mail, much less that it was inspecting its mail for malware. By then, government agencies were already screening emails for spam; the intrusion detection network simply extended that concept to other unwanted packets. What's more, since roughly the 1980s, these computers had been displaying warnings to users that government systems are subject to monitoring.

But privacy groups were spoiling for a fight. They portrayed the proposal as the second coming of Big Brother.

"I think this is a very frightening proposal," an ACLU representative told ZDNet News.[1]

"We feel the government should spend its resources closing the security holes that exist, rather than to watch people trying to break in," said a counsel for the Center for Democracy and Technology.[2]

"I think the threats (of network vulnerability) are completely overblown," said the general counsel for the Electronic Privacy Information Center, adding that claims of a security threat is leading to "'a Cold War mentality' that threatens ordinary citizens' privacy."[3]

In the end, civil liberties resistance was so strong that only the Defense Department was allowed to build an intrusion detection network. For years thereafter, the civilian agencies experienced intrusions that could have been prevented by the intrusion prevention system proposed by President Clinton. But once burned was twice shy. The privacy groups had thoroughly tainted the idea of intrusion prevention on the Hill, and there was real reluctance to revisit the issue. When the Bush administration wrote its cybersecurity strategy, it did not even try to revive the idea.

Finally, though, five years later, the Bush administration decided to force the issue. Mike McConnell, the director of National Intelligence, had been my boss at NSA, and he had spent the years after leaving NSA building a cybersecurity practice at a large consulting firm. A quiet, self-deprecating Southerner with a talent for briefing higher-ups, McConnell was determined to move cybersecurity to the front burner.

He didn't have to work too hard to persuade DHS to take on the challenge. We were alarmed at the ease with which attacks were being launched against civilian agencies. With the backing of President Bush and Mike McConnell, we again proposed an intrusion detection network for civilian agencies. And civil libertarians once again renewed the fight to stop us—as though nothing had changed in ten years. Without the slightest evidence of irony, they again raised privacy objections to the government monitoring its own communications.

We got further than President Clinton did, but not much. Congress appropriated funds for the project, but it had not been fully implemented when Barack Obama was elected president. Spooked by the privacy outcry, the Obama administration postponed full implementation of intrusion monitoring so that it could again examine all of the privacy issues. Pilot projects are underway, but final decisions about how, when, and whether to implement effective intrusion monitoring are still awaiting consensus among the lawyers.

Meanwhile, attacks similar to those that compromised the Dalai Lama's network are continuing. The privacy debate had caused ten years of delay, and it may yet kill an effective intrusion prevention system.

It's remarkable when you think about it. Right now, this minute, agents of an authoritarian government are covertly turning on cameras and microphones in homes and offices all across America, spying on the unsuspecting and the innocent. They're recording our every thought, our every keystroke, as we prepare private documents or visit websites.

And they're able to do that today thanks to the hard work of *privacy* advocates.

How did the privacy community end up facilitating surveillance and espionage on an unprecedented scale? History, mainly, and a lack of imagination.

The men and women who built the computer industry grew up in a very different era from those who pioneered the air travel industry. Air travel enthusiasts first launched commercial flights between the two world wars, when government was big and military risks were on everyone's mind. The pioneers were children of their age. They foresaw a world in which air travel was used for military and espionage purposes; they understood that unregulated flights could lead to disaster as the skies filled up. To manage those risks, they helped the government fashion a comprehensive regulatory scheme for pilots, airlines, and airplanes.

Computer technology, in contrast, was born in the wake of World War II, at a time when the challenge of totalitarianism was on everyone's mind. The men and women who built the earliest computers were children of a different era. They most feared that their machines would be misused by authoritarian governments. Unlike an earlier generation of technologists, they struggled to limit government's role in their industry. And they succeeded. From electronic intercepts to information processing practices, for the next forty years, laws on information technology were aimed as much at regulating the government as at regulating the industry.

By the time the threat of widespread computer misuse finally arrived, the privacy groups already had a narrative fixed in their mind. They could not imagine any threat to computer users' privacy that could be worse than the one they saw in the United States government. Saying no to the government was their default position.

By the end of the Bush administration, DHS was used to the idea that even the most obvious security measures would be opposed by privacy groups. We still had an obligation to do what we could to head off the building security risks. We also knew intrusion prevention, valuable as it was, wouldn't do that by itself.

We needed a broader strategy. In mid-2008, the Homeland Security Council asked DHS to provide options for a set of long-term strategy questions. The policy office was assigned to pull them together.

We found a lot of tough tactical questions that needed to be answered, but the real problem was our strategic posture. And only two ideas that offered any hope of curing our strategic vulnerabilities—attribution and regulation.

Attribution

Here's our strategic security problem in a nutshell: We are attacked every day by an imaginative, highly motivated, and anonymous adversary. We can prevail only if we mount near-perfect defenses. And, since there's no penalty for mounting an attack, the adversary simply tries again and again until something works.

This defensive strategy is, quite simply, too hard. A wholly passive strategy almost never works in the real world.

Take burglary. We certainly spend money on defense. A good lock on your door can keep burglars out of your home. But the lock isn't all that good by itself. We take it for granted that burglars can't sit on our doorsteps day after day, studying our lock and trying new lock picks every evening to see what works. If they could, they'd find a way in sooner or later.

Burglars don't sit on your doorstep because they're afraid of being busted. It's the threat of the police that makes your lock as effective as it is.

Defending networks is the same kind of problem. Security measures are all well and good, but unless we can also identify and deter attackers, defense alone will never do the job.

We have a lot of ways to punish attackers once we identify them. It's identifying them that's hard.

We began by trying to use the tools of law enforcement to identify the attackers. Practically all computer attacks are crimes, after all. They usually violate fraud, extortion, and computer abuse laws. Many attacks would be deterred if the perpetrators faced a realistic risk of arrest and prosecution.

But crossing international boundaries on the Internet is easy. Attackers discovered very early that they could cover their tracks by breaking into lightly guarded computers in several countries and hopping from one to the next before launching an attack on their real target. That way, the police would have to track them back from country to country before discovering their real location. And doing that would require subpoenas valid in each country.

That wasn't easy. To get one country to enforce another country's subpoena requires patience and lengthy legal analysis. The country that's being asked to enforce the subpoena will only do so if it too views computer attacks as crimes. It has to have the ability to carry out the search very quickly. Otherwise the logs will be overwritten and the evidence gone. Indeed, unless the information can be gathered nearly instantaneously, the attackers will always have the advantage. They can compromise new machines and add new hops to their route faster than the police can serve subpoenas to track them.

This problem has been obvious for more than two decades. The United States began encountering it in the 1980s and, by 1989, it had persuaded the Council of Europe to propose work on an international cybercrime convention to streamline the identification process. Getting that far took great effort. The Justice Department had to explain over and over to less computer-savvy governments why it needed such an agreement.

Not until late 2001 was there actual agreement in principle on a few very basic steps—making computer hacking a crime and naming a contact point to handle subpoena requests quickly. And that simply marked the start of a long, slow, international law-making process. The cybercrime convention didn't come into effect until 2004, when a grand total of three countries ratified it. As of 2009, fifteen countries had fully ratified and acceded to the convention, and twenty-eight more were in various stages of adopting it. As international efforts go, that is a considerable success (although the numbers are inflated by the European Union, which has pressed its twenty-seven members to join, along with EU satellites like Liechtenstein).

And what does the convention do to solve the attribution problem? In essence, the members of the convention have agreed that they will adopt a common set of computer crimes and that they will assist each other in investigating these crimes.

That's it. A good thing, no doubt, but hardly likely to stop the massive attacks we see today. Hackers have compromised hundreds of thousands, sometimes millions, of machines. If they chose to hop from one of those to the next before launching an attack, the authorities would need to serve hundreds of thousands of subpoenas in dozens of countries—and to do it as fast as the hackers could move from one machine to the next. The hackers can move at the speed of light—literally. The governments can move at the speed of paper, courts, and sealing wax. It's no contest.

At best, the convention offers a partial solution to computer crime as it existed in the 1980s. But building a consensus for even its limited measures took more than a decade. And even then, the consensus was distinctly limited in geographic reach. Neither Russia nor China has shown any inclination to adopt the convention. Nor, for that matter, have thoroughly wired countries like South Korea, Brazil, Nigeria, Singapore, and Australia. So even if we still lived in the 1980s, there would still be plenty of places in the world for hackers to hide.

The only alternative to the convention that the international community has found is worse—and in thoroughly predictable ways. Led by Russia, the United Nations has recently been touting the idea of "disarmament talks" for cyberspace.

There are several possible motivations for such a proposal. One possibility is that the Russians genuinely believe that an arms control treaty for cyberspace would be good for all concerned, demilitarizing and taking the fear of disaster out of the networks on which the world relies. Unfortunately, that's not particularly likely. You can't have a real arms control agreement unless you can verify compliance. But as we've seen, a principal feature of computer attacks is the difficulty of attribution. If attacks continued after "disarmament" how would we know that anyone had disarmed?

The Russians' models seem to be the multilateral chemical and biological weapons conventions that were negotiated in Geneva during the Cold War. By the usual standards of the international community these are wildly successful agreements, adopted by more than

150 countries. They proved wildly successful from the Soviet point of view as well, since the United States actually abandoned its chemical and biological weapons after signing the conventions while the Soviets kept theirs in place. Even more remarkably, the United States managed to get a black eye in the process, because it had the temerity in 2001 to tell the international community that the convention was unverifiable, that it could not prevent proliferation of biological weapons, and that there was no point in establishing intrusive inspection regimes that would not work.

From the Russian point of view, replaying this drama has no downside. If an agreement is reached, the United States, with its hyper-compliant legal culture now fully integrated into military planning, will undoubtedly adhere to any ban the new agreement imposes. But countries that want to use the tools of cyberwarfare will be free to do so, relying on the anonymity that cloaks attackers today. If the United States sees that trap and refuses to accept an unenforceable agreement, the international community will replay the drama that accompanied the U.S. refusal to negotiate an unenforceable biological weapons protocol.

Just agreeing to consider the proposal, as the new administration seems to have done, allows Russia to divide us from our allies in Europe—who always seem eager to put new international legal limits on warfare, even if the limits can't actually be enforced.

In the end, then, our inability to solve the problem of attribution and anonymity poses severe threats not just to our pocketbooks but also to our national security and our international standing. We thought that it was foolish to solve the problem with what Harvard law professor Larry Lessig once called "East Coast code"—laws and treaties. Instead, we thought, the answer would prove to be "West Coast code"—software and hardware design. In the long run, we needed an architecture that automatically and reliably identifies every machine and person in the network.

I knew that privacy groups would melt down if anyone proposed to do that for the Internet. Anonymity has become (wrongly in my view) equated with online privacy. Any effort to cut back online anonymity will be resisted strongly by privacy groups. And they'd be able to find popular support, at least for a time. Practically everyone does something online that he's ashamed of.

At the same time, practically everyone spends large parts of the day on a network where his every action *is* identified and monitored. Most corporate networks have robust attribution and audit capabilities, and the insecurity of the public networks is forcing private networks to study the conduct of their users ever more closely in the hopes of identifying compromised machines before they can cause damage.

In trying to chart a broad network security strategy, I thought we needed more research and incentives to improve audit and attribution capabilities in hardware and software. And we needed architectural and legal innovations to encourage one secure and attributable network to link up securely with another. In the long run, and perhaps in the short run, that sort of organic linking among attributable systems may be the only way to build a network on which identification is rapid and sure.

That doesn't mean the old, anonymous Internet has to disappear. But I suspect we'll have to create a new network that coexists alongside the old one. Users who value security—who want an assurance that their financial assets and their secrets will not be stolen by hackers—will choose the secure alternative, at least most of the time.

The policy office at DHS put that idea forward as an option for consideration by the Homeland Security Council.

Regulation

Cybersecurity regulation had been talked about for years. The Bush administration floated the possibility in 2002. Or, to be more precise, Richard Clarke floated the idea.

Clarke was a flamboyant bureaucratic warrior camouflaged by the dress and haircut of a high school math teacher. A career official with a knack for building empires—and making enemies—he had risen to take charge of both cybersecurity and terrorism policy in President Clinton's National Security Council. He later became famous briefly for his scathing denunciation of the Bush White House's response to terrorism warnings. But in 2000 he was better known as the man who had sponsored the failed Clinton administration plan to build a monitoring network.

Clarke was held over by the Bush administration, with the same two portfolios he had held under President Clinton—terrorism and cybersecurity. But he never seemed to gain the same support in the new administration as he had in the old one. After the attacks of 9/11, pushed out of the terrorism job, he poured himself into his cybersecurity role, spending much of 2002 drafting a strategy for the new administration.

Always a hard-charger, Clarke had high ambitions for his new effort. He planned a grand event to unveil the strategy in September of 2002. Reportedly, the strategy sidled up toward new mandates for industry, calling on technology companies to contribute to a security research fund and pressing Internet service providers to bundle firewalls and other security technology with their services. But just days before the event, Clarke's wings were publicly clipped. His long and elaborate strategy, with its nods toward imposing regulatory requirements, was rapidly and harshly cut down. Anything that could offend industry, anything that hinted at government mandates, was stripped out. It was finally unveiled, not as a final document, but as a simple draft for further comment.

For Clarke it must have been the final straw. He'd already been pulled off the terrorism account with brutal swiftness after 9/11, and now his year of effort on cybersecurity had ended in a public rejection of his work.

He stayed in the White House just long enough to produce a final strategy document that was as tepid as the draft. Then he quit.

Industry had claimed another scalp in its long campaign to head off federal mandates aimed at improving computer security. The president (though not industry) eventually paid a heavy price for Clarke's resentment. The one-time security adviser became a harsh Bush critic, in testimony before the 9/11 Commission and in his other writings.

I thought of Clarke's fate as we put together the report for the Homeland Security Committee. Regulation had become an electrified third rail. Especially in a generally business-friendly administration, advocating more regulation was not likely to be career enhancing.

But the status quo clearly wasn't working. Moore's law was working against us. We had to find a way to change incentives, to get information technologists to start building security into the foundation of our networks. It's not that I thought regulation was always going to be the right answer. But I was sure that it had to be on the table. Especially because regulation didn't have to mean classic command-and-control Federal Register rulemaking.

Government doesn't have to issue mandatory rules to influence private sector behavior. It can use a variety of incentives to encourage security. So the policy office laid out a range of approaches, ranging from soft to hard.

Soft regulation

The softest option was to nudge industry toward security measures by offering liability protection in exchange. This is the most comfortable form of regulation for business, because instead of punishing bad behavior it rewards good behavior. This is something we understood at DHS, where we administered the Safety Act[4]. That act provides liability protection to companies that manufacture and sell qualified antiterrorism technology.

The idea behind the act is simple. Some anti-terrorism technologies work well but not perfectly; they reduce risk but don't eliminate it. Unfortunately, after a terrorist incident, the people who have been fully protected by the technology will be grateful, and the people who haven't been fully protected will sue, claiming that the technology was defective, since it didn't protect them from all harm. That's not a recipe for encouraging the deployment of new technology.

So, to keep fear of liability from squelching advances in technology, the Safety Act sets a cap on liability for approved technologies. There are a lot of conditions built into the act. Companies must, for example, carry whatever level of liability insurance DHS considers necessary to compensate people who may be harmed in a terrorist attack. But in return, the threat of open-ended, company-killing liability is taken off the table.

We thought that DHS could use the Safety Act itself to encourage companies to adopt some cybersecurity technologies. The protections of the act aren't limited to physical products; they also cover services and information technology. We thought the act could even be applied to security services and processes, vulnerability assessments, and cybersecurity standards.

But the Safety Act wasn't perfectly adapted to cybersecurity tools. Most hackers are not terrorists. In addition, network security measures work in layers. There is no single magic bullet that provides all security needs. If many security products fail to prevent an attack, and not all of them are covered by the act, sorting out which ones caused the damage could require endless, expensive lawsuits. And, because network threats change so often, products designated under the act would have to be updated frequently. Even with regular updates, the extent to which a particular technology provides protection will likely erode over time as attackers seek ways around the defense. At what point should protection be modified or withdrawn, we wondered, and who will press for that change? Finally, the insurance market for cybersecurity products remains at best a work in progress, so it wasn't clear that adequate coverage was available. For these reasons, we concluded, the Safety Act was probably better as a model of what could be done without regulation than as a tool that could be used immediately to encourage broad cybersecurity measures.

We also noted a second "soft" way to influence business—government purchasing standards. Many critical infrastructure companies do business with the U.S. government. The government has great weight as a buyer of technologies, and it can influence the market for security by the standards it sets for its purchases. The government cannot, however, dictate terms to suppliers of technology. The government may be the single largest buyer of some technology, but it is far outweighed in the aggregate by private sector purchasers. Further, without new policies, the government wouldn't really act as a "single" buyer. IT procurement is divided among many agencies, and these agencies would fight security standards that raise costs or reduce competition.

We wanted the government to consider a more unified approach to its procurement of information technologies. We thought the government could establish government-wide contract models that incorporated preferred technologies and security practices requirements into federal contracts. In fact, some steps on this road had already been taken. Federal purchases are required by law to meet certain federal information security standards.

We knew, though, that using procurement to enhance commercial IT security is easier said than done. The U.S. government's first efforts to leverage its procurement power for IT security began in the 1970s, when the government established the Trusted Computer Security Evaluation Criteria—the "Orange Book"—and began to evaluate commercial products that were submitted for review. The idea, then as now, was to use federal contracts as an incentive for vendors to incorporate security measures in their products.

The scheme never had as big a security impact as hoped; the commercial market for computers rapidly outpaced the government market, and private purchasers came to perceive their security needs as different from those of the government. Sellers and buyers alike complained that security evaluation slowed adoption of current IT hardware and software.

For all those reasons, the procurement process has not so far turned out to be an effective way to influence network security.

Hard regulation

And what about the "hard" option—just plain regulating? You know, just putting network security requirements into the Federal Register?

We couldn't ignore that option, I thought. In fact, a lot of the most critical industries were already subject to government regulation. These included financial institutions, energy, and telecommunications. And some of these industries were already subject to cybersecurity regulation. Financial institutions, for example, must follow a unified set of cybersecurity rules. But even financial regulators don't require particular security measures. The rules are largely procedural, resembling the instructions on a bottle of shampoo: Institutions must study their vulnerabilities, cure them, assess the effectiveness of the cure, and repeat.

It's hard to write rules that go beyond such procedural steps, because the attackers change tactics faster than regulations can be amended. What's more, the cost of mandatory security would be very high; it would slow innovation and productivity growth severely.

Even so, there's a case for mandating particular security measures for regulated industries. It's the Howard Crank problem all over again. Every year, the exponential growth of information technology makes our lives a little better, our businesses a little more efficient and profitable. And every year it makes us a little more vulnerable to a military strike on our infrastructure that could leave us without power, money, petroleum, or communications for months.

Large parts of the country could find themselves living like post-Katrina New Orleans—but without the National Guard over the horizon. Protecting against that risk isn't part of most companies' balance sheets. It's not hard to see that as the kind of market failure that requires regulation.

But even if there is a market failure, the government still isn't well-equipped to solve it. At a minimum, the regulatory agencies would have to find a way to coordinate and issue standards much faster than they now write regulations. Today, the practical speed limit is eighteen months from new idea to final rule. There's not much point in replacing a predictable market failure with an equally predictable government failure.

And what about all the vulnerable IT networks that are not in the hands of regulated industries? If they are compromised, the harm goes beyond the users of those networks. The compromised machines can be used to attack others, including government systems. To set standards in that world would certainly require new legislation.

Industry, we knew, wouldn't like any talk about regulation. But they were fighting the last war. New security legislation had in fact already been enacted, though in an odd, and mostly unfortunate, way. Laws have been adopted in all but five states that require companies to disclose any security breaches that lead to the disclosure of sensitive customer data. The more the federal government has dithered over security rules for industry, the more aggressively the states have moved into the opening. Their breach notification laws are becoming de facto security regulations for all companies. First, they punish bad security by forcing companies that are compromised to admit that fact, as long as some personal data was accessed. Second, in a crude way, they recognize that good security measures can make notification unnecessary, and that encourages companies to invest in technologies that are so recognized. For example, many state laws recognize that encrypted data may be safe even if the system it is stored on has been compromised. So, naturally, many companies have expanded their use of encryption to avoid embarrassing breach notifications.

The problem with these laws is that they don't necessarily point companies in the direction of real security improvements. Because they only punish companies for breaches that disclose personal data, they have encouraged the companies to lock up or discard certain kinds of customer data—rather than focusing on keeping hackers out of systems that control their most critical functions.

The problem is particularly acute in the area of stolen and lost laptops. Thousands of business laptops are lost or stolen every day. Usually, the thief wants the laptop, not the data. But if there is personal data in the laptop, that data has technically been compromised, thus forcing companies to send embarrassing notices to everyone concerned. After a few such cases, companies begin to divert their security budget to double-locking laptop drives with passwords and encryption. Those measures won't keep Ghostnet out of their networks, but they get the highest investment priority because of the peculiarities of state law.

By the same token, state laws expressly recognizing encryption of data as a defense have artificially heightened the priority that security offices assign to the deployment of encryption, even though it too does little to block a sophisticated attack. There are many measures other than encryption that may be equally effective at providing a defense in depth, but state legislatures have not been able to draft laws that reward more comprehensive security.

Finally, state laws vary substantially, creating great tension for law-abiding companies, which find they cannot actually comply with all of them. For all those reasons, there is growing support for a federal law that would set a single breach disclosure standard. Such a law could also create incentives for higher cybersecurity standards. In fact, replacing inconsistent state notification laws with a security-minded federal law would be a victory for both security and innovation.

The Report

By the time we finished the report, I realized that we hadn't just touched the third rail, we were tap-dancing on it. By candidly treating the end of online anonymity and the adoption of tough security regulation as options, we were goring some of the noisiest oxen in Washington.

Well, what the hell, I thought. Maybe the time was right for a reconsideration of security regulation, especially after the hodgepodge the states were making of the issue.

I was wrong.

Memories of Dick Clarke's fate were too fresh, and by mid-2008 the administration was running out of time. I showed a draft of the report to the front office and sent the Homeland Security Council a copy. Not much later I got a call. The council didn't want to even raise regulation as an option in the interagency discussions. They feared that industry and Congress would kill the little progress that had been made if regulation were even treated as an option. In fact, they wanted to bury the report. Instead of thinking about the future, they'd focus only on tasks that could be done in the waning months of the Bush administration.

This was disappointing but understandable. Chertoff, who'd been a rock in other disputes, was now focused only on fights he could win and changes he could implement in six months or less. And we had reached that point in an administration where accomplishing even the simplest and most obvious tasks had become nearly impossible. Energy was draining out of the Bush team, and what remained was soon focused on a cascading financial crisis that left no time for next year's threats.

I thought that there might be value in letting the Obama administration consider these issues without explaining that it was reviewing options proposed under President Bush. The new administration might have more leeway to consider the attribution and regulation issues with an open mind.

I was wrong about that, too.

The Obama administration brought a flurry of energy and apparent determination to the problem. As well it should have. Barack Obama and John McCain, after all, had been the first presidential candidates whose campaign networks were systematically penetrated and exploited by foreign intelligence-collectors. And candidate Obama had pledged that cybersecurity would be a top national security priority in his administration. Nevertheless, the new administration's resolution seemed to waver within weeks of the inauguration.

The new administration did produce a cybersecurity strategy only a few months into the term, but White House watchers learned a lot from what it said and how it was edited. The draft was reportedly produced on the schedule set by the president—within sixty days of his request. But it didn't go to him on that schedule. Instead, it went through a new set of edits, as office after office protected itself, its prerogatives, or its constituencies by removing controversial passages.

The result was mostly pabulum—pabulum of a sort that would have been familiar to the Clinton and Bush White Houses, of course, since they too had blinked when faced with hard choices over cybersecurity.

For example, the strategy paper recognized that improving authentication of people and machines is a key to improving cybersecurity. While much of its attention was focused on just making sure that federal networks can properly identify users, it acknowledged as a goal the creation of a "global, trusted eco-system" that could form the basis of a secure network. But it called for that system to be built by working with "international partners" and by building an ecosystem that is seen to protect "privacy rights and civil liberties." Hard experience tells us that if building a secure network depends on the full support of the international and privacy communities, it will never happen.

Business too was fully protected from the specter of security regulation in the Obama administration's strategy document, which mentioned regulation just once—to declare that it would be considered only "as a last resort."

By the time the editing was done, Washington knew that nothing dramatic would come from the cybersecurity initiative—or the new cybersecurity coordinator job the president had announced with fanfare. Indeed, the position remained unfilled for nearly a year, until Howard Schmidt agreed to take the job in late December 2009.

Three presidents in a row had tried to change course and head off the worst consequences of Moore's law for our national and personal security.

All three had failed.

None had been able to defy the privacy and business lobbies, inside and outside government, that guarded the status quo.

11 Invested in Insecurity

The city of Dubai leaps straight out of the flat sands and flat seas of the Arabian Peninsula. One minute you're driving through scrubless desert, the next you're cruising an elevated freeway past a phalanx of thirty-story skyscrapers, most built in the last ten years. Today, with a mountain of debt, Dubai has the look of last year's boomtown; the newest skyscrapers lack tenants and construction has nearly ceased. But during its heyday from 2005 to 2009, Dubai's ambition seemed as unbounded as the desert that it sprang from. And part of its plan was to become the great transshipment port of the Middle East—just as Singapore is the great entrepôt of the Far East. By 2006, with several bustling modern ports, it had largely succeeded.

That's when it encountered—and transformed—the Committee on Foreign Investment in the United States, first handing DHS its best tool for combating network security threats and, eventually, taking that tool out of the department's hands.

The success of the port of Dubai was due in no small part to Dubai Port World, a company owned by the royal family. DPW, as it was called, was the principal terminal operator in Dubai. Its success there led it to branch out, purchasing terminals in many other ports.

Running a port is a lot like running a small city. The government usually provides police, fire protection, and perhaps utilities, while the terminal operators carry out the main economic activity—storing goods and moving them from ship to land and back. To do that, the terminal operator leases land in a port and then builds a pier for ships, cranes to unload the ships, a parking lot for the cargo to rest, plus perhaps a small management office. The operator makes its money lifting containers out of ships and holding them for shippers to pick up. The terminal operator is thus a lot like a store owner in a city—economically vital but responsible mainly for his own property.

Operating a terminal was once a local business, just like a store. But globalization has come to the industry, and the top five operators in the world now handle more than a quarter of all trade. None of the biggest operators is an American company; in fact, even in the United States, four out of five terminals are operated by foreign companies.

So it didn't exactly set off alarms when one of these foreign terminal operators decided to buy another foreign terminal operator.

Soon we would wish that it had.

The buyer was DPW. The seller was P&O—the Peninsular and Oriental Steam Navigation Company, a two-hundred-year-old British firm that also had terminal operations in much of the world, including the United States. P&O leased terminals in six U.S. ports, and DPW would be getting those along with the rest of the company.

DPW asked the Committee on Foreign Investment in the United States, or CFIUS, to approve the transaction. Created by executive order in 1975, CFIUS conducts national security reviews of foreign investments in U.S. companies. As long as we are running fiscal and balance of payments deficits, the United States pretty much has to keep selling many of its assets to foreign buyers. But we also have to fence off some companies and sectors for national security reasons. We would not let an adversary—Iran or North Korea, say—purchase a major defense contractor. The opportunities for espionage and sabotage are too tempting. But defense contractors are not the only companies that create opportunities for espionage and sabotage. We would not want, say, major U.S. telephone companies to fall into the hands of countries that might use the companies to spy on Americans.

At bottom, CFIUS was charged with deciding which transactions posed unacceptable national security risks. The committee has broad but vague powers. In essence, any foreign company buying a

U.S. company has the option of notifying CFIUS of the transaction. If CFIUS doesn't do anything within thirty days, then the transaction can go forward. If CFIUS has questions, it can launch an investigation. In theory, the investigation is completed in forty-five days and a recommendation is made to the president, who has fifteen days to decide whether to block the transaction on national security grounds.

That's the theory. When Congress first set rules for CFIUS in 1988, it imagined a fairly quick ninety-day process with a sharp yes-or-no decision at the end. Congress took pains to avoid delaying investments. In addition to the short decision deadlines, Congress allowed companies to skip the CFIUS process completely.

Why do companies go through the CFIUS process if they don't have to? It's simple; they want certainty. If they notify a transaction to CFIUS and get no objection, then the United States can't overturn the deal later on national security grounds (unless the information supplied by the parties was false or misleading). So if the parties to a transaction have even a tiny concern about whether the deal will raise national security objections, it's a good idea to make a CFIUS filing. Most investors want to find out about national security objections early, when the deal can still be unwound. If the concerns arise later, one party or the other may be hurt badly. It's almost impossible to unscramble the eggs once a deal has been finalized, and the effort to do so would put both companies at risk.

When we were at DHS, we estimated that only about 10 percent of large transactions received CFIUS review. The rest didn't raise even modest national security concerns. Of that 10 percent, the vast majority were approved without comment. Only about 10 percent of submitted cases led to further action by the committee, meaning that the committee devotes almost all of its attention to roughly 1 percent of all the investments made by foreigners in U.S. companies.

But the stakes for that 1 percent can be enormous. Congress gave the president authority to block any foreign acquisition of a U.S. company if the committee found credible evidence of a threat to national security.

Whether to seek CFIUS approval for the Dubai Port World transaction must have been a close question. Neither company was based in the United States, after all. But CFIUS still could exercise some authority over the transaction. Six U.S. terminals would be getting a new foreign owner.

At the same time, asking for approval didn't look like a big risk. No one in CFIUS had ever raised a national security concern about the ownership of terminals in U.S. ports. And the banks that back these transactions are notoriously risk-averse; if there were a CFIUS issue, they'd want to know right away, not after the deal was done. So DPW decided to go for the certainty of a committee approval. Since DHS was the recognized expert in port security and one of the toughest security advocates on the committee, DPW consulted us early.

I had just taken over as head of policy, and CFIUS had just been assigned to my office. I had no staff of my own, but I wasn't a stranger to CFIUS. After leaving NSA, I had many clients with CFIUS concerns, and I had negotiated some of the detailed agreements that the Justice and Defense departments insisted upon when foreign companies acquired large interests in U.S. telecommunications companies. I knew how valuable CFIUS could be in protecting security, and I was pleased that DHS had already established itself as a leader on the committee.

While the Defense Department had long worried about foreign investments involving its contractors and its technology, its main concern was military threats to our security. But on 9/11 al Qaeda had used civilian technology to kill more Americans at home than any foreign military attack had ever done. So from the start, DHS focused on ways in which foreign ownership might expose the home front to unconventional attacks. Because national security was not defined narrowly, DHS had no trouble fitting this approach into the statute, and in 2007, Congress ratified DHS's approach by explicitly including homeland security and critical infrastructure protection in the new definition of national security.

DHS's broad view of national security covered a lot of ground. But our top worry was sabotage and espionage in the information technology sector. We knew that there were some governments that routinely asked their companies to help spy on other countries. And any technology that allowed spying could be used for sabotage. Once a hostile nation has compromised a computer, it is up to that nation whether to exploit the computer or shut it down. That was too big a risk to take, DHS argued. Some companies and some countries just couldn't be trusted. They shouldn't be allowed to control U.S. networks.

The federal government doesn't have authority to set cybersecurity standards generally for the private sector. It doesn't even have authority to exclude from U.S. markets companies and products that are likely to be used for espionage. It can prosecute spies and companies that conspire with them, of course, but only after the damage is done, and a successful prosecution depends on compiling proof beyond a reasonable doubt and, often, on extradition or other cooperation from the government that ordered the spying. It's not much of a weapon.

CFIUS, however, offers real authority to protect telecom and IT security, and DHS moved quickly to ensure it was used for that purpose. When a company or country with a questionable reputation filed to acquire a U.S. IT or telecom company, DHS often asked the intelligence community whether either had engaged in espionage against the United States or others. (This practice was eventually institutionalized for all applicants.) Even if the company or country hadn't actually been caught in the act, DHS would assess whether the transaction increased U.S. vulnerability to the kind of cyberattacks we knew were likely in the long run.

A number of transactions did increase U.S. vulnerability. The telecom industry is globalizing at the same time that it is shifting from big, specialized telephone switches to Internet technologies. The IT industry has been globalized for decades, but opportunities to compromise components and complete products continue to grow, particularly as companies diversify their software as well as their hardware supply chains. DHS paid special attention to foreign investment in computer security products and services. Just as terrorists hoping to assassinate an official are most likely to succeed if they can gain control of the official's security detail, so attackers hoping to compromise a network are most likely to succeed if they can gain control of the network's security system.

The terminal deal that DPW was proposing, though, had nothing in common with the transactions that most threatened U.S. interests. In telecommunications and information technology transactions, we knew there was a risk that foreign buyers might use their new acquisition as a base for espionage or network attacks. But why would Dubai want to sabotage a U.S. port? And even if it did, how would owning a terminal make that more likely?

The terminals that DPW was buying were just plots of land and warehouses inside six U.S. ports. Their security was overseen by the port authorities, the local governments, and the Coast Guard.

I polled the DHS components responsible for ports and found no concerns about the transaction; they all said that the current owner cooperated fully and voluntarily in all our security programs, and they had no reason to think that DPW would act differently. None of the other CFIUS agencies took even a passing interest in the deal.

Even so, there was one more thing we could do. I knew that companies had entered into "mitigation agreements" with CFIUS agencies in the past. In fact, I'd negotiated them. Could we get one here, I wondered?

Mitigation agreements weren't anything that Congress had created. When Senator J. James Exon and Representative James Florio drafted the Exon-Florio Amendment[1], they expected CFIUS to ask a straightforward question about a foreign takeover: "Will this transaction put national security at risk?" And the answer, they thought, would be binary: either yes or no.

In the world of real transactions, though, it is rarely that simple. Suppose a company we don't fully trust wants to buy a company that sells software. Most of the software is plain vanilla consumer stuff—spreadsheets, word processing programs, and the like. But one of the products is a centrally managed security service that screens all the packets that flow in and out of the user's computer. We might be able to live with the risk of compromise to the consumer products, but if the security service is ever compromised, every user's machine will be owned by a foreign intelligence agency from the day they install the software. That's too great a risk. We decide to oppose the transaction.

When it learns of our objection, though, the buyer says something that neither Senator Exon nor Representative Florio expected.

"Actually, we aren't interested in the security service. We've been planning to sell it. Can you approve the deal if we spin it off?" the buyer asks.

The sensible thing is to agree. We'll get everything we want without blocking the deal.

But what if there really isn't time to sell the security company before the CFIUS statute requires us to say yes or no to the transaction? We have only thirty days, after all.

"Well, will you approve the deal today if we *promise* to sell the subsidiary as soon as possible?" the buyer asks next.

Again, the sensible thing is to agree, as long as we know the buyer's promise will be kept. But to make sure it is, we need a strict agreement that can be enforced long after the transaction has been approved.

That simple example shows why CFIUS found itself forced to invent what became known as a "mitigation agreement." If the buyer entered into a binding agreement that mitigated any security risk in the transaction, the committee would approve the deal. It was good for everyone. The buyer and seller got what they wanted. And so did CFIUS—in fact, it got what it wanted without saying no to a foreign investment, something that can give a country a bad name in investment circles.

But a mitigation agreement doesn't have to be limited to something as clear-cut as the sale of a subsidiary. Sometimes the buyer wants to keep a subsidiary but has no interest in running it. It may solve a security concern by promising to leave the current American management in place. Before CFIUS can rely on that promise, though, the company has to put it in writing and agree to be legally bound by it.

DPW had been telling us it had no interest in changing the management or practices of the U.S. terminals. I decided that we would ask DPW to put that in writing. After all, there was at least a small risk that the new owners would want to reduce costs by cutting security. A mitigation agreement would lock them in to their promises.

It turned out to be an easy sell. DPW agreed that it would stay in the voluntary security programs that P&O had joined. For good measure, DPW agreed to an open-book arrangement with DHS, allowing the department to inspect its records and obtain employee security data at will. These were incremental improvements in security, and DPW was willing to provide them in order to smooth the way for the transaction.

DHS did not need to get the approval of CFIUS to negotiate these provisions; we were the only agency on the committee with the slightest interest in this transaction. Once DHS was satisfied, the rest of the committee quickly okayed it.

By mid-January, CFIUS had finished its thirty-day review, DPW and DHS had signed the mitigation agreement, and the deal had cleared. According to the law, DPW was fully protected by the safe harbor provision of CFIUS. The United States could not legally overturn the deal.

A week went by, then another. Although CFIUS approval was in place, DPW was still in a bidding war with another purchaser. Not until February 11, when its rival bowed out, was DPW's victory announced in the business press. The contest was over.

Or, rather, it would have been but for a small company in Miami. Eller & Company had two joint ventures with P&O. For some reason, Eller didn't want DPW to take over that relationship. So it hired Joe Muldoon, a retired lobbyist and polo player, to get the deal overturned somehow. In the end, Muldoon turned out to be one of the great overachievers in history. Not since Andrew Jackson fought the Battle of New Orleans has anyone won such an influential victory after the war was over. And never has such a public fuss been unleashed on behalf of such a tiny commercial interest.

Muldoon had never handled a CFIUS matter, and he probably didn't know that the approval was already final. He also didn't know—or perhaps didn't care—that terminal operators don't have much to do with port security. He just started telling anyone who would listen that national security was somehow at stake in the transaction. Finally, two weeks after the deal had been approved, someone heard him.

On Sunday, February 12, a story by the Associated Press claimed for the first time that the deal raised security issues, a twist raised by Senator Charles E. Schumer, who said that the transaction would "outsource . . . sensitive Homeland Security duties."

I assumed he was repeating things he heard from Muldoon. They weren't true.

But that didn't matter.

By the end of Sunday, the blogs were buzzing. And the administration's rapid response team was silent. For one good reason. They had no idea what Senator Schumer was talking about. The transaction had set off no alarms as it wended its slow way through CFIUS. The lobbyist and politicians now complaining had said nothing while the deal was being reviewed.

And the review process had been over and done with for a month. For policymakers, that might as well have been eternity. Whatever whisper of worry they might have heard at the time of approval had long ago been crowded out by more pressing matters. Not until the working staff who had dealt with the case came to work on Monday were we able to gather the information we needed to respond.

By then it was too late. On Tuesday, February 14, the press had launched a story line that treated the transaction as the sale—lock, stock, and barrel—of six large American ports to an Arab company. That was the line taken that day by the Associated Press, which headlined the story "Arab firm may run 6 U.S. ports."[2] Soon, the *Washington*

Times had the same slant: "Some of the country's busiest ports—New York, New Jersey, Baltimore and three others—are about to become the property of the United Arab Emirates."[3] By Friday morning, a *Washington Post* writer channeling administration critics was frothing: "The management of major U.S. ports taken over by an Arab-owned company? What was the Bush administration thinking when it allowed such a thing?"[4]

For a couple of weeks, that was the nicest thing anyone said about us. No one listened when we tried to explain that port security is the job of the port authority and DHS, not the terminal operators.

It was a full-fledged Washington panic, of a kind seen only rarely, when a brand-new issue breaks suddenly and politicians have to wing it, with only their jangling switchboards for guidance.

The talk shows and blogs had a field day. So did the partisans. The issue let Democrats get to the president's right on national security by demanding that Arabs not be allowed to run the security of American ports. Congressional Republicans, who couldn't afford to seem soft on national security, rushed to condemn the deal as well. Congressmen of both parties launched crude attacks on Dubai and the United Arab Emirates to which it belongs. Congress held hearing after hearing to condemn the administration and to demand that the deal be overturned. In the end, the company buckled, promising to sell off its U.S. port properties.

A Washington panic is a funny thing. It seems to take Washington by the throat. No one can think or talk about anything else. Congress is suddenly ready to enact legislation in days, not weeks or months.

And then, like a tropical monsoon, the panic lifts. The clouds part. Politicians blink a bit shamefacedly in the sun. And everything goes back to normal.

That's what eventually happened with the DPW case. Though you couldn't have guessed from the hearings, our message slowly got through: DPW wasn't buying American ports, we patiently repeated. It wasn't going to be responsible for security. It had signed an unprecedented mitigation agreement that addressed any reasonable security concerns. And Congress's noisy performance was undermining the U.S. reputation as a good place to invest—as well as CFIUS's reputation for raising only serious national security concerns.

Behind the bluster, Congress started to get nervous. It began looking for an exit. When DPW finally bowed to political reality and agreed to get rid of P&O's U.S. facilities, Congress was eager to claim the scalp and move on. Muldoon had earned his fee, at great cost to America's credibility in world financial markets.

The monsoon had passed. The sun was out again. But the DPW affair would hang over CFIUS for the rest of President Bush's second term. For a time, fear of another CFIUS eruption would allow DHS to turn the committee into a powerful bulwark against new computer and telecommunications insecurities. In the end, though, it would create a business backlash that showed the limits of security regulation even in a time of great and growing vulnerability.

For DHS, the fight over Dubai ports was a distraction from the real security risks posed by globalization of telecommunications and networks. The insecurity of U.S. networks wasn't just an organized crime problem. It was the result of deliberate policies adopted by countries that viewed us as an intelligence target. If they could get their companies to compromise U.S. networks, they'd do it in a heartbeat. So allowing foreign companies to take up critical positions in U.S. computer and telecommunications networks, either as suppliers or as service providers, raised serious national security issues. At the same time, globalization was relentless. The old days, when AT&T provided local and long distance service—and made all the equipment on the network—were long gone. And the collapse of the high-tech bubble had transformed the industry that emerged from AT&T's breakup. The Baby Bells were consolidating; long distance was disappearing as a separate business; wireless was displacing land-lines; and the equipment companies that had dominated North America for a century were in trouble. We couldn't just say no when foreign companies came courting. In that context, mitigation agreements became a way to say yes to globalization without completely surrendering to foreign espionage. The agreements became a kind of company-specific network security regulation. We began to insist on a mitigation agreement in any transaction that posed even a modest threat. Each agreement created an ad hoc regime designed to curb foreign government infiltration of U.S. telecommunications and information technology.

The toughest agreements created a wall between the foreign owner and U.S. production facilities. This was common where CFIUS wanted to approve a deal in which the acquired company had sensitive government contracts. The wall was meant to keep the contracts free from foreign influence. The same thing was occasionally done for highly sensitive commercial contracts.

Another common security measure was to insist that the government (or an approved third party with technical skills) be guaranteed the right to inspect the buyer's hardware designs and processes, its software source code and testing results, and any other part of the production process that might reveal a deliberate compromise. To make sure that data was not shipped abroad and compromised there, some mitigation agreements required that data about Americans be kept in the country; sometimes the agreements required special security measures for the data.

The agreements also established a host of procedural security safeguards. These often included a government-approved security officer with broad powers and an obligation to report any suspicious incidents to the U.S. government. They also included regular audits by the government or a third party designated by the government. Personnel with access to sensitive data typically had to be screened; this sometimes included limits on outsourcing. Workers usually had to be trained in the security requirements and encouraged to report violations; and whistleblowers had to be protected from retaliation.

We were acutely aware that these measures weren't perfect. The substantive requirements were at best a mixed bag as far as security went. In theory, access to source code and hardware designs would allow our experts to find any Trojan horse built into the product. But few government workers have the expertise to find these needles in a haystack of products. Unless we insisted that the companies pay for very expensive outside experts to check their work, or we received an intelligence tip about corporate misbehavior, we had only a modest chance of catching a really clever compromise.

The same was true of the procedural safeguards. Reporting obligations and whistleblower protections couldn't guarantee that we'd hear about an attempt at compromising U.S. products. They just increased the chances that someone would blow the whistle.

Still, imperfect as they were, mitigation agreements were well ahead of whatever was in second place. They were in fact our only good tool for policing foreign efforts to build insecurity into U.S. networks.

There was just one difficulty. The law didn't actually authorize mitigation agreements. No one knew how to enforce them, or even whether they could be enforced. If we were going to turn mitigation agreements into a kind of regulatory regime, we'd have to make sure they got the same respect as other regulatory measures.

Practically the first case I saw when I came on board was a small transaction that raised just this concern. The confidentiality of the process prevents me from providing details unless the companies have made them public, so I will not name the foreign buyer or the U.S. target. But both sold computer security products, so trust was critical. If you can't count on the loyalty of the company that provides your security, you have no security. *Quis custodiet ipsos custodes*—who will guard the guards themselves?—and all that.

As it happened, the foreign buyer of the security company had already entered into a mitigation agreement with DHS. An earlier transaction had been flagged for review, but the company had persuaded the government that negotiated safeguards would protect the national interest. The new case was tougher, but it became easier as we looked more closely. It turned out that no one had closely followed up as the company implemented the earlier agreement. The company had sent the government letters putting forward self-serving interpretations of the agreement, and no one in government had responded. Now, as we took a close look, we didn't like what we saw. We were sure that the company had deliberately misread—and then violated—the mitigation agreement.

That was that. Why would we trust the company a second time if it hadn't lived up to the first set of promises? DHS took the lead in fighting the transaction. We ruled out another mitigation agreement. The transaction had to be rejected, we insisted. After a long period of disbelief that DHS truly intended to block the deal, the foreign buyer ultimately withdrew from the transaction.

That was the right result. The risk of foreign ownership can hardly be higher than in the area of security services. If we couldn't rely on the company's promises we couldn't find a middle ground.

I knew that the decision would enhance compliance with mitigation agreements. Before this, lawyers could tell their foreign clients that compliance with mitigation agreements was, if not optional, at least negotiable. After all, they might not even be enforceable, and for sure the government would have to sue to get compliance. If so, what was the harm in adopting an unreasonably narrow reading of the agreement? As long as its reading sounds plausible to a judge, the client would suffer no harm from defying the intent of the agreement.

But we didn't want to be forced to go to court over every misreading of the agreement, as though a security agency was just another party with a contract claim. Now we wouldn't have to. We had made it clear that companies would suffer very severe consequences indeed if they failed to live up to a reasonable reading of their mitigation responsibilities. We had taken a big step toward making CFIUS mitigation agreements a credible regulatory regime.

Still, I wasn't completely happy with DHS's performance. Not one member of CFIUS had taken responsibility for making sure the mitigation agreements that protected our security were actually being followed. How could we expect companies to take these mitigation agreements seriously, I asked, if the government agencies that negotiated them didn't seem to care?

In one sense, DHS was the last agency that should have been responsible for enforcement of mitigation agreements. We were brand-new members of CFIUS, and the Policy office, which had been assigned to handle CFIUS, didn't exist until late 2005 and had not yet been staffed. Even so, we decided to take the lead in reviewing and auditing all of the mitigation agreements that DHS had signed. I hired Stephen Heifetz, a lean, sharp lawyer whose instincts and work habits had been honed in private practice. He could handle anything that the big-firm lawyers on the other side of the table threw at him.

Once he had his team assembled, I sent Heifetz out to audit the companies that had signed mitigation agreements with DHS. The team gave notice that they were coming, but not too much. When they arrived, they demanded records showing compliance and also insisted on reviewing all emails relating to the agreement. If the companies had been deliberately skirting their obligations it would have been hard to hide.

As we expected, most companies were complying, but we also saw clearly that they had become less than vigilant over the years. Heifetz said that email records told the same story in almost every company. Once the deal was done, months might go by without any special attention to the mitigation requirements. Then, suddenly, there would be a spike in high-level attention to compliance. The companies would launch internal reviews to make sure their performance was up to snuff. The spike almost always occurred a day or two after we had sent notice that our audit team was coming out for an inspection.

That was exactly what we hoped to achieve. It is human nature not to follow inconvenient rules when no one is watching. Every regulator knows that. If you want your rules followed, you have to remind companies that you're watching. That's what our audits did. Never again would the companies feel that DHS didn't care whether they complied with mitigation agreements. We were on our way to creating a successful cybersecurity enforcement regime.

This was not our only step to ensure that mitigation agreements were respected. We began to include financial penalties in the agreements. And to make sure that the buyer could never treat fines as simply a cost of doing business, we tied the size of the penalties to the value of the target company. The bigger the transaction, then, the higher the price would be for violating the agreement.

We soon had an opportunity to show we meant business when it came to assessing fines. One buyer of highly sensitive equipment had agreed to spin off a particular portion of the business within a few months of the closing. As the deadline grew nearer, though, the company began coming in regularly, explaining how hard it was working to find a buyer, and how much trouble it had encountered. It was clearly angling for an extension. We agreed, but we also declared that we'd begin imposing fines if the next deadline was missed. What's more, the fines would get bigger every month.

After agreeing to those terms, the company missed the next deadline, too. It asked us to forgo the fines. We refused. The penalties kicked in. As they began to mount, the company quickly found a way to spin off the business.

In a handful of cases, where the national security stakes were very high, we went even further. As the North American equipment market collapsed, the dominant supplier, Lucent, began to hemorrhage. The company put itself up for sale, and Alcatel won the bidding. For us, the stakes could not have been higher.

Alcatel manufactures telecommunications equipment and has been quite close to the French government for years. The French government had frequently been accused of carrying out espionage against U.S. targets. Lucent may have fallen on hard times, but it still manufactured and maintained the switches that carry most of North America's telephone calls. It was the home of the storied Bell Laboratories, whose Nobel-winning research had developed technologies from the transistor and the laser to the Unix operating system. Even the slightest risk that Lucent's capabilities might be turned against the United States was unacceptable.

I thought hard about saying no to the transaction, but the more we looked at the market, the more convinced we became that Lucent couldn't survive on its own. Vetoing the deal would put Lucent on a road to rapid decline. (That judgment still looks correct in hindsight; at the time, Nortel, the other North American telecom manufacturer, looked a bit healthier and chose to stay independent as the industry consolidated. That strategy turned out worse than Lucent's. In 2009, Nortel declared bankruptcy and was sold off in pieces.)

To salvage what we could from a bad set of options, DHS and other national security agencies decided to approve the deal and negotiate the toughest security measures ever imposed under CFIUS. We wanted above all to make sure that there would be no cheating on the deal. To make sure that the agreement would be scrupulously observed, the committee decided on the harshest penalty for breach that had ever been proposed.

If Alcatel breached the agreement in a way that threatened U.S. security, we insisted, the committee could reopen the acquisition. In other words, if there was a breach, the United States could require that Lucent be disgorged and restored to independence. This was called the "evergreen" provision because CFIUS's right to disapprove the transaction would remain in effect forever.

Alcatel and Lucent were nearly slack-jawed when we put this proposal on the table. How could that possibly work, they wanted to know. Five or ten years after the transaction had closed, Lucent would be deeply integrated into Alcatel; undoing the merger at that point could be a death sentence for both companies.

They weren't wrong. No one was sure how the companies could be pried apart at that stage. For that reason, some doubted that the United States would ever invoke the remedy. But the committee members believed that the risk was enormous—a compromise of Lucent's switches could disclose all of the government's wiretaps and make Americans subject to foreign wiretaps at home. If those were the stakes for U.S. national security, we needed to do everything possible to deter a violation of the network security measures.

A death sentence, we thought, should provide a measure of corporate deterrence.

In the end, Alcatel and Lucent accepted the agreement, including the evergreen clause. They decided that the risk created by the clause was material to their future prospects and disclosed it publicly to their investors (which is why I can discuss it publicly). In some ways, the Alcatel-Lucent deal was a high-water mark in the effort to make CFIUS a bulwark against subversion of U.S. information and telecommunications networks. It was public, it was demanding, and it was clearly going to be enforced. Indeed, other agencies, particularly Justice and the Treasury, began imitating DHS and bulking up their audit and enforcement capabilities at about the time we signed the Alcatel-Lucent agreement.

The tough new CFIUS regime benefited from the fallout from the Dubai port debacle. No policymaker wanted to be caught asleep at the switch if another transaction raised national security concerns. Agencies that had shown little interest in CFIUS before DPW now understood its importance, and they were reluctant to second-guess the security agencies. At least at first.

The same was true of investors, who had come to think of CFIUS as something of a paper tiger. CFIUS filings had hit an all-time low in 2003, but by 2006 and 2007 they had rebounded to levels not seen since Exon-Florio was enacted. (Part of that was DHS's doing; we began actively monitoring new transactions and requiring the parties to bring their deals—no matter how small—to CFIUS for review.)

Mitigation agreements also increased. DHS had signed seven such agreements in 2004 and 2005. In 2006 and 2007, after DPW, DHS signed an average of fifteen mitigation agreements a year. And many of the strongest enforcement measures for mitigation agreements were adopted in the same time frame.

For all the value we got from mitigation agreements, we weren't kidding ourselves that we'd solved the cybersecurity problem. CFIUS and its mitigation agreements were an unsatisfying way to address a broader problem. CFIUS made it harder to compromise U.S. networks by buying a U.S. company. But foreign governments have other ways to compromise U.S. networks. They can provide subsidies so their own companies can underbid U.S. suppliers. If their price and quality are right, sooner or later the foreign companies will end up with a big share of the U.S. market—without ever making an investment that CFIUS can review. And if a company never makes a CFIUS filing, it will never have to sign a mitigation agreement, leaving some markets half-regulated.

Even more difficult to police is the supply chain. IT hardware and software are assembled from components made all over the world. A foreign government seeking to compromise U.S. computers doesn't need to buy Dell, or Intel, or Microsoft. It could buy a hard drive maker, a motherboard assembler, a modem supplier, even a keyboard manufacturer. Any of those components can be the source of computer security compromises. Again, without an investment in a U.S. company, CFIUS can do nothing about a "supply chain attack."

Even so, we had made a start, and a good one. Partial as they were, CFIUS mitigation agreements were still the best tool in our toolkit. They helped to close off the quickest and most obvious route that foreign governments might follow to compromise U.S. communications and data. Best of all, we seemed to have strong popular support for careful scrutiny of foreign acquisitions. If anything, the public had been convinced by the Congressional and media flap over DPW that CFIUS review was too lax.

In the end, though, DPW was poisoned fruit. The unjustified abuse that Congress had heaped on DPW eventually spurred a backlash. But when it came, it was aimed not at the worst Congressional offenders but at DHS.

Using CFIUS to reduce cybersecurity vulnerabilities was DHS's key strategy. As we turned mitigation agreements into a regulatory tool, we were drawing fire. And from some of the same forces that opposed us when we used new tools to deal with the risk of jet travel—business and the international community.

These forces slowly turned the DPW case into a millstone around the necks of the security community. At first, they concentrated on stopping the congressional effort to enact legislation that would make CFIUS tougher. Business groups quietly communicated their concern about the bill's effect on investment. After the initial burst of enthusiasm, work on the bill slowed. Nothing had been enacted by the midterm elections of 2006, in which Democrats took control of both the House and Senate. Although they had been loud in condemning the DPW deal while out of power, by the time they took control, those calls had muted.

Congress was now hearing from other governments as well as business. Other governments have no reason to encourage the United States to protect its national security through CFIUS. In fact, some governments have a direct interest in precisely the opposite. But even for our friends, there's no reason to praise CFIUS. The safest—and most conservative—stance was disapproval, and the DPW case certainly offered plenty of fodder for that position.

Many governments claimed to see a protectionist motive in CFIUS. For some, the accusation of protectionism was clearly a projection of their own inclinations. France, famously, had decided in 2005 that a French yogurt company was a "jewel" of French industry and therefore could not be sold to Pepsi. The Germans had refused to let foreigners buy into their auto industry. But the best defense is a good offense, the Europeans had learned; so European and other trade negotiators began to criticize U.S. CFIUS practice, hinting that it would have to be negotiated away in the next round of trade talks.

In the United States, unease about CFIUS spread to businesses that depended on foreign companies—from Wall Street investment banks to K Street lawyers. They too began quietly campaigning against the new regulatory push. They didn't want to see the United States opened further to espionage or sabotage, of course. But couldn't we do that without cutting off their deal flow?

The Alcatel-Lucent "evergreen" clause added to the tumult. From a foreign investor's point of view, the one good thing about CFIUS was its certainty; once a deal cleared, it was cleared for good. It was a safe harbor against future storms. By adding an evergreen clause to the mitigation agreement, though, we had torn down the breakwater, leaving Alcatel and perhaps others exposed to future national security storms.

For foreign investors and their lawyers, the evergreen clause offered a second issue to rally round. In our view, the furor over the provision was out of all proportion to how often it was likely to be used. The fines and other enforcement measures that DHS had introduced were almost always tough enough to keep companies on the straight and narrow. Evergreen clauses were worthwhile only when normal incentives might not be enough to ensure compliance (usually when we feared that a foreign government could force the foreign company to take actions without regard for the company's own financial interests).

Part of the problem was perception. We couldn't talk about individual cases, and we didn't tell the parties to the transaction what our intelligence said about the buyer. So from the outside, our decisions did not look consistent or predictable. Sometimes we'd oppose a deal fiercely because intelligence revealed dangers that weren't obvious to outside observers, or even the parties. To outsiders, the role of intelligence in CFIUS was deeply frustrating, because it deprived them of the opportunity to rebut the charges.

They weren't wrong to be concerned. Intelligence is never perfect, and it should always be challenged before it is relied upon. Some of the CFIUS agencies didn't have a broad understanding of intelligence, and they sometimes gave it too much credence. (From time to time, I would propose audits or inspections of foreign buyers as a way of checking what the intelligence agencies were saying, but it was not easy to get the buyers to agree. Perhaps they didn't understand that an inspection might help them by providing a check on the intelligence—or perhaps they feared that it would confirm what the intelligence was telling us.)

The backlash against CFIUS was also aided from within. CFIUS has a peculiar structure that is almost guaranteed to spur bitter conflict. Originally established as a committee of cabinet members headed by the treasury secretary, the committee has gradually added members from the White House bureaucracy. So, in addition to cabinet departments like Defense, State, DHS, Justice, and Commerce, the table is cluttered with representatives from the U.S. trade negotiating office, the Office of Science and Technology Policy, the National Security Council, the National Economic Council, and so on and so on. I say cluttered because these offices could talk but did not vote on transactions.

The White House offices are, in theory, at the table to protect the president. The idea is that their advice will be conveyed confidentially to the president if and when the committee makes a formal recommendation. That's the theory. In fact, the White House agencies all have turf struggles with each other, and they're often at the table to fight their rivals, or in the hope of influencing the debate before it reaches the White House.

White House staff didn't vote in CFIUS cases. But that hardly mattered, because votes were rarely useful. CFIUS is not an agency, and the Treasury Department, though it chairs the committee, is little more than first among equals. The purpose of the committee is to make a recommendation to the president. If one cabinet secretary wants to say something to the president, and another secretary is adamant that something else must be said, the treasury secretary will not be able to resolve the dispute. Both messages will be delivered.

And, given the institutional interests of the departments, it was almost inevitable that disagreements would arise. The State Department, for example, is always concerned about the reaction of foreign nations to our CFIUS decisions, and foreign nations never welcome a tough CFIUS regime. So State invariably opposed for as long as it could any effort to put conditions on transactions. The Office of the U.S. Trade Representative (USTR) was, if anything, even more predictable in opposing the use of CFIUS for cybersecurity purposes.

DHS, in contrast, was among the most likely to propose mitigation agreements or outright vetoes of risky deals. With Justice and the Defense Department, DHS formed the heart of CFIUS's national security wing. Less predictable, at least over time, were Treasury and Commerce. Treasury is deeply sensitive to the mood of foreign investors, and that tended to push it toward the State Department. But it also had a large security role in stopping terrorist finance, and it was constrained by the need to act as chair of the committee, muting its natural sympathies. The Commerce Department speaks for U.S. business interests; some of its leaders thought that was enough to determine their position in CFIUS cases. Under other leadership, though, Commerce would sometimes give weight to its own national security arm, the office that oversees export controls on high technology and recognizes the risk posed by potential compromises.

There was a deep divide between the "national security" agencies and the "trade" or "economic" agencies. And, because Treasury could never force a decision over an impassioned dissent, arguments at CFIUS, particularly at the lowest levels, had a kind of well-worn vitriol to them. Everyone knew that the dispute would go higher. The only reason to pull back was fear that your boss wouldn't support you. At DHS, that was never a problem. We had short lines of communication and decisive leaders at the top. The secretary and deputy secretary could absorb new information and pass judgment on a course of action in minutes. Other agencies with less certainty of their boss's views were less willing to hold firm, and that sometimes helped us advance our cybersecurity agenda.

In the long run, though, the DPW flap hurt us badly. As the panic wore off, policymakers all across the government began to realize that they had been foolish to make such an issue of the DPW investment. That had been DHS's view all along. We thought the DPW case was a distraction from the greater dangers in telecom and information technology. For the business and international interests that opposed those measures, though, DPW was a godsend. Everyone knew that DPW had been a serious overreaction, and it was easy to lump everything together and argue that CFIUS was being abused.

As that idea took hold, CFIUS meetings grew more divided. Decision makers at the top of the Commerce Department or the U.S.

Trade Representative's office might not know much about cybersecurity, but they were happy to take a stand against CFIUS abuse. They began to back their lower-level officials more frequently on that basis. And so a logjam of unresolved conflict over CFIUS issues began to creep higher up the decision chain.

Deadlock became the norm. Trade agencies in particular would exercise a "bureaucrat's veto" by insisting that nothing could be done without their agreement and then asking for more paper, more process, and more debate before that agreement could be granted. They didn't say no, they just asked for more time.

Everyone in government is familiar with this tactic. The power to delay is often the power to prevent a policy decision. It was one more weapon in the arsenal of the institutional conservatives trying to prevent new policies from being adopted.

But delay had unexpected costs. The thirty-day deadline for decisions on most transactions was increasingly ignored. Too often, CFIUS would launch forty-five-day "investigations" simply to give the contending agencies more time to resolve their differences. Or it would strong-arm companies into "withdrawing" their applications and refilling them, starting the clock over again.

Much of this delay was caused by a growing determination on the part of the trade agencies to fight over the terms of mitigation agreements. But from the outside, all that the parties knew was that CFIUS was slowing their deal. For the trade agencies, this was a twofer. Their stalling tactics made it harder to get tough new mitigation agreements. And the delays brought the entire CFIUS process into disrepute, which increased the business backlash against strong CFIUS review.

Of course, the delay was hard on the companies involved in the transaction, but the trade agencies only occasionally seemed bothered by that. In fact, while DHS was viewed from the outside as the principal source of CFIUS scrutiny, and thus of delays, we were often the only voice arguing that the process should move more quickly to protect investors' need for certainty and promptness.

Officials who joined the administration after DPW also brought with them views shaped by the public debate but not informed by the intelligence that had driven our decisions in particular cases. Without access to that information, they tended to assume that all CFIUS decision making had been as irrational as the DPW case.

The National Security Council in particular suffered from this effect, and by 2007 it had abandoned any pretense of being an honest broker in CFIUS disputes. It became instead the principal combatant, working relentlessly to cut back the tough new security regime that we had introduced to CFIUS.

The critical showdown would come over who could negotiate and sign mitigation agreements. There was a long tradition of agency autonomy in this area. For years, mitigation agreements had been viewed as agreements with individual CFIUS members, not with CFIUS as a whole.

"This proposed mitigation agreement is between you and DHS," we used to tell companies when we tabled a draft. "It is meant to address the concerns that DHS has about your transaction. If we negotiate a satisfactory agreement, DHS will not oppose the transaction. We're not speaking for CFIUS, so there's always a possibility that the committee will disapprove the deal notwithstanding this agreement. And if we don't reach agreement, your deal may still be approved. You are simply taking the risk that DHS will oppose the deal and that we'll be able to persuade CFIUS not to approve it."

Because we were negotiating only for DHS (and sometimes for other agencies with similar concerns), it was easy for us to agree on tactics, priorities, and reach agreement on a deadline. That autonomy and flexibility is what allowed DHS to sign the quick mitigation agreement with DPW that was the administration's best defense during the Washington panic over the case.

For the trade agencies, though, that was all history. As far as they were concerned, DHS's authority to sign mitigation agreements had to be taken away. First, they argued that DHS and other agencies negotiating mitigation agreements should keep the rest of CFIUS informed about the progress of the talks; then they argued that DHS should take their views into account in negotiating the agreements. Both of those positions sounded perfectly reasonable, but we accepted them with foreboding.

In theory, consultation with other agencies may provide useful new perspectives or avoid problems. In government practice, however, a consultation requirement is just a first step; it allows the consulted agency to second-guess and interfere, because it gives the agencies a chance to probe for weak spots. That is what happened in CFIUS. The trade agencies had little interest in helping the security agencies improve their mitigation agreements. Their principal interest was gaining enough information to argue that no mitigation agreement was necessary. Some of the more extreme agencies even violated the spirit and perhaps the letter of the CFIUS confidentiality requirements by "coaching" parties, suggesting arguments they should make when negotiating with DHS and then seconding those arguments in internal debates.

Eventually, the trade agencies began to insist that they weren't being consulted in good faith if DHS reserved the right to sign an agreement while the trade agencies were still asking questions. Consultation, in other words, couldn't end until the trade agencies agreed that all their questions had been answered. Of course, that formulation simply meant that the trade agencies could stall an agreement for as long as they could think up new questions. Or, more commonly, for as long as they could find new ways to ask the same old questions.

Impatient with this effort to undercut DHS's authority in a backdoor fashion, DHS simply continued to sign mitigation agreements. The parties usually were happy to do the deals, and the quicker the better. They had no interest in the ideological issues being raised by the trade agencies; they just wanted to move on. The trade agencies believed that the willingness of the parties to accept DHS's terms was irrelevant. They thought the parties were simply knuckling under because they needed to get their deals done quickly. They thought it was bad policy to use the leverage of CFIUS approval to extract security agreements that would not apply to everyone in the industry. And they found DHS's refusal to be cowed more and more frustrating. Even at the deputy secretary level, conflict grew intense as CFIUS pressed DHS to give up its traditional authority to execute mitigation agreements.

By early 2007, the trade agencies and Treasury decided to take their frustration to Congress. The new Congress was led by Democrats, and they had made CFIUS reform a priority. But they were also listening to the business groups and foreign countries that had begun complaining about DHS's tough scrutiny. At a hearing to which DHS was not invited, its mitigation agreements were roundly criticized. Witnesses repeatedly bemoaned the fact that the number of mitigation agreements required by DHS tripled in 2006 from the previous three-year average (up from 4.5 to 15).

One witness expressed concern "that some agencies are taking undue advantage of the leverage inherent in CFIUS. CFIUS should not be a fishing expedition for a single agency to address comprehensive industry objectives on a "catch-as-catch-can" basis merely because they have leverage over one industry participant. ... [I]f the Department of Homeland Security perceives a vulnerability in our telecommunications infrastructure, it should address that vulnerability across the sector, without regard to the ownership of firms."[5] Others made similar complaints.

Congress continued to insist that it wanted to make CFIUS tougher, but its actions said something else. Throughout the hearings and debates, congressmen touted the new bill as strengthening CFIUS and security. But when the television lights were turned off, the drafters sat down with the Treasury Department, and the committee leadership added language designed to undercut the authority of any agency to enter into a mitigation agreement on its own.

The new bill took the long overdue step of acknowledging the need for mitigation agreements, and it called for a "lead agency" in each case to negotiate the mitigation agreement. At the last moment, though, the House financial services committee leadership slipped in an amendment to the bill, requiring that any mitigation agreement be negotiated "on behalf of the committee."[6] The effect of this modest phrase was dramatic. It would allow Treasury and the trade agencies to insist that they had to supervise the negotiation of any mitigation agreement now that the talks were being conducted "on behalf of" the entire committee. That meant that no negotiation could occur without a consensus among all CFIUS members. And that in turn meant that the trade agencies could use the "bureaucrat's veto" of endless delay to kill mitigation agreements even over the objection of the agency negotiating them.

The new CFIUS law[7] also contained a provision requiring that mitigation agreements be based upon a "risk-based analysis" of the threat to national security of the proposed transaction. The same manager's amendment described above also added language to this provision to specify that this analysis must be "conducted by the committee." This amendment gave the trade agencies a hand in analyzing national security threats and determining the level of appropriate mitigation. Once again, the committee leadership had reduced the security provided by CFIUS.

The House didn't exactly advertise the fact that it was weakening the hand of the security agencies. That wouldn't have been consistent with the dominant narrative in the press, where Congress was still loudly proclaiming the need to strengthen CFIUS because the administration hadn't given enough weight to security in the DPW case. Still, it seems likely that Congress knew exactly what it was doing. The business witnesses had asked that agency autonomy be abolished or constrained in the name of encouraging foreign investment, and as the Congressional Research Service noted, the amendment was adopted because the earlier bill, which lacked it, "could have delayed and discouraged foreign investment."[8]

International and business groups, in short, seem to have persuaded the committees that the real problem with CFIUS was not that it was too weak but that it was too tough. Needless to say, that wasn't a change of mind that Congress was eager to shout from the rooftops.

After the bill was enacted, the National Security Council wasted little time turning the "on behalf of" language into precisely what DHS had feared—a radical restriction in the authority of the security agencies. In fact, it built an entire edifice of obstruction on those few words. Under the executive order[9], the lead agency must achieve consensus within CFIUS before it can even propose a mitigation agreement. To do this, the agency must prepare a written statement that (1) identifies the national security risk posed by the transaction, including potential threats, vulnerabilities, and consequences, and (2) sets forth the mitigation measures, which must be "reasonably necessary" to address the risk.

After jumping through these hoops just to propose a mitigation measure, the lead agency must also get committee approval before negotiations can begin. It must keep the committee fully informed of its activities and must notify the Secretary of the Treasury in advance of any proposed major action, allowing time for the committee to consult and direct the lead agency about how it should act.

By the time the order was fully written, the lead agency was less a leader than an indentured servant. It might sit in the driver's seat, but every member of CFIUS would have a hand on the steering wheel and a foot on the brakes of the negotiations. The trade agencies were happy to use the brakes. No negotiations could occur, they would insist, until a final position had been agreed to by all agencies. This made the old tactic of delay and refusal to agree a potent weapon again. Security agencies were ordered not to even tell the parties to the transaction what their concerns were until they had the consent of the other agencies.

This quickly led to absurd results. In one case, when DHS expressed concerns about what might happen after the merger, the parties promised to take action after the merger that would completely resolve the worry. DHS suggested to the committee that the promise be put in writing so that the assurance was binding. Some members objected and the assurance was never formalized.

In another case, the deadlock in the committee went on so long that the parties wrote letters to all members of the committee begging to be told what DHS wanted, arguing that it would much rather agree to reasonable mitigation conditions than wait for the committee to finish its internecine bureaucratic war. Nothing doing. The trade agencies were determined to make the United States safe for foreign investment no matter how many foreign investors they had to hurt in the process.

The most ironic note was sounded toward the end of the administration, when another foreign purchase of port facilities was submitted for approval. DHS proposed a modest mitigation agreement, similar to the DPW agreement that so many in Congress had condemned as inadequate during the panic. This time, though, under the law that Congress had enacted in reaction to DPW, even this modest agreement could not be imposed. The trade agencies refused to accept it, and Congress had made their consent a necessary condition to any mitigation agreement.

The counterattack on behalf of business and the international community had come a long way against heavy odds. The new law had been so trimmed and twisted that in the end the one part of the DPW affair that could not be repeated was the one part that contributed to security—the mitigation agreement.

The effect was felt quickly. In 2008, the number of mitigation agreements fell dramatically, and they became even more rare in 2009.

In the end, though, much of what DHS did to make CFIUS a force for network security endured. Even in the waning days of the administration, long after the new CFIUS law and executive order took effect, a new transaction raising severe security concerns came to CFIUS. Working with the other security agencies, DHS made the case against the deal. Faced with evidence of grave risk, the trade agencies folded; they did not oppose our recommendation that the transaction be rejected. Had the security agencies been willing to execute a mitigation agreement, they would have accepted that recommendation as well.

The lesson of that transaction was that the trade agencies would not fight the security agencies when the chips were down. Security is the mission of DHS, Defense, and Justice. If those agencies say with confidence that a transaction will raise serious security concerns, it is hard for an agency like USTR to second-guess them. And at the highest levels, each agency tends to take a broader view than simply its own bureaucratic interest. This means that, for transactions that raise the greatest concern, the new law is not fatal to the reforms that DHS pioneered.

Still, the story shows how hard it is to regulate even the most dangerous cybersecurity threats. CFIUS dealt with the particularly overt and troubling threats, and in most cases it had found a way to allow investments to go forward, though with safeguards.

Even so, the nations and companies that opposed any regulation had successfully advocated for a law and executive order that undermined the security agencies, at least somewhat. That they accomplished their mission in the teeth of noisy public demands for tougher CFIUS security standards is a testament to their formidable clout.

12 Smallpox in the Garage

In January 1970, a German electrician fell ill after a trip to Pakistan. He was hospitalized with what appeared to be typhoid fever. He had been isolated for several days when the doctors realized that he didn't have typhoid fever.

It was smallpox.

Fear riffled through the hospital, and the community beyond. Smallpox has probably killed more human beings than any other disease. And it kills them with particular cruelty. After starting out like a bad flu, after a few days the disease attacks the victim's skin. Tiny spots appear, spread, and then harden into pus-filled blisters. Gradually, with excruciating pain, the blisters pull the outer layer of skin away from the under-layers. Sometimes the skin pulls loose in sheets. Sometimes the blisters attack not just the skin but the eyes, the throat, and every other orifice, ripping loose skin inside the body as well. Desperate with thirst, the victims can't drink; swallowing is just too painful.

Throughout it all, the victim remains fully conscious. A third or more of the victims die. Those who survive are often permanently scarred, or blind or both.

The electrician lived. But many who came into contact with him were infected. Several died.

What was most frightening was how the virus spread. One victim spent only fifteen minutes in the hospital. All he did was ask directions, briefly opening a door that led to a corridor thirty feet from the patient's room. That was enough. He came down with smallpox.

Three other victims were even farther away—two floors above the electrician's isolation ward. It was January, but tests revealed that opening the hospital windows just a crack allowed currents of air to drift between rooms on different floors. The virus had floated out the patient's window and along the outside wall; it then slipped into three different rooms two stories above, infecting patients in each room.

Seven years later, in 1977, Ali Maow Maalin also fell ill with smallpox. This time, though, it turned out to be good news.

Maalin was a cook from Merca, Somalia—where smallpox was making its last stand. Vaccination was slowly tightening a noose around the disease. Because smallpox reproduces only in humans, widespread vaccination left fewer and fewer places for the virus to reproduce and spread.

The first vaccination for smallpox—or indeed for any disease—came in 1796. That was when Edward Jenner realized that milkmaids who caught cowpox seemed to be protected from smallpox, to which cowpox was related. Jenner's vaccine based on cowpox marked the beginning of man's counterattack on smallpox. By the 1970s, vaccinations had gradually reduced the disease's natural range to the wilds of Somalia and Ethiopia.

The World Health Organization hoped to make Ali Maow Maalin the last victim of smallpox in history. It quickly vaccinated everyone who had been in contact with him, then held its breath. Would other cases flare up?

WHO waited.

A year.

Two years.

Three.

At last, after three years with no natural cases of smallpox, the World Health Assembly declared victory. It triumphantly called a special 1980 meeting.

"[T]he world and all its peoples have won freedom from smallpox," the assembly declared. This was "an unprecedented achievement in the history of public health." Together, the nations of the assembly had "freed mankind of this ancient scourge."[1]

Copies of the virus were locked away in Atlanta and Moscow for research purposes, but the disease was gone from nature. Vaccinations stopped. Few Americans born after the 1960s have the dimpled scar on their arm that is the last trace of mankind's worst nightmare.

It had taken a bit less than two centuries for vaccination to free the world from "this ancient scourge."

Today, the likelihood that the world will remain free from this ancient scourge is close to zero.

Smallpox is back, or nearly so.

Within ten years, any competent biologist with a good lab and up-to-date DNA synthesis skills will be able to recreate the smallpox virus from scratch. Millions of people will have it in their power to waft this cruel death into the air, where it can feed on a world that has given up its immunity.

How can I be so sure? Easy. I've seen the same thing happen already, and so have you. The very same revolution that made possible the explosion of information technology—and set the table for network attacks—is now transforming biology, with consequences that are both exalting and frightening.

The same relentlessly exponential improvement in technology that gave us Moore's Law and that democratized the computer is now democratizing the technology of life. It is empowering an army of biologists to tinker with biology in ways that will help us all live longer and more comfortable lives.

And then, unless we do something, it will kill us in great numbers.

"Synthetic biology" blends biology, chemistry, and engineering. The field really began to take off when it moved from laboriously replacing a single gene to building whole stretches of the genome from scratch.

DNA is organized like a spiral staircase, and each step on the stairs is called a base pair. Linking base pairs together into longer sequences allows researchers to make more complex genes—and ultimately more complex organisms. So progress in synthetic DNA is measured by how many base pairs have been successfully strung together. In recent years, progress has been exponential.

In 2002, after a two-year effort, a team of researchers announced that they had assembled the entire polio virus. To do that, the team had to assemble 7,500 base pairs of DNA, precisely in order. The next year, scientists managed to knock years off the process, assembling a bacteriophage with 5,300 base pairs in just two weeks.

Two years later, in 2005, researchers' capabilities had tripled. A team managed to synthesize an influenza virus with 14,000 base pairs. Just a year later, they had surpassed that mark by a factor of ten, synthesizing the Epstein-Barr virus, with 170,000 base pairs.

Smallpox has 180,000.

By 2005, whether smallpox would be synthesized was simply a matter of choice, not of capability.

The following year, the outgoing secretary general of the United Nations, Kofi Annan, grew alarmed. He pointed to researchers' successes in building an entire virus from scratch and said, "In the right hands, and with the appropriate safety precautions, these are sound scientific endeavours that increase our knowledge of viruses. But if they fall into the wrong hands, they could be catastrophic."[2]

Too late. By 2009, the state of the art had left 180,000 base pairs in the dust. A team of researchers announced that it had assembled a bacterial genome with 583,000 base pairs. Creating smallpox from scratch was no longer even an interesting challenge.

Nor were these capabilities confined to a few specialty laboratories. Foundries sprang up to sell made-to-measure DNA, at ever-declining prices that put Moore's Law to shame. Synthesizing DNA cost $10 per base pair when George W. Bush ran for president in 2000. By the time of his second inauguration, the price was $2 per base pair. When he left office in 2009, the price was down to about 25 cents. For those who don't want to use a foundry, DNA synthesizers are available for sale on eBay.

Kofi Annan was wrong. This technology isn't going to fall into the wrong hands. Just like jet travel and powerful computers, it's going to fall into *everybody's* hands. The Mayo Clinic. Hezbollah. Pfizer. Al Qaeda. Apple. Ted Kaczynski, Timothy McVeigh, and the Fort Hood shooter.

They won't need their own labs to build bugs to order. Even today, it's possible to obtain long sequences of synthetic DNA simply by sending a message to the private "foundries" that assemble DNA to order.

Struggling to survive in a new market with thin margins, the foundries' sense of responsibility for what they make is, well, limited. The *Guardian* newspaper in Great Britain demonstrated this when one of its journalists successfully ordered a lightly modified piece of the smallpox genome over the web. The order was mailed to his home, no questions asked. When a dozen foundries were asked whether they screened DNA orders to see whether they were providing sequences that terrorists could turn into weapons, only five answered "yes."

As many as half the foundries questioned by journalists did not routinely screen their orders to make sure that they were not helping terrorists construct a dangerous virus. The order came in, and they filled it, often with no questions asked.

If current trends continue, anyone who can get his hands on a computer virus today will soon be able to get his hands on a custom-built biological virus.

And who can get his hands on a computer virus today? In an age of drop-down-menu malware attacks, the answer is simple.

Anyone who wants to.

Perhaps it isn't completely fair to assume that exponential growth in biotechnology will democratize biological terror in the same way that computer technology democratized computer crime. After all, unlike computer hackers, bio-hackers can't pretend that releasing pathogens is a good way to demonstrate their skills or to dramatize the need for better biosecurity. So perhaps biological malware will arrive more slowly than its computer counterpart. That's good.

So far, the terrorists who've tried to use biological weapons have turned out to be more hapless than terrifying. A cult that wanted to win an election in rural Oregon poisoned the local salad bar to suppress turnout. A Japanese group experimented with anthrax and ended up spreading a harmless, non-virulent vaccine strain around Tokyo. The anthrax-laced letters sent to prominent journalists and politicians in 2001 included a warning to take antibiotics and thus dramatically reduced casualties. Al Qaeda tried to acquire biological weapons before 9/11, but its efforts never really got off the ground.

Maybe large-scale bioterrorism is harder than it seems. Or maybe we're just in that golden era we also experienced in computer technology; maybe the bad news just hasn't caught up with the good news. Much the same thing happened with jet travel for that matter. Apart from some Brazilian military officers who commandeered a civilian flight in 1959 to further their coup attempt, there were no notable hijackings of a commercial flight before 1968, even though they had been possible since at least the 1950s. Early that year, though, an El Al plane was seized by Palestinian terrorists and a U.S. flight was hijacked and diverted to Cuba. Then the deluge began. By the end of 1968, there had been half a dozen hijackings to Cuba alone, and the stage was set for decades of ever more spectacular hijackings.

The lag between good news and bad owes something to the surprisingly conservative nature of terrorism. Terrorists don't like to fail; failure doesn't inspire fear. But once a new tactic has been pioneered, and it has become clear that governments don't know how to respond to it, everyone piles on. Suicide bombings were virtually unknown until the early 1980s, when they were used in the Lebanese and Sri Lankan conflicts. The tactic is now widely used by terror groups in many countries. We may be only one or two successful attacks away from a similar wave of bioterrorism.

When those attacks will occur, however, is anyone's guess. All we can say is that every year biological attacks become more probable, just as biotechnology becomes ever more democratized. And, of course, if disaster becomes more probable every year, then sooner or later disaster will happen, though it may show up late. That's a lesson financial markets learned again in 2008 (as did New Orleans residents in 2005). Sooner or later, the inevitable does happen.

One cabinet-rank official summed it up a little differently after I gave him a briefing on the topic.

"Maybe," he said, "the human race isn't meant to survive."

I understood how bad the threat was. I had been briefed on it while investigating U.S. intelligence agencies' work on Iraq's WMD program. The agencies were eager to tell us how much they knew about other nations' nuclear weapons programs. We got briefing after briefing. Nukes were a major concern, and the agencies had scored many successes in penetrating other nations' programs.

On biological weapons, the intelligence community was noticeably less voluble. Everyone acknowledged that biological weapons were a terrible threat. Worse than nuclear weapons in some ways. They could kill as many people. And the aftermath would be worse. The day after a nuclear weapon goes off in an American city, a hundred nations will order their airlines to fly to the United States, carrying assistance until the crisis has passed. The day after a biological weapon is used in an American city, a hundred nations will order their airlines to stop flying to the United States until the crisis has passed.

But, with a few exceptions, intelligence operatives and analysts seemed almost to have lost hope of understanding other nations' biological weapons programs. The programs are easier to hide and require less in the way of investment than nuclear weapons. The equipment and training that supports them have many innocent commercial uses in the pharmaceutical and pesticide industries.

And the agencies' track records were not good. The Soviet Union—and Russia thereafter—had maintained a truly loathsome biological weapons program for decades after the United States gave up its program. It treated the disappearance of smallpox, and the worldwide end of smallpox vaccinations, as an invitation to devise more potent weapons using its stores of the pathogen. The Soviet program was discovered only when defectors began to talk about their work on artificial new diseases that were proof against existing countermeasures, or that responded to treatment by changing into something even worse.

The same was true in Iraq. Saddam Hussein maintained a biological weapons program for years, hidden from both U.S. intelligence and UN inspectors. (If you're wondering why no such program was found after the U.S. invasion, the answer is that Saddam Hussein finally dismantled the program after his son-in-law defected and disclosed it to the West in 1995. Saddam admitted the existence of the program and announced that it had been shut down; intelligence agencies, shocked by what they had missed, credited Saddam's admission but doubted his claim that the easy-to-hide program had ended.)

Intelligence gaps on biological weapons raised our concern about anonymous attacks. Like computer malware, biological agents are hard to tie back to an individual or group. Ambiguity about attribution has already prevented the United States from taking effective retaliatory action against computer attackers. It's quite possible that we won't do any better against attackers armed with biological weapons. The best test of our capabilities came in the 2001 anthrax attacks. The FBI used great ingenuity and massive resources to question, search, and investigate all the likely suspects. It finally announced, to some skepticism, that it had identified the guilty man in 2008—seven years after the attack.

When I got to DHS, I asked my staff what we could do to cut the risk of biological terrorism. They described two new programs launched after the 2001 anthrax attacks. The first was to develop countermeasures—vaccines, treatments, etc.—for the most threatening pathogens. The second was to get a better picture of who actually had access to such pathogens inside the United States. These were large programs, funded by a Congress that feared another attack was imminent. But as the years went by without an attack, the programs had slowly been bent to fit the institutional inclinations of the agencies that got the money.

Take the countermeasures program. This is an absolutely essential step. Unlike nuclear weapons, biological weapons can be defeated even after the attack. That is, if we have a smallpox vaccine and can distribute it quickly, we can stop an infection in its tracks, greatly limiting the harm done by the disease. We could take the weapon out of terrorists' hands. A biological attack that is met by quick, effective countermeasures is like a bomb that has been defused before the blast.

But our countermeasures strategy has serious flaws. It requires a massive investment in medicines that often have no civilian use. We will never have a need for smallpox vaccine except to defend ourselves against attack. The doctors and researchers of the National Institutes of Health (NIH) were not used to battling human adversaries. They were scientists who wanted to do pure research, not something that felt like military work. Like any industry facing a market change, the traditional research community resented the funding that went to countermeasures research, and they didn't have much trouble turning that resentment into an ideological and personal campaign against the program. (The debate broke into the open when traditional NIH researchers launched a smear campaign against Tara O'Toole, the Obama administration's nominee to head DHS's science office. Her success at building a countermeasures research program led to her being labeled an alarmist and a female Dr. Strangelove by traditional researchers, delaying her confirmation for months.)

More troubling was the way business as usual in other parts of the Department of Health and Human Services threatened our ability to actually use the countermeasures that had been developed at such great cost. For example, getting approval for such countermeasures is staggeringly expensive. A host of regulatory hurdles has been set up for new drugs. The regulations assume that the drugs are being championed by private companies hoping to make billions in profits if they are approved. But the private sector will not spend billions to get regulatory approval for a product that may never be deployed.

Even if government pays that cost, most countermeasures, such as vaccines, have side effects that may be rare but can be quite serious.

Even faced with the threat of an occasionally deadly H1N1 influenza in 2009 and 2010, many Americans refused to be vaccinated. It would be nearly impossible to persuade them to be vaccinated against anthrax or smallpox on the chance that these pathogens would be unleashed by terrorists.

So the countermeasures will sit in warehouses, waiting for an event. Once smallpox or anthrax is released in a vulnerable population, the countermeasures will have to be deployed on a massive scale in a matter of days, even hours. At DHS we knew that this would be a logistical nightmare. After all, we'd lived through the errors and delays as government tried to improvise in the wake of Hurricane Katrina. An incident of biological terrorism would create the same problems, except the victims might be desperately sick, not just hungry and thirsty, and the rescuers would be delayed longer by fears for their own safety.

Imagine a biological attack in which terrorists release a large cloud of anthrax in an urban area without telling anyone. Even with air sampling equipment in place it might take a day or two to confirm the attack. If everyone who'd been exposed took antibiotics within three days, practically all of them could be saved. The weapon could be defused. But if it took five or six days to start antibiotics, we could lose half the population. That's an enormous difference, making every hour of logistical delay a matter of life and death.

So how were we planning to deliver antibiotics? The postal service. That's right. The aggressively unionized postal service workforce would be asked to show up and drive into anthrax-contaminated areas to distribute antibiotics. Of course, they would want armed protection, so law enforcement agents would somehow meet up with the postal workers and they'd both go around delivering antibiotics. To me, this sounded, well, unlikely. Getting the workers to show, hooking them up with their armed escorts, making sure they and their escorts had started antibiotics, verifying the routes, making sure they weren't swamped by people who couldn't stay home for their antibiotics, keeping others from trailing them to steal antibiotics from mailboxes, all of this would have to be done for the very first time under unbelievable time pressures.

There was a way to cut through this mess. If everyone had their own medical kit of antibiotics at home, all they'd have to do is open it and start taking antibiotics as soon as the attack was discovered. We'd save days of delay and avoid the chaos of distribution. Even if only one-fourth of the exposed population had antibiotics, that would take a load off the distribution system. And in a pinch, people could share their antibiotics, so they wouldn't need government distribution until a week into the course of treatment. That would buy us time and ease the crisis no matter how many people had the home med kits. Not only that, it would leave people in charge of their fate. Instead of being helplessly dependent on government action, they could actively plan for and assist in the emergency.

That's also why the bureaucrats of Health and Human Services hated it. Government officials rarely doubt their own capacity to direct the lives of ordinary citizens. Doctors too seem to have vast confidence in their own judgment, at least as compared to patients. So it shouldn't be a surprise that government doctors have no faith whatsoever in the great unwashed mass of citizens. The Public Health Service has, basically, one piece of advice for the public in any health emergency: sit tight and wait for our instructions. We'll decide who should get vaccines or antibiotics, and in what order. If it's a close question, we'll send you to your family doctor, and he or she will tell you what to do. On no account should you do anything to help yourself. If you try to buy antibiotics, you'll be "hoarding" medicines that are needed more by others, like, uh, medical professionals.

When the first anthrax attacks occurred, that's exactly what government doctors said, and their guidance was posted on government and American Medical Association Web sites. Anyone trying to obtain Cipro or other antibiotics was seen as ignorant or selfish or both. In addition to the fear that medicines wouldn't be rationed in accord with government priorities, medical professionals were understandably concerned about the overuse of antibiotics, which has encouraged the evolution of antibiotic resistance. So letting ordinary people have antibiotics in their homes was considered too risky. They might take it for a headache.

So the med kit idea met a wall of medical and bureaucratic resistance, even though both the secretary and deputy secretary of Health and Human Services eventually became supporters of the idea. Unable to defy their superiors, the bureaucrats who worked for them slow-rolled the idea. Eager to prove that you and I can't be trusted, and to wait out their bosses, they insisted on a large-scale test, putting emergency kits in the hands of citizens and telling them not to open the kits except in a government-announced emergency. I was delighted when they had to report back to the interagency that only one person had opened the kit improperly—an elderly woman who heard an official tornado emergency announcement and opened her package in the hope that it might offer some guidance.

Since the study hadn't turned out quite the way the bureaucrats expected, it was clear that what we needed was, well, more studies. The leaders of DHS and Health and Human Services pushed hard for a better set of plans to distribute med kits and use other methods to avoid the postal service option. In the month before the election, despite concerns that we'd look as though we were spreading fear, the two departments announced a number of steps that would make med kits possible. But time had run out; the efficacy of med kits was still being studied (in a Minnesota pilot project) when the Bush administration left office.

A year later, the bureaucrats won. An unimaginative bioterror strategy was released by the White House in December 2009.[3] It contains an inevitable section, beloved of bureaucrats, setting out everyone's "Roles and Responsibilities." Such documents are beloved of bureaucrats because that's where all the turf wars are fought.

Now, you and your family probably didn't hire anyone to participate in those turf wars on your behalf.

Believe me, it shows.

Because when the document sets out your roles and your responsibilities (*i.e.*, the roles and responsibilities of "Individuals and Families"), here's what it says:

> There is a critical role for families and individuals in reducing the risks from biological threats. Individual contributions to community resilience can undermine motivations for biological threats by reducing their effectiveness. We will encourage individuals and families to undertake the following:
>
> - Following general guidance for disaster preparedness, such as keeping supplies of food and other materials at home—as recommended by authorities—to support essential needs of the household for several days if necessary;
> - Being prepared to follow public health guidance that may include limiting their mobility throughout the community for several days or weeks, or utilizing designated evacuation routes; and
> - Informing appropriate authorities when they encounter or observe suspicious or unusual activities.[4]

This language was surely meant to resolve the bureaucratic battle conclusively against do-it-yourself preparedness. It says individuals are supposed to "follow guidance" about keeping food and other materials at home. But in case you didn't understand the first time that you're only supposed to do what the government tells you, the bit about keeping materials at home gets an added and quite redundant qualifier. While you're following government guidance about keeping materials at home, remember that you're only to keep materials "as recommended by authorities."

And how will you get, say, antibiotics in an emergency? That shoe dropped a few weeks later. The Obama administration decided to make a big bet on the postal service's nimbleness, sense of urgency, and dedication to duty. In a Christmas week executive order[5], it announced plans to bet your life on the postal service having all those qualities and more.

Stop for a moment to imagine the scene. Postal workers will be asked to drive into contaminated neighborhoods even though they can't be sure their countermeasures will work against whatever strain has been spread there. The neighborhoods will be full of people desperate to get antibiotics, so for protection, the postal workers will first have to meet up with guys with guns whom they've never seen before. They also have to collect antibiotics from pickup points that they may or may not have seen before. They'll meet the guys with guns there, or someplace else that may have to be made up at the last minute. Then they'll start out on routes that almost certainly will be new to them. As they go, they will be expected to seamlessly and fairly make decisions about whether to deliver the antibiotics to homes where no one is present, to rural mailboxes that may or may not be easily rifled, to people on the street who claim to live down the way, to the guys with guns who are riding with them and have friends or family at risk, and to men in big cars who offer cash for anything that falls off the truck.

And this will put antibiotics in the hands of every single exposed person within forty-eight hours, from a no-notice standing start?

No way. It will be a nightmare. And that's not a knock on the postal service, which may, in fact, be as good a public agency as any for getting antibiotics into the hands of an exposed population.

That said, no one but an idiot would bet his life or his children's lives on flawless execution from a public agency doing something it's never done before.

So here's what I did—and what you should do, too. I asked my doctor for an emergency supply of antibiotics that would get me through the first week or so of a crisis. I promised not to take the antibiotics irresponsibly for colds or other viral infections. And I was ready to change doctors over the issue.

I got the prescription.

Some public health officials may try to make you feel guilty about "hoarding" antibiotics or contributing to antibiotic resistance. Poppycock. If you buy while supplies are plentiful, you're actually creating a bigger market for these products and contributing to the maintenance of production capability. And if you don't take them in response to a tornado warning, you won't affect resistance.

In fact, you're being socially responsible. If we do suffer an anthrax attack and the postal service has trouble keeping up, a sure bet if ever there was one, you can defer your delivery in favor of someone who has no stash. You'll take a bit of strain off a system that is going to need all the relief it can get.

And for those who'd like to recapture their youth, in addition to the glow of virtue, you might even feel a bit of leftover sixties civil disobedience thrill. When I tried to give this home stockpile advice in a speech toward the tail end of the last administration, the lawyers at Health and Human Services told our lawyers that I'd be violating the law—because advocating an unapproved use of prescription medicine is a criminal offense under the federal food and drug laws. And, while taking antibiotics for an anthrax attack is an approved use, getting antibiotics in case of an anthrax attack is not. If the Health and Human Services lawyers were right, then this part of the book would be a felony. I think they're full of it, or I wouldn't be writing this. But if I'm wrong, well, power to the people.

The new policy is a throwback to an era of government-knows-best. There's a big role for government in countering terrorism, but this isn't it. This is like telling passengers that the best response to an air hijacking is to sit tight and wait for the authorities to arrive.

It's insufferably paternalistic. And it's bad advice.

So the bad news is that the administration isn't going to help you prepare a home med kit. No standard packaging and labels, no encouragement for doctors to prescribe the kits responsibly, no sober discussion of the risks. You're officially discouraged from worrying your sweet head about such things.

The good news is, no one will listen.

At least, not if I can help it. In fact, since no one in government has followed through on the claim that my advocacy of home med kits is illegal, you've got an easy response if government doctors try to discourage you from getting a home stash. Just tell them you're adhering to the roles and responsibilities in the administration's bioterrorism strategy: You're keeping material at home "as recommended by authorities"—two of them, the authority of this book and of your own common sense as an independent citizen.

The other government program to thwart biological terrorism is based on the Willie Sutton principle. Sutton robbed banks "because that's where the money is." If you want to prevent the release of pathogens, probably the best place to start is where they are. And the people who ought to get the earliest scrutiny are those who have regular access to those pathogens. Because history tells us that bugs in the lab have a way of ending up in the wild.

In February 1978, Christmas break was a distant memory for the cadets of the U.S. Air Force Academy near Colorado Springs, Colorado. They were grinding their way through the bleakest stretch of the academic year. Suddenly, in less than three hours, five hundred of them had lined up outside the academy's clinic. They had the flu, and within days, three-fourths of the student body had fever, sore throats, headaches, and weakness.

Yet the faculty suffered no ill effects. They lectured to nearly empty rooms. Later, researchers pieced together the flu's origins. It was an H1N1 virus, very like one that had circulated in 1950. That explained why the cadets fell ill while the faculty did not. The older instructors had already been exposed. The younger ones had not. Still, the older faculty's resistance seemed surprisingly complete.

The reason for that soon became clear. The virus that hit the academy wasn't just similar to the 1950 version. It was identical. Now, nature doesn't usually repeat herself so precisely. But human researchers do. Many scientists think the 1977-78 influenza was released from a store of the 1950 strain—in error or otherwise. We still don't know.

Twenty-three years later, though, there wasn't much doubt that someone could release a pathogen from an existing store. According to the FBI, Bruce Ivins exploited his status as a biodefense worker at Fort Detrick in Maryland to obtain enough anthrax to kill seven people.

Fears of an inside job led Congress to adopt the "select agent" program in 2002. Its purpose was to keep the worst pathogens out of the wrong hands. It called on the Department of Health and Human Services to identify truly dangerous pathogens such as Ebola, plague, and anthrax. Researchers who wanted to work with these agents had to register their facilities, name an officer who was responsible for security, and prepare both a security and a safety plan for the agents. Those who worked with the agents had to undergo background checks; they were to be listed in a database and checked against criminal and immigration records. Foreigners who passed a background check could work with the agents if they did not come from a country that sponsors terrorism. All shipments and handling of these materials had to be tracked, and exports were subject to control.

DHS didn't exist when the select agent program was created. But we thought we had something to offer. The program was trying to solve a problem that looked a lot like the problem we faced at the border. Most lab workers, like most travelers, are entirely innocent; we want them to keep doing exactly what they're doing. So we needed a way to separate the great mass of ordinary researchers from a few risky ones. In the travel arena, the key was good data about travelers. If we knew who was coming to the United States, and we had a good idea who was risky, we could concentrate our attention on the tiny minority of risky travelers.

The same was true of researchers. In fact, that was the theory behind the select agent rules already enacted. Anyone with access to highly dangerous pathogens would be identified and investigated by the FBI. If the bureau had reason to think the researcher was a risk, access to the pathogens could be denied. But the FBI is at heart a criminal investigative enterprise. It doesn't make the kind of screening decisions DHS has to make every day at the border.

So DHS maintained electronic databases that offered up-to-date information about who was coming to the United States and who was a security concern. The select agent records, in contrast, were kept in paper files, or at best were frozen electronic pictures of documents rather than easily searched electronic data. This meant that the FBI performed a one-time check on each researcher, using this paper record. Once that person was cleared, there was no good way to go back and look at his or her record without doing a paper search. As a result, the records simply sat in file cabinets for years. If a new fact showed up that made a researcher seem more risky—calls to a known terrorist, for example, or a decision to overstay his visa illegally—the federal government might never know that he also had access to an extraordinarily dangerous biological agent, at least not without getting out the paper files and checking names.

That didn't seem sufficient to us; we thought that researchers with access to the most deadly biological agents on the planet should get at least as much scrutiny as sleepy tourists arriving from Munich or Bangkok. We offered to put the files into a modern database or spreadsheet format so that they could be cross-checked automatically on a regular basis. We knew that even this would not be a foolproof system. A well-organized terrorist group could recruit people with clean records to work at pathogen research facilities. But it's almost always a mistake not to do something about terrorism risks just because you don't have a 100 percent guarantee of success. Terrorists are human, too. Sometimes they can be discouraged by measures that might not hold up to extended testing. And sometimes their efforts to evade and test your systems will backfire, drawing attention to the plot. The more information you have, the more likely you are to spot these efforts.

Since our approach to the problem of biotechnology involved learning more about researchers, we could expect privacy objections. But all we were proposing was to digitize records that had already been given to the government for purposes of background checks. You wouldn't think that privacy groups would object to government doing a better job with data it already had. At least that's what DHS thought. But in the end we didn't get a chance to find out how they'd react.

DHS was the new boy. The FBI and Health and Human Services had been given responsibility for the select agent program by

Congress before DHS was even created. They didn't get along particularly well, but they agreed on this much: They didn't need a third agency involved in the program, no matter what improvements the agency was willing to pay for. When we asked HHS which research labs held select agents, something we'd have to know to perform any review—or to plan a rescue if a flood, hurricane or earthquake struck the laboratory—HHS staff simply refused to provide the data. Even after the secretary of HHS twice promised our secretary that the data would be sent, his staff refused.

To justify their stonewalling, both the FBI and HHS played the privacy card. They told us they couldn't give DHS access to the background check data because, conveniently, they hadn't mentioned such information sharing when they wrote the privacy statement explaining how the data would be used. They'd have to publish a new privacy statement, then take comments on the change, then respond to the comments, they said, and maybe, maybe then, they could give us access.

We'd been down that road before. Even routine changes to a privacy statement take a year-and-a-half. And that's assuming the agency wants to make the change. If the agency didn't want to do it, the opportunities for delays and detours were endless. The FBI began the process, but I wasn't surprised that it hadn't been completed by the time we left office.

Maybe it never will be. One of the open secrets of the federal government is that privacy concerns can often be a useful way to advance bureaucratic interests without sounding parochial. ("We're not turfy; we're civil libertarians.") No agency likes to share information with another. The other agency may use the information successfully but not share credit. Or it may use the information to second-guess the operations of the agency that gathered it. That's one reason the wall was so difficult to eradicate. Privacy claims simply reinforced a natural bureaucratic instinct to hold information close. In 2001, that mix of turf and privacy constraints had cost us dearly. For a while, it had receded as we counted the cost. But this was a different threat, and as we turned the reins over to a new administration, all the old instincts had revived.

And just like the fight over the wall in 2001, privacy groups had won this fight without even having to show up. The rest of us had lost.

That was frustrating; it was also just the beginning of our difficulties. The select agent program was based on an assumption that wouldn't be true much longer. Congress had assumed that we knew where the pathogens were. It hadn't prepared for a world where pathogens could be assembled from the blueprints of life.

History had already demonstrated that even the workers in government labs couldn't be fully trusted to keep pathogens under lock and key. What were we going to do when anyone with access to the DNA sequence of a pathogen could simply build it—or, even more simply, order it from a foundry?

We probably had a few years to find a way to head off this nightmare, but we needed a plan. I began to consult biotech experts, looking for someone who understood the technology, the risks, and perhaps some of the opportunities.

Craig Venter is a bald man with a beard and the tanned, bulky fitness of a sixty-year-old defying his years. He leans across the DHS conference room table as though he owns it. But the meeting isn't going quite as smoothly as Venter expected.

Venter is used to government meetings. He'd been a government researcher himself, long ago. But now he is a kind of biotech rock star, famous for sequencing the human genome in a bitter, elbow-throwing race between the National Institutes for Health and an upstart private company he created. Venter's company caught the NIH from behind, and the drama of the chase helped Venter raise a billion dollars for his company.

Venter learned then that sizzle sells, and he's a master at creating a narrative that catches journalists' imagination. In a second biotech undertaking, he sailed around the world, dipping into the ocean and parsing the DNA he found there. Now he's launched on his third—a private effort jump-started with government funds that has already assembled nearly 600,000 base pairs to make the chromosome of a bacterium. He hopes to create an artificial organism that will make hydrogen or ethanol for industrial fuels.

If anyone represents the promise of biotech, it is Venter. He sees engineered organisms as the key to progress and riches on a vast scale. So he can't be comfortable with the theme of the meeting.

I am pressing him on risks, not promise. Venter knows more about biotech than almost anyone. If there's a way to avoid the dangers that come with democratizing genetic engineering, Venter should have it at his fingertips.

"What will stop terrorists from inventing new diseases?" I ask. Even if they're afraid of blowback that infects their supporters, plenty of pathogens affect different ethnic groups differently; and some viruses cause genetic mutations. Won't we see groups or individuals trying to engage in a kind of DIY eugenics—improving the species by killing off disfavored racial or ethnic groups or by introducing new genetic material to make future generations more peaceful and compliant?

They wouldn't even have to succeed to cause a disaster, it seems to me. A badly coded biological virus probably won't act like a badly coded computer virus. Bad computer code usually does more or less nothing. The computer's default state is inactivity. But in the biological world, the easiest way to build a new organism is to start with one that already exists and then change a few genes. That means using one that's been honed by billions of years of evolution to survive—to feed and breed at all costs. Even if the new gene turns out to be defective, the resulting organism could find a way to keep on feeding and breeding. We don't know what it will feed on or how quickly it will breed, but any surprises on this front are likely to be bad ones.

I'm thinking of what happened in 2001, when an Australian research project went frighteningly wrong. The researchers were trying to create a rodent contraceptive from the mousepox virus. They spliced a gene into the mousepox virus. They didn't want to hurt the mice, so they injected the engineered virus only into mice bred for resistance to mousepox. And, adding suspenders to their belt, they vaccinated some of the mice for mousepox before administering the injection.

As a contraceptive, it turned out, the new virus was an overachiever. Dead mice don't have sex, and dead mice were what the virus produced. The new gene turned the formerly mild mousepox virus into a killer, overriding the genetic resistance of every unvaccinated mouse. And then it turned on the vaccinated mice, killing half of *them* for good measure. If just one researcher made just one mistake as bad as that with human subjects, I tell Venter, even nations that had stockpiled vaccines would be destroyed. How do we know, I say, that well-intentioned hobbyists, not to mention hapless terrorists, won't produce pathogens that are far more lethal and contagious than they intended?

Truth be told, this is turning into a bit of a rant, but I'm still not done. I'm not going to have another chance to get biotech advice from a rock star. Perhaps mistakes and terrorism aren't even the worst we have to fear, I offer. Computer viruses became ubiquitous only when hackers realized that they could make money from the infections. They had invented a new form of organized crime. Why couldn't the same thing happen in biotech? If we don't know who has released a pathogen, couldn't some crooked business, somewhere in the world, be tempted to design a disease, patent a cure, and then let the disease loose upon the world? Even if others suspected wrongdoing, the sick would still pay whatever it costs to get well, and with the proceeds, a company could buy a lot of protection from its government. What can we do to keep foreign businesses from trying such a tactic?

I pause. That's a lot to put on the table. But at least I've laid out all my concerns. I'm hoping Venter can see something I've missed, some reason why democratizing this technology won't ultimately empower the worst in human behavior as well as the best. Or at least some way to keep his beloved technology from putting humanity at risk.

I wait. Venter leans in, clears his throat. He smiles the winning smile that has charmed reporters and government funders for more than a decade.

"My, my, don't *you* have an imagination," he beams.

That's how it goes with many of the biotech leaders I consult. They know what the risks are. They just don't like to talk about them.

Rob Carlson is a principal at Biodesic and one of the industry's most astute observers. A physicist by training, he's spent years studying biotechnology as a business and a human undertaking.

Carlson has close-cropped hair and a genial, wonkish air. He's an eager teacher. But he grows distinctly uncomfortable when I turn the conversation to bioengineered pathogens.

Carlson wants to talk about where the industry is going. Biotech has already produced enormous improvements in productivity, he says. Drugs developed with recombinant DNA already have sales of $65 billion a year, and biotech products already account for 2.5 percent of GDP growth. One company has modified yeast into a bug that can transform sugar into everything from malaria drugs to jet fuel and gasoline. Production will begin in 2010. And many companies expect to build bugs that can produce other chemicals out of petroleum. The chemical industry could be transformed by bioengineering, Carlson argues, but these changes cannot be achieved without making the tools for bioengineering cheaper and more efficient.

So, cheaper they will get. And bioengineers everywhere will benefit. Already, the foundries that assemble small bits of DNA into large stretches have been driven by competition into fully automating the process from code to gene sequence. Even so, the biggest bottleneck in industry is the time engineers spend waiting around for foundries to send back the sequences they've ordered. The engineers don't want to wait. Carlson thinks the chemical industry's need to experiment quickly with many different genes and organisms will continue to force the pace of automation until the process can be performed in a single machine that can be run by the engineers on premises. That machine will grow cheaper and smaller at an exponential rate because of the returns and the integration of semiconductor processes. The result will be desktop DNA synthesis, Carlson predicts, and perhaps very soon.

When that happens, he sees a golden age of bioengineering. Bugs will eat our waste—literally, feasting on municipal sewage—producing raw materials that other bugs will turn into plastics and chemicals. Energy independence may come to any nation with modern sewers. The opportunities are astonishing.

I interrupt. Yes, I know. Biotech is irresistible. But that desktop DNA synthesizer—who's going to use it besides chemists? What about all the bad things that will come from putting this power into everyone's hands?

Carlson blinks. Well, sure, there could be bad things. Terrible things, maybe. But with technology like this in our hands, we can devise countermeasures faster and make them more effective than we ever dreamed possible. A revolution is coming. Why do you insist on looking at the downside?

He pauses and returns to the emerging economic opportunities. The industry is already global, and the business logic of bioengineering is already established. It's a fantastic new technology that will transform our lives for the better. Surely we'll be able to handle the risks in that transformed world.

After all, I think, who wants to be the voice of doom when everyone else is hoping to be the Steve Jobs and Steve Wozniak of biotech, playfully hacking genomes and starting a global empire in the garage?

Silicon Valley and the computer revolution is exactly what Rob Carlson and the rest of his generation hope to emulate. A growing "DIY bio" movement shows bio-hackers how to extract and modify DNA on their own, using household equipment. There's a *Biotech Hobbyist* magazine with a "series that will show you how to grow your own skin culture and suggest some very cool projects you can do with it."

There's even a biotech version of the Linux open source operating system. "Biobrick" prizes are awarded to teams that create standardized open-source DNA parts that perform predictable biological functions and can be combined in new ways.

Today, colleges hold lighthearted competitions for the best biological design. MIT's winning team in 2006 re-engineered *Escherichia coli*—an organism that lives in the human gut and helps to give our waste its distinctively foul smell. When the students were done, the redesigned E. coli smelled like wintergreen.

Biotech: it's cute, it's fun; and then you get rich.

I remember when the computer software geeks first came to Washington in the early 1990s. They were shocked to hear that the government wouldn't let them offer strong encryption to the world. The government feared that unbreakable encryption would allow criminals, terrorists, and pedophiles to hide evidence and communicate without fear of wiretaps. The technologists dismissed the fears. Encryption would be necessary to do business on the Internet, a development that was inevitable, they said, sounding a lot like Rob Carlson. Government would just have to get out of their way.

Carlson and other biotech industry representatives have none of the software industry's in-your-face contempt for government. After all, many of them are funded by NIH and hope to develop treatments that will pass muster with the Food and Drug Administration. Instead of defiance, they offer deflection, simply gliding past the risks and averting their gaze. It's the way most of us deal with the animal experiments that make new drugs possible: They're unfortunate, tragic even, but that's the price of progress; now, can we talk about something else, please?

Sixty-five years ago, with a bright flash and a mushroom cloud, the nuclear age was born in the New Mexico desert. Robert Oppenheimer was a prime mover in the first nuclear test, and he later told how the scientists reacted:

> We knew the world would not be the same. A few people laughed. A few people cried. Most people were silent. I remembered the line from the Hindu scripture, the *Bhagavad Gita*. Vishnu is trying to persuade the prince that he should do his duty and to impress him takes on his multi-armed form, and says, "Now I am become death, the destroyer of worlds." I suppose we all thought that, one way or another.[6]

Nuclear technology came into the world burdened by a sense of original sin. Before it became a source of cheap, carbon-free energy, it would kill and wound two hundred thousand people in Hiroshima and Nagasaki. For nuclear scientists even their most satisfying work was alloyed with tragedy.

It's a long way from that sober sense of guilt to the spirit that gave the world E. coli that smells like wintergreen. That's because, with nuclear technology, the deaths came first. With biotech, as with jet travel and computer networks, it's the delight, and the profits, that have come first.

It's odd. No one in the industry denies the risks, and some can be eloquent about the need to address the problem. But a curious disconnect remains between their intellectual acceptance of the danger and their response to it. At a visceral level, many of the biological and medical researchers who are leading the revolution simply cannot believe their technology may end up causing more harm than good. Some of them seem convinced that doctors, or at least medical researchers, just aren't the kind of people who would do such a thing. And so they fight restrictions on their work with the fervor of men and women who are determined to make the world a better place—no matter what the bureaucrats say.

DHS had no authority to force the foundries to screen their orders. Many of them were overseas, and none were subject to direct regulation. But we decided to press them anyway. We might not have regulatory authority, but we could make noncompliant foundries uncomfortable. We met with some of the DNA synthesis companies and told them they had a responsibility to prevent misuse of their products. They should know each customer and whether the customer was a legitimate business. And they should make sure the string of code they were building was not dangerous—the string of code that gives a pathogen its virulence, say, or the insertion of a toxin into the gene for an edible plant. If they got a suspicious order, they should report it to the government.

The purpose of this screening wasn't just to keep terrorists from building pathogens. We were also thinking about attribution after an attack. If we are attacked with an agent that might have been engineered, we will quickly find the resources to review every synthetic DNA order in recent years—and to interview every purchaser whose orders resemble the pathogen. But if the foundry doesn't keep records, we can't review them later. Quickly identifying the attacker is one of the great challenges of biological terrorism; if we can do that, we will deter many future acts and we will reassure our citizens that their government is not helpless in the face of what could be a devastating attack.

Measured against the horrors and risks that come with exponential biotechnology, that may not seem like much of a response. But it was a start; it reflected a core strategy of expanding the information needed to identify risky people, either before or after an event. And if it seems like too little too late to you (as it does to me), there were plenty of officials who were prepared to fight even these modest steps.

Some of the American and European foundries were responsive. A few had already begun screening customers and keeping records. They were in business for the long haul, and they couldn't afford to acquire a reputation for irresponsibility. That was worth something, but if other foundries refused to screen orders, then we'd just be moving the risky customers to the irresponsible suppliers.

DHS's proposal to press the foundries to engage in screening met with a tepid reaction at the lower levels of HHS. The NIH, in particular, was so sure that basic research in biology was a boon to mankind that it refused even to keep track of who was accessing the research on dangerous pathogens that it published on the Internet. Researchers who blithely published work that could be used both for weapons development and energy production would be widely condemned as dangerously irresponsible; but unrestricted publication of biological research is still an article of faith, even though such research can also be used both for commercial and military purposes.

Only after members of the industry and two independent biosecurity boards had made similar recommendations did NIH agree in principle to do something about foundry screening. NIH proposed to tell its grantees that they should send orders only to foundries that engaged in screening.

For other countries, controlling biotechnology was simply not on the agenda. Biotech expertise had spread throughout the world. Nations that missed the information technology boom were rushing to stake a claim in the next hot field. Commercial DNA foundries can be found in California, New York, and Massachusetts, of course, but also in Pretoria, Moscow, Dalian, and Tehran. Where we saw a global risk requiring oversight, these capitals saw a chance to catch and pass the United States in the exploitation of biotechnology. They still chafed at the role that Intel and Microsoft played in information technology. Why couldn't the Microsoft of biotech be Chinese or Singaporean or Dutch, they asked? If the United States wanted to hobble its researchers with elaborate restrictions, well, fine. That was an opportunity not to cooperate with the United States but to steal a march on it.

If pressed for cooperation, international diplomats argue that the key is enforcing the Biological Weapons Convention. This is an example of just how wedded to the status quo international diplomacy can be. The Biological Weapons Convention is modeled on treaties to control nuclear weapons that can trace their roots back to the 1940s, when U.S. policymakers hoped to move from nuclear weapons to the peaceful production of nuclear power. The nuclear weapons convention adopted in the 1970s seeks to follow the same pattern; it offers a simple bargain to countries that lack nuclear weapons: Abandon military use of nuclear technology and the countries that have weapons will teach you how to use nuclear technology for peaceful purposes. Every five years, the nuclear haves and have-nots get together in Geneva. There, the have-nots press the haves to abandon nuclear weapons before they get down to the less high-minded task of demanding more aid and more technical assistance in using nuclear technology.

The Biological Weapons Convention more or less borrowed the same model when it was adopted in the 1970s, even though it was never a good fit. The nuclear convention makes at least some sense because there is a vast difference between building a nuclear power plant and building a nuclear weapon. Information about the peaceful uses of nuclear technology is not easily used in a weapons program. So it's possible to transfer peaceful-use technology without dramatically increasing the risk of weapons proliferation.

That's not true for biological technology. There's no real difference between a bioengineering facility meant to cure disease and one meant to cause it. Facilities can be switched from one purpose to another with little more than a long weekend and a few gallons of bleach. Inspections to catch cheaters would have to be deeply intrusive, could easily become a cover for the theft of intellectual property, and would almost certainly fail to catch countries that were serious about maintaining an illicit program. The advent of synthetic DNA, with its radical empowerment of all researchers, makes the model even less relevant.

If ever there were a doubt about the dysfunctional conservatism of international forums, the persistence of the Biological Weapons Convention surely should put an end to it. The risks of biotech are novel and pressing. But the solution posed by internationalists is to draw on a model that was adopted for nuclear weapons in the 1970s and hasn't been a notable success in the forty years since. Finding a new response to a new problem seems to be simply beyond the capability of the international community.

In short, we were on our own. DHS kept pressing for action on foundry screening. A year after we left office, five of the biggest DNA foundries agreed on a common screening protocol that they would apply to every synthetic gene order; they also agreed to keep customer records for eight years.

This was progress, if it actually survived scrutiny by the European privacy bureaucracy. (European members of the group did not explain how they would square this new practice with the EU requirement that order data be destroyed when no longer needed for commercial purposes.) But at best, it covered only 80 percent of the foundries by market share.

Domestically, in 2009, HHS issued voluntary guidelines meant to encourage and set standards for screening of foundry orders. But the incentives to follow the guidelines remained limited. Exponential growth in the market has made NIH's standards less important. Today, NIH grantees probably account for no more than 10 percent of the foundries' business. Foundries that find the standards constraining can simply limit their sales to customers who aren't using NIH money. And if the United States tries to make the rules mandatory, they can take their facility elsewhere; biotech firms are likely to be welcomed in other countries with open arms and less demanding laws.

In a globalized world, where regulations may be put on the block to get an edge in the international competition for new industry, is there any way to prevent a race to the bottom on synthetic DNA? Perhaps, but only over the opposition of privacy, business, and other governments. If the United States really wants to ensure that biotechnology researchers and developers meet biosafety and biosecurity standards, it can use the one piece of government leverage that still counts in that world.

For biotech firms, the road to riches is intellectual property. A patent entitling firms to a royalty on the exploitation of some new biotech technique or drug is the key to most startups' business plans. And U.S. patents are particularly important because, in the absence of government medical price controls, the U.S. market probably pays a disproportionate share of the development costs for new drugs.

If all companies seeking patents derived from biotech research were required to demonstrate compliance with reasonable safety and security measures, the requirements would likely be observed globally, since even companies located in deeply hostile nations, such as Cuba, have sought U.S. patents for their research. (Despite sanctions and a bitter war of words between the two countries, Cuba has been granted more than seventy-five U.S. patents in the last thirty-five years.)

Of course, the governments that would be bypassed by such a measure can be counted on to protest, as will the business interests that want intellectual property protection without regard to their security record. And, since the most obvious biosecurity measures include detailed records of who is performing what kinds of research, we can expect other nations and the business community to cloak their interests in a cloud of privacy objections.

Requiring biotech companies to demonstrate that they have met biosecurity standards in order to get patent protection might well work, but it's guaranteed to trigger hostility from business, privacy, and international interests, and that's why it probably won't happen, at least not until the ever-steepening curve of biotechnology produces a disaster.

PART FOUR

THE PRIVACY PROBLEM

13 What's Wrong with Privacy?

One question still nags at me. It's easy to understand why business interests fight any government action that might slow or redirect the exponential path of their industry. It's even understandable that for many countries the default position is opposition to U.S. initiatives. In each case, it's a cold calculation of self-interest.

But why are privacy groups so viscerally opposed to government action that could reduce the risks posed by these exponential technologies? The cost of their stance was made clear on September 11, 2001. That tragedy might not have occurred if not for the aggressive privacy and civil liberties protection imposed by the FISA court and OIPR; and it might have been avoided if border authorities had been able to use airline reservation data to screen the hijackers as they entered the United States.

But even after 9/11, privacy campaigners tried to rebuild the wall and to keep DHS from using reservation data effectively. They failed; too much blood had been spilled.

But in the fields where disaster has not yet struck—computer security and biotechnology—privacy groups have blocked the government from taking even modest steps to head off danger.

I like to think that I care about privacy, too. But I had no sympathy for privacy crusaders' ferocious objection to any new government use of technology and data. Where, I wondered, did their objection come from?

So I looked into the history of privacy crusading.

And that's where I found the answer.

In the 1880s, Samuel Dennis Warren was near the top of the Boston aristocracy. His father was a self-made paper-manufacturing tycoon. His wife, Mabel Bayard Warren, was the daughter of a U.S. senator and secretary of state.

Warren himself was no slouch. He had finished second in his class at Harvard Law School. He founded a law firm with the man who finished just ahead of him, Louis Brandeis, and they prospered mightily. Brandeis was a brilliant, creative lawyer and social reformer who would eventually become a great Supreme Court justice.

But Samuel Dennis Warren was haunted. There was a canker in the rose of his life. His wife was a great hostess, and her parties were carefully planned. When Warren's cousin married, Mabel Warren held a wedding breakfast and filled her house with flowers for the event. The papers described her home as a "veritable floral bower."

No one should have to put up with this.

Surely you see the problem.

No? Well, Brandeis did.

He and Warren both thought that, by covering a private social event, the newspapers had reached new heights of impertinence and intrusiveness. The parties and guest lists of a Boston Brahmin and his wife were no one's business but their own, he thought.

And so was born the right to privacy.

Angered by the press coverage of these private events, Brandeis and Warren wrote one of the most frequently cited law review articles ever published. In fact, "The Right to Privacy," which appeared in the 1890 *Harvard Law Review*, is more often cited than read—for good reason, as we'll see. But a close reading of the article actually tells us a lot about the modern concept of privacy.

Brandeis,[1] also the father of the policy-oriented legal brief, begins the article with a candid exposition of the policy reasons why courts should recognize a new right to privacy. His argument is uncompromising:

> The press is overstepping in every direction the obvious bounds of propriety and of decency. Gossip is no longer the resource of the idle

> and of the vicious, but has become a trade, which is pursued with industry as well as effrontery . . . To occupy the indolent, column upon column is filled with idle gossip, which can only be procured by intrusion upon the domestic circle. The intensity and complexity of life, attendant upon advancing civilization, have rendered necessary some retreat from the world, and man, under the refining influence of culture, has become more sensitive to publicity, so that solitude and privacy have become more essential to the individual; but modern enterprise and invention have, through invasions upon his privacy, subjected him to mental pain and distress, far greater than could be inflicted by mere bodily injury . . . Even gossip apparently harmless, when widely and persistently circulated, is potent for evil . . . When personal gossip attains the dignity of print, and crowds the space available for matters of real interest to the community, what wonder that the ignorant and thoughtless mistake its relative importance . . . Triviality destroys at once robustness of thought and delicacy of feeling.[2]

What does Brandeis mean by this? To be brief, he thinks it should be illegal for the newspapers to publish harmless information about themselves and their families. That, he says, is idle gossip, and it distracts "ignorant and thoughtless" newspaper readers from more high-minded subjects. It also afflicts the refined and cultured members of society—like, say, Samuel Dennis Warren and his wife—who need solitude but who are instead harassed by the fruits of "modern enterprise and invention."

What's remarkable about "The Right to Privacy" is that the article's title still invokes reverence, even though its substance is, well, laughable.

Is there anyone alive who thinks it should be illegal for the media to reveal the guest-list at a prominent socialite's dinner party or to describe how elaborate the floral arrangements were? Today, it's more likely that the hostess of a prominent dinner party will blog it in advance, and that the guests will send Twitter updates while it's under way. For most socialites, what would really hurt is a *lack* of media coverage. To be blunt, when he complains so bitterly about media interest in a dinner party, Brandeis sounds to modern ears like a wuss.

Equally peculiar is the suggestion that we should keep such information from the inferior classes lest they abandon self-improvement and wallow instead in gossip about their betters. That makes Brandeis sound like a wuss *and* a snob.

He does sound quite up-to-date when he complains that "modern enterprise and invention" are invading our solitude. That is a familiar complaint. It's what privacy advocates are saying today about Google, not to mention the NSA. Until you realize that he's complaining about the scourge of "instantaneous photographs and newspaper enterprise." Huh? Brandeis evidently thinks that publishing a private citizen's photo in the newspaper causes "mental pain and distress, far greater than could be inflicted by mere bodily injury."

If we agreed today, of course, we probably wouldn't have posted 3.5 billion photographs of ourselves and our friends on Flickr.

Anachronistic as it seems, the spirit of Brandeis's article is still the spirit of the privacy movement. The right to privacy was born as a reactionary defense of the status quo, and so it remains. Then, as now, new technology suddenly made it possible to spread information more cheaply and more easily. This was new, and uncomfortable. But apart from a howl of pain—pain "far greater than . . . mere bodily injury"—Brandeis doesn't tell us why it's so bad.

I guess you had to be there.

Literally. Unless you were an adult when photography came to newspapers, you'll probably never really understand what the fuss was about. We've all been photographed, and most of us aren't happy with the results, at least not all the time. But that's life, and we've learned to live with it. Most of us can't imagine suing to prevent the distribution of our photographs—which was the tort Brandeis wanted the courts to create.

We should not mock Brandeis too harshly. His article clearly conveys a heartfelt sense of invasion. But it is a sense of invasion we can never share. The sensitivity about being photographed or mentioned in the newspapers, a raw spot that rubbed Brandeis so painfully, has calloused over. So thick is the callous that most of us would be tickled, not appalled, to have our dinner parties make the local paper, and especially so if it included our photos.

And that's the second thing that Brandeis's article can tell us about more contemporary privacy flaps. His brand of resistance to change is still alive and well in privacy circles, even if the targets have been updated. Each new privacy kerfuffle inspires strong feelings precisely because we are reacting against the effects of a new technology. Yet as time goes on, the new technology becomes commonplace. Our reaction dwindles away. The raw spot grows a callous. And once the initial reaction has passed, so does the sense that our privacy has been invaded. In short, we get used to it.

At the beginning, of course, we don't want to get used to it. We want to keep on living the way we did before, except with a few more amenities. And so, like Brandeis, we are tempted to ask the law to stop the changes we see coming. There's nothing more natural, or more reactionary, than that.

Most privacy advocates don't see themselves as reactionaries or advocates for the status quo, of course. Right and left, they cast themselves as underdogs battling for change against the entrenched forces of big government. But virtually all of their activism is actually devoted to stopping change—keeping the government (and sometimes industry) from taking advantage of new technology to process and use information.

But simply opposing change, especially technological change, is a losing battle. At heart, the privacy groups know it, which may explain some of their shrillness and lack of perspective. Information really does "want to be free"—or at least cheap. And the spread of cheap information about all of us will change our relationship to the world. We will have fewer secrets. Crippling government by preventing it from using information that everyone else can get will not give us back our secrets.

In the 1970s, well before the personal computer and the Internet, privacy campaigners persuaded the country that the FBI's newspaper clipping files about U.S. citizens were a threat to privacy. Sure, the information was public, they acknowledged, but gathering it all in one file was viewed as vaguely sinister. The attorney general banned the practice in the absence of some legal reason for doing so, usually called an investigative "predicate."

So, in 2001, when Google had made it possible for anyone to assemble a clips file about anyone in seconds, the one institution in the country that could not print out the results of its Google searches about Americans was the FBI. This was bad for our security, and it didn't protect anyone's privacy either.

The privacy campaigners are fighting the inevitable. The "permanent record" our high school principals threatened us with is already here—in Facebook. Anonymity, its thrills and its freedom, has been characteristic of big cities for centuries. But anonymity will also grow scarce as data becomes easier and easier to gather and correlate. We will lose something as a result, no question about it. The privacy groups' response is profoundly conservative in the William F. Buckley sense—standing athwart history yelling, "Stop!"

I'm all for conservatism, even in unlikely quarters. But using laws to fight the inevitable looks a lot like Prohibition. Prohibition was put in place by an Anglo-Saxon Protestant majority that was sure of its moral superiority but not of its future. What the privacy community wants is a kind of data Prohibition for government, while the rest of us get to spend more and more time in the corner bar.

That might work if governments didn't need the data for important goals such as preventing terrorists from entering the country. After September 11, though, we can no longer afford the forced inefficiency of denying modern information technology to government. In the long run, any effective method of ensuring privacy is going to have to focus on using technology in a smart way, not just trying to make government slow and stupid.

That doesn't mean we have to give up all privacy protection. It just means that we have to look for protections that work with technology instead of against it. We can't stop technology from making information cheap and reducing anonymity, but we can deploy that same technology to make sure that government officials can't misuse data and hide their tracks. This new privacy model is partially procedural—greater oversight and transparency. And it is partly substantive—protecting individuals from actual adverse consequences rather than hypothetical informational injuries.

Under this approach, the first people who should lose their privacy are the government workers with access to personal data. They should be subject to audit, to challenge, and to punishment if they use the data for improper purposes. That's an approach that works with emerging technology to build the world we want to live in. In contrast, it is simple Luddism to keep government from doing with information technology what every other part of society can do.

The problem is that Luddism always has appeal. "Change is bad" is a slogan that has never lacked for adherents, and privacy advocates sounded alarm after alarm with that slogan as the backdrop when we tried to put in place a data-based border screening system.

But would we really thank our ancestors if they'd taken the substance of Brandeis's article as seriously as its title? If, without a legislature ever considering the question, judges had declared that no one could publish true facts about a man's nonpolitical life, or even his photograph, without his permission?

I don't think so. Things change. In an odd way, privacy is a lot like clothing. Like clothing fashions, privacy standards evolve—and not just in one direction. Skirt lengths or necklines that are fashionable in one decade look slutty in the next. Americans grow less private about their sex lives but more private about financial matters. Today, few of us are willing to have strangers living in our homes, listening to our family conversations, and then gossiping about us over the back fence with the strangers who live in our friends' homes. Yet I'll bet that both

Brandeis and Warren tolerated without a second thought the limits that servants put on their privacy.

Why does our concept of privacy vary from time to time? Here's one theory: Privacy is allied with shame. We are all ashamed of something about ourselves, something we would prefer that no one, or just a few people, know about. We want to keep it private. Sometimes, of course, we should be ashamed. Criminals always want privacy for their acts. But we're also ashamed—or at least feel embarrassment, the first cousin of shame—about a lot of things that aren't crimes.

We may be ashamed of our bodies, at least until we're sure we won't be mocked for our physical shortcomings. Privacy is similar; we are often quite willing to share information about ourselves, including what we look like without our clothes, when we trust our audience, or when the context makes us believe that our shortcomings will go unnoticed. Most of us would rather be naked with our spouse than a random stranger. And we would not appear at the office in our underwear, even if it covers more than the bathing suit we wore at the beach on the weekend.

For that reason, enforced nudity often feels like a profound invasion of our privacy. At least at first. In fact, though, we can get used to it pretty quickly, as anyone who has played high school sports or served in the army can attest. That's because the fear of mockery is usually worse than the experience. We often fear mockery because we're self-absorbed; we don't realize that, to others, our private shortcomings are not that unusual and not that interesting. So when we discover that being naked in a crowd of other naked people doesn't lead to mockery and shame, we begin to adapt. We develop a callous where we once were tender.

The things that Brandeis considered privacy invasions are similar. Very few of us are happy the first time we see our photograph or an interview in the newspaper. At first, we're surprised and embarrassed at how big our nose looks or how inarticulate we sound. We're unhappy in a way that Brandeis would find quite familiar. But pretty soon we realize it's just not that big a deal. Our nose and our style of speech are things that the people we know have already accepted, and no one else cares enough to embarrass us about them. The same is true when we Google ourselves and see that a bad review of our dinner-theater performance is number three on the list. Our first reaction is embarrassment and unhappiness, but the reaction is oddly evanescent.

If this is so, then the zone of privacy is going to vary from time to time and place to place—just as our concept of physical modesty does. The "zone of privacy" has boundaries on two sides. We don't care about some information that might be revealed about us, probably because the revelation causes us no harm—or we've gotten used to it. If the information is still embarrassing we want to keep it private, and society may agree. But we can't expect privacy for information that society views as truly shameful or criminal.

Over time, information will move into and out of the zone of privacy on both sides. Some information will simply become so unthreatening that we'll laugh at the idea that it is part of the privacy zone. Photographs long ago entered that category, despite Brandeis's campaigning. Similarly, in 1948, George Orwell could shock Britons by imagining that the government would install cameras in our homes. Today, it's the homeowners who are buying and installing the cameras so they can broadcast their activities. Some information will move from criminal evidence into the zone of privacy, as sexual preference has. Or it may move in the other direction: Information that a man beats his wife is no longer protected by a zone of familial privacy, as it once was; now it's viewed as evidence of a crime.

The biggest privacy battles will often be in contexts where the rules are changing. (The subtext of many Internet privacy fights, for example, is whether some new measure will expose the identities of people who download pornography or copyrighted music and movies. Society is divided about how shameful it is to download these items, and it displaces that moral and legal debate into a fight about privacy.)

The contextual nature of privacy shows up everywhere. Divorce litigation is brutal in part because information shared in a context of love and confidence ends up being disclosed to the world in a deliberately harmful way. The unspoken agreement under which the information was shared has been broken: "I am telling you about my alcohol abuse so that we can fight it together, not so you can tell my employer and the rest of the world." A lot of privacy law is an attempt to translate that sense of betrayal into a doctrine that the courts can enforce.

That's another odd thing about privacy that makes it so contextual. Privacy isn't really about keeping data completely hidden from view. It's about making sure that the information isn't used in an unexpected and harmful way. Often the activity in question (like making a telephone call or a credit card purchase) is something that the individual does freely, with clear knowledge that some other people (his bank or his phone company) know what he is doing. Sometimes the activities are proudly public in nature—protests against government policy, for example.

In those cases, the privacy concern is not that the bank or the phone company (or our spouse) actually *has* the information but rather what it will do with the information it has—whether it will use the data in ways we didn't expect or give the data to someone who can harm us. We want to make sure the data will not be used to harm us in unexpected ways.

And that helps explain why privacy advocates are so often Luddite in inclination—because modern technology keeps changing the ways in which information is used. Once, we could count on practical obscurity—the difficulty of finding bits of data from our past—to protect us from unexpected disclosures. Now, storage costs are virtually nil, and processing power is increasing exponentially. It is no longer possible to assume that your data, even though technically public, will never actually be used. It is dirt cheap for data processors to compile dossiers on individuals, and for them to use the data in ways we didn't expect.

Some would argue that this isn't really "privacy" so much as a concern about abuse of information. However it's defined, though, the real question is what kind of protection it is reasonable for us to expect. Can we really write a detailed legislative or contractual pre-nup for each disclosure, setting forth exactly how our data will be used before we hand it over? I doubt it. Maybe we can forbid obvious misuses, but the more detailed we try to get, the more we run into the problem that our notions of what is private, and indeed of what is embarrassing, are certain to change over time. If so, does it make sense to freeze today's privacy preferences into law?

In fact, that's the mistake that Brandeis made—and the last lesson we can learn from the odd mix of veneration and guffawing that his article provokes. Brandeis wanted to extend common law copyright until it covered everything that can be recorded about an individual. The purpose was to protect the individual from all the new technologies and businesses that had suddenly made it easy to gather and disseminate personal information: "the too enterprising press, the photographer, or the possessor of any other modern device for rewording or reproducing scenes or sounds."[3]

This proposal is wacky in two ways. First it tries to freeze in 1890 our sense of what is private and what is not. Second, it tries to defy the gravitational force of technology.

Every year, information gets cheaper to store and to duplicate. Computers, iPods, and the Internet are all "modern devices" for "reproducing scenes or sounds," which means that any effort to control reproduction of pictures, sounds, and scenes becomes extraordinarily difficult if not impossible. In fact, it can't be done.

There is a deep irony here. Brandeis thought that the way to ensure the strength of his new right to privacy was to enforce it just like state copyright law. If you don't like the way "your" private information is distributed, you can sue everyone who publishes it. One hundred years later, the owners of federal statutory copyrights in popular music and movies followed this prescription to a T. They began to use litigation to protect their data rights against "the possessor[s] of any other modern device for . . . reproducing scenes or sounds," a class that now included many of their customers. The Recording Industry Association of America (RIAA) sued consumers by the tens of thousands for using their devices to copy and distribute songs.

Unwittingly, the RIAA gave a thorough test to Brandeis's notion that the law could simply stand in front of new technology and bring it to a halt through litigation. There aren't a lot of people who think that that has worked out well for the RIAA members, or for their rights.

Brandeis wanted to protect privacy by outlawing the use of a common new technology to distribute "private" facts. His approach has fared no better than the RIAA's. Information that is easy to gather, copy and distribute will be gathered, copied, and distributed, no matter what the law says.

It may seem a little bit odd for me to criticize Brandeis and other privacy campaigners for resisting the spread of technology. After all, the whole point of this book is that we can't simply accept the world that technology and commerce serve up.

True, we can't. The risk is too great. But neither can we defy gravity.

It's one thing to redirect the path of technological change by a few degrees. It's another to insist that it take a right angle. Brandeis wanted it to take a right angle; he wanted to defy the changes that technology was pressing upon him. So did the RIAA.

Both were embracing a kind of Luddism—a reactionary spasm in the face of technological change. They were doomed to fail. The new technologies, after all, empowered ordinary citizens and consumers in ways that could not be resisted. If the law tries to keep people from enjoying the new technologies, in the end it is the law that will suffer.

But just because technologies are irresistible does not mean that they cannot be guided, or cannot have their worst effects offset by other technologies. That is the message of this book: The solutions I'm advocating will only work if they allow the world to keep practically all the benefits of the exponential empowerment that new technology makes possible.

14 Privacy for the Real World

By now you may be asking, "Okay, Mister-I'm-a-privacy-advocate-too, what's *your* solution to the tension between information technology and our current sense of privacy?"

That's a fair question. The short answer is that we should protect privacy, but not by defying the course of technology or by crippling government when it investigates crimes. We can do it by working with technology, not against it. In particular, we can use information technology to make sure that government officials lose *their* privacy when they misuse data that has been gathered for legitimate reasons. Information technology now makes it easier to track every database search made by every user, and then to follow any distribution of that data outside the system. In other words, it can make misuse of the data in government files much more difficult and much more dangerous.

But before talking about what might work, let's take a closer look at some of the ideas that don't. Privacy campaigners have a limited repertoire; they usually roll out one of three basic solutions to the privacy problem. Unfortunately, these three solutions either don't protect our privacy in any meaningful way or they make it so hard to catch terrorists and criminals that they will end up getting thousands of us killed. Or both.

Their first privacy solution is one we've already seen. It's the Brandeisian notion that we should all "own" our personal data. That has some appeal, of course. If I have a secret, it feels a lot like property. I can choose to keep it to myself, or I can share it with a few people whom I trust. And I would like to believe that sharing a secret with a few trusted friends doesn't turn it into public property. It's like my home. Just because I've invited one guest home doesn't mean the public is welcome.

But in the end, information is not really like property. Property can only be held by one person at a time, or at most by a few people. But information can be shared and kept at the same time. And those with whom it is shared can pass it on to others at little or no cost. If you ever told a friend about your secret crush in junior high you've already learned that information cannot be controlled like property. As Ben Franklin is credited with saying, "Three may keep a secret if two of them are dead." The redistribution of information cannot be easily controlled in the best of times, and Moore's Law is making the control of information nearly impossible.

The recording and movie industries discovered the same thing. If these industries with their enormous lobbying and litigation budgets cannot control information that they own as a matter of law, the rest of us are unlikely to be able to control information about ourselves. Gossip is not going to become illegal simply because technology amplifies it.

That's why Brandeis's proposal never really got off the ground, at least not as he envisioned it. Buoyed by Brandeis's prestige, the idea that private facts are private property lingered on in the courts for years, but what survived of his proposal is scarcely recognizable today.

In fact, so transformed is Brandeis's privacy doctrine that it is now described, accurately, as a "right of publicity," which surely would have him turning in his grave. Currently, most states honor Brandeis by allowing lawsuits for unauthorized commercial use of a person's likeness, either by statute or judge-made law.

Over time, courts lost sight of Brandeis's purpose. They began to take the analogy to property literally. Brandeis wanted to treat private information like property because that was the only way to give a remedy for the "mental pain and distress, far greater than could be inflicted by mere bodily injury," that he thought a man suffered when his photo was published without permission. But as people got used to having their pictures taken, the mental pain and distress slowly drained out of the experience.

All that was left was the property analogy. And so judges began shrinking the right until it only had bite in the one set of circumstances where the right to control one's image actually feels like a property right—when the image is worth real bucks. Thus, the courts require disgorgement of profits made when a celebrity's name, face, voice, or even personal style is used without permission to sell or endorse products. As a result, the right to exploit a celebrity's image really is property today; it can be sold, transferred, and even inherited.

There's only one problem with this effort to turn privacy into property. It hasn't done much for privacy. It simply protects the right of celebrities to make money off their fame. In fact, by monetizing things like celebrity images, it rewards those who have most relentlessly sacrificed their privacy to gain fame.

The right of publicity is well named. It is the right to put your privacy up for sale. Not surprisingly, a lot of people have been inspired to do just that. Ironically, Brandeis's doctrine has helped to destroy the essence of what he hoped to preserve.

Oh, and in the process, Brandeis's approach has stifled creativity and restricted free speech—muzzling artists, social commentators, and businesspeople who want to make creative use of images that are an essential part of our cultural environment. It's a disaster. Slowly, courts are waking up to the irony and limiting the right of publicity.

The same "private information as property" approach has also made a modest appearance in some consumer privacy laws, and it's worked out just as badly. At bottom, consumer privacy protection laws like the Right to Financial Privacy Act[1] treat a consumer's data like a consumer's money: You can give your data (or your money) to a company in exchange for some benefit, but only if you've been told the terms of the transaction and have consented. Similarly, the Cable Communications Policy Act of 1984[2] prevents cable providers from using or releasing personal information in most cases unless the providers get the customer's consent.

The fruit of this approach is clear to anyone with a bank account or an Internet connection. Everywhere you turn, you're confronted with "informed consent" and "terms of service" disclosures; these are uniformly impenetrable and non-negotiable. No one reads them before clicking the box, so the "consent" is more fiction than reality; certainly it does little to protect privacy. Indeed, it's turning out a lot like the right of publicity. By treating privacy as property, consumer privacy protection law invites all of us to sell our privacy.

And we do. Only for most of us, the going price turns out to be disconcertingly cheap.

The second way of protecting privacy is to require what's called a "predicate" for access to information. That's a name only a lawyer could love. In fact, the whole concept is one that only lawyers love.

Simply put, the notion is that government shouldn't get certain private information unless it satisfies a threshold requirement—a "predicate" for access to the data. Lawyers have played a huge role in shaping American thinking about privacy, and the predicate approach has been widely adopted as a privacy protection. But its value for that purpose is quite doubtful.

The predicate approach to privacy can be traced to the Fourth Amendment, which guarantees that "no Warrants shall issue, but upon probable cause." Translated from legalese, this means that the government may not search your home unless it has a good reason to do so. When the government asks for a search warrant, it must show the judge "probable cause"—evidence—that the search will turn up criminal evidence or contraband. Probable cause is the predicate for the search.

Lawyers spend a lot of time thinking about the Fourth Amendment. Every law student spends weeks exploring its intricacies. Evidence from an illegal search cannot be used in a criminal prosecution. So millions of defendants have made claims under the Fourth Amendment after being convicted, giving the courts many opportunities to apply the amendment. All problems look like a nail to someone who has only a hammer.

And all privacy problems tend to look like the Fourth Amendment to lawyers who have grown up parsing its protections.

It's been applied to cops on the beat, for example. A traffic stop is pretty close to an arrest, and a pat-down is even closer to a full-fledged search. But requiring warrants and probable cause would make it impossible to pat down rough customers in a bad part of town or to stop drivers just to check license and registration. So the courts came up with a new predicate for such intrusions on our freedom—"reasonable suspicion."

When a flap arose in the 1970s over the FBI practice of assembling domestic security dossiers on Americans who had not broken the law, the attorney general stepped in to protect their privacy. He issued new guidelines for the FBI. He was a lawyer, so he declared that the FBI could not do domestic security investigations of Americans without a predicate.

The predicate wasn't probable cause; that was too high a standard. Instead, the attorney general allowed the launching of a domestic security investigation only if the bureau presented "specific and articulable facts giving reason to believe" that the subject of the investigation may be involved in violence.

Actually, the story of the FBI guidelines shows why the predicate approach often fails. The dossiers being assembled by the FBI were often just clippings and other public information. They usually weren't the product of a search in the classic sense; no federal agents had entered private property to obtain the information. Nonetheless, the FBI guidelines treated the gathering of the information itself as though it were a kind of search.

In so doing, the guidelines were following in Brandeis's footsteps—treating information as though it were physical property. The collection of the information was equated to a physical intrusion into the home or office of the individual. Implicitly, it assumes that data can be locked up like property.

But that analogy has already failed. It failed for Brandeis and it failed for the RIAA. It failed for the FBI guidelines, too. As clippings became easier to retrieve, clippings files became easier to assemble.

Then Google made it possible for anyone to assemble an electronic clips file on anyone. There was nothing secret about the clippings then. They were about as private as a bus terminal.

But the law was stuck in another era. Under the guidelines, the FBI and the FBI alone needed a predicate to print out its Google searches. You have to be a pretty resilient society to decide that you want to deny to your law enforcement agencies a tool that is freely available to nine-year-old girls and terrorist gangs. Resilient but stupid. (Not surprisingly, the guidelines were revised after 9/11.)

That's one reason we shouldn't treat the assembling of data as though it were a search of physical property. As technology makes it easier and easier to collect data, the analogy between doing that and conducting a search of a truly private space will become less and less persuasive. No one thinks government agencies should have a predicate to use the White Pages. Soon, predicates that keep law enforcement from collecting information in other ways will become equally anachronistic, leaving law enforcement stuck in the 1950s while everyone else gets to live in the twenty-first century.

I saw this lawyerly affinity for predicates up close at DHS. The issue was laptop searches at the border. The government has always had the right to search anything crossing the border without probable cause. Smugglers are smart and highly motivated; they would find a way to exploit any limitations on the authority to conduct searches. The first Congress knew that quite well, and in 1789, two months before it sent the Fourth Amendment to the states for approval, Congress gave the customs service "full power and authority" to search "any ship or vessel, in which they shall have reason to suspect any goods, wares or merchandise subject to duty shall be concealed."[3]

Obviously, DHS and its border predecessors didn't search laptops in 1789. But they did search books, papers, correspondence, and anything else that could store information. That was the law for two hundred years, with one exception. The Supreme Court has ruled that a few extraordinarily intrusive techniques—body cavity searches and forced x-rays—require a "reasonable suspicion."[4]

Laptops are treated like books and papers. They are searched whenever border officials think that such a search is likely to be productive. And even the famously liberal Ninth Circuit, the court of appeal that includes California, has had no trouble approving that practice.[5]

For good reason. Laptop searches pay off.

Take *United States v. Hampe*, triggered by a 2006 border search at Bar Harbor, Maine. The search turned up a laptop with numerous images of child pornography; officers also found "children's stickers, children's underwear, children's towels or blankets with super heroes printed on them," as well as "12-15 condoms" and "a container of personal lubricant." The lawbooks are full of unsuccessful appeals by convicted pedophiles and child porn smugglers, claiming that the laptops holding the evidence against them should not have been searched without a predicate.[6]

After 9/11, we used laptop searches to find possible terrorists. That's in part because investigators famously failed to inspect the laptop of one of the 9/11 conspirators, Zacarias Moussaoui, when it might have done some good. Found early enough, the information on his laptop might have helped uncover Moussaoui's ties to al Qaeda. Having learned that lesson, we began using laptop searches more often when terrorism was a risk.

In 2006, for example, border officials at the Minneapolis-St. Paul airport referred a suspect traveler to secondary inspection. There they found that his computer contained video clips of IEDs being used to kill soldiers and destroy vehicles and a video on martyrdom. He was also carrying a manual on how to make improvised explosive devices, or IEDs—a weapon of choice for terrorists in Afghanistan and Iraq.

Despite two hundred years of history and precedent, as well as the proven value of searching electronic media, privacy groups launched a campaign against laptop searches toward the end of the Bush administration. This was a strange and unhappy era in the debate over privacy. By 2005, privacy advocates had found a growing audience for claims that the Bush administration had abandoned all limits in pursuing terrorism—that it had swung the pendulum violently away from privacy and in favor of government authority.

By attacking alleged privacy violations in the war on terror, the privacy groups found that they could tap a passionate core of support. But apart from adoption of the USA PATRIOT Act, there hadn't been that many domestic legal changes after 9/11. But the privacy groups weren't about to stop shooting just because they were running out of targets. Instead, the rights groups started attacking security practices that had been established in the 1990s or earlier. I watched the return to pre-September 11 thinking with dismay. But even I was surprised to find groups seriously proposing to swing the pendulum back, not to September 10, 2001, but to July of 1789. (Perhaps I didn't realize, said one colleague, just how long the ACLU thought the Bush administration had been in power.)

The privacy advocates' solution to the laptop issue was the lawyer's favorite—a predicate requirement. Laptops should not be searched at the border, they argued, unless the border official could articulate some specific reason for conducting the search. That argument was rejected by both the Bush and the Obama administrations after careful consideration.

We rejected it for two reasons. It wouldn't have protected privacy in any meaningful way. And it would have helped pedophiles and terrorists defeat our border defenses. Other than that, it was jim-dandy.

Why wouldn't it help protect privacy? Because as a practical matter, no border official today searches a laptop without some reasonable suspicion about the traveler. The exponential increase in commercial jet travel and the unforgiving thirty-second rule mean that only one traveler in two hundred is sent to secondary inspection for a closer look. Once there, many travelers quickly satisfy the officials that they don't deserve more detailed inspection.

Everyone at the border is busy; there's another jet or another bus arriving in minutes. Border officers don't have the luxury of hooking up the laptops of random travelers for inspection without a good reason. Officers who waste their time and DHS's resources that way are going to hear from their supervisors long before they hear from the travelers' lawyers.

Okay, you may say, the rule wouldn't do much good. But surely it can't hurt, can it? If border officials only search laptops today when they have a good reason to do so, why not make that a requirement? What harm can it do to make reasonable suspicion a predicate for laptop searches at the border?

Plenty. Requiring reasonable suspicion before a laptop search will open every border search to litigation. And in court, it may be hard to justify even some very reasonable judgments.

Sometimes, the primary inspector will send the traveler to secondary simply because the inspector is not comfortable with the traveler. Remember Mohamed al Kahtani—the twentieth hijacker? He was sent to secondary inspection on the basis of intuition—there was no evidence of illegality in the fact that he did not speak English and hadn't filled out his arrival forms. But the inspector's intuition was dead right. Kahtani deserved all the scrutiny he got, and more. Still, if the inspector had opened the terrorist's laptop on the basis of his intuition, could he have been sure the courts would agree that he had a reasonable suspicion? That uncertainty would undermine the effectiveness of border procedures, perhaps giving a free ride to wealthy travelers or those who threaten legal action if they are delayed.

Inevitably, enforcement of a predicate requirement for border searches will produce litigation. The litigation will focus on the motives of the border officials. The courts will tell those officials that some reasons are not good enough. Defense lawyers will want to see the personnel records of border officials, hoping to show that they've inspected a disproportionate number of laptops belonging to minorities, or to Saudis, or to men, or any other pattern that might get the case thrown out. Border officials will have to start keeping detailed records justifying each laptop search. New paperwork and new procedures will clog the inspection process, backing up travelers and penalizing any inspector who searches a laptop.

A predicate requirement would mean that every official who inspects a laptop will get to spend quality time on the stand with a defense counsel dedicated to questioning the officer's motives and painting the officer as a racist, sexist, or whatever else the lawyer thinks might work. In close cases, it's inevitable that border officials will be slow to conduct a search that brings with it a host of paperwork and the chance to be cross-examined. And that inevitably means that we'll catch fewer criminals and terrorists.

Wait a minute, you might ask, what if those officials really are racists or sexists? Shouldn't we do something about that? Surely my laptop shouldn't be searched because of prejudice?

A lot of academics and lawyers are too quick to assume that law enforcement is full of racists or sexists; disliking cops is about the only form of prejudice that is still respectable in their circles.

But let's assume that their prejudice is right, at least sometimes, and that there are biased officials at work on the border. Surely there's a better way to find them and get them off the job than to count on criminal defense lawyers exposing them on the witness stand years after the event.

By now, notice, we're not even talking about privacy anymore. The "predicate" solution has, in effect, changed the subject. We're talking about the motives of border officials, or ethnic profiling, or something; but it isn't privacy. We're also moving the whole discussion into territory that lawyers find comfortable but that ordinary people might question.

The Fourth Amendment approach to privacy assumes that privacy is best protected by letting criminals challenge the search that produced the evidence against them. But before adopting that solution, we ought to be pretty sure that we're going to get benefits that match the cost of letting guilty defendants go free, something that isn't obvious here.

The predicate solution also creates more litigation and gives lawyers new power to discomfit officials. It's easy to see why that would appeal to lawyers, but American litigation is surely the most costly policymaking process on the planet—and not exactly democratic, either. Again, we'd need to foresee real benefits that can't be achieved in some other fashion before buying into that approach. And, for all the reasons I've given, there are very few benefits to be gained from the "predicate" approach to most privacy problems.

That leaves the third approach to privacy, one we've already seen in action. If requiring a predicate is the lawyer's solution; this third approach is the bureaucrat's solution. It is at heart the approach adopted by the European Union: Instead of putting limits on when information may be collected, it sets limits on how the information is used.

The European Union's data protection principles cover a lot of ground, but their unifying theme is imposing limits on how private data is used. Under those principles, personal data may only be used in ways that are consistent with the purposes for which the data were gathered. Any data that is retained must be relevant to the original purposes and must be stored securely to prevent misuse.

The EU's negotiating position in the passenger name records conflict was largely derived from this set of principles. The principles also explain Europe's enthusiasm for a wall between law enforcement and intelligence. If DHS gathered reservation data for the purpose of screening travelers when they cross the border, why should any other agency be given access to the data? This also explains the EU's insistence on short deadlines for the destruction of PNR data. Once it had been used to screen passengers, it had served the purpose for which it was gathered and should be promptly discarded.

There is a core of sense in this solution. It focuses mainly on the consequences of collecting information, and not on the act of collection. It doesn't try to insist that information is property. It recognizes that when we give information to others, we usually have an expectation about how it will be used, and as long as the use fits our expectations, we aren't too fussy about who exactly gets to see it. By concentrating on how personal information is used, this solution may get closer to the core of privacy than one that focuses on how personal information is collected.

It has another advantage, too. In the case of government databases, focusing on use also allows us to acknowledge the overriding importance of some government data systems while still protecting against petty uses of highly personal information.

Call it the deadbeat-dad problem, or call it mission creep, but there's an uncomfortable pattern to the use of data by governments. Often, personal data must be gathered for a pressing reason—the prevention of crime or terrorism, perhaps, or the administration of a social security system. Then, as time goes on, it becomes attractive to use the data for other, less pressing purposes—collecting child support, perhaps, or enforcing parking tickets. No one would support the gathering of a large personal database simply to collect unpaid parking fines; but "mission creep" can easily carry the database well beyond its original purpose. A limitation on use prevents mission creep, or at least forces a debate about each step in the expansion.

That's all fine. But in the end, this solution is also flawed.

It, too, is fighting technology, though less obviously than the predicate and property approaches. Data that has already been gathered *is* easier to use for other purposes. It's foolish to pretend otherwise. Indeed, developments in information technology in recent years have produced real strides in searching unstructured data or in finding relationships in data without knowing for sure that the data will actually produce anything useful. In short, there are now good reasons to collate data gathered for widely differing purposes, just to see the patterns that emerge.

This new technical capability is hard to square with use limitations or with early destruction of data. For if collating data in the government's hands could have prevented a successful terrorist attack, no one will congratulate the agency that refused to allow the collation because the data was collected for tax or regulatory purposes, say, and not to catch terrorists.

What's more, use limitations have caused great harm when applied too aggressively. The conflict with the EU is a reminder that the "wall" between law enforcement and intelligence was at heart a use limitation.

It assumed that law enforcement agencies would gather information using their authority, and then would use the information only for law enforcement purposes. Intelligence agencies would do the same. Or so the theory went. But strict enforcement of this use limitation ended up preventing cooperation that might have thwarted the 9/11 attacks.

Like all use limitations, the "wall" between law enforcement sounded reasonable enough in the abstract. While no one could point to a real privacy abuse arising from cooperation between the intelligence and law enforcement agencies in the United States, it was easy to point to the Gestapo and other totalitarian organizations where there had been too much cooperation among agencies.

What was the harm in a little organizational insurance against misuse of personal data, the argument ran. The rules allowed cooperation where that was strictly necessary, and we could count on the agencies to crowd right up to the line in doing their jobs. Or so we thought. In fact, we couldn't. As the pressure and the risk ratcheted up, agents were discouraged from pushing for greater communication and cooperation across the wall. All the Washington-wise knew that the way to bureaucratic glory and a good press lay in defending privacy. Actually, more to the point, they knew that bad press and bureaucratic disgrace were the likely result if your actions could be characterized as hurting privacy. Congress would hold hearings; appropriators would zero out your office; the second-guessing arms of the Justice Department, from the inspectors general to the Office of Professional Responsibility, would feast on every detail of your misstep. So, what might have been a sensible, modest use restriction preventing the dissemination of information without a good reason became an impermeable barrier.

That's why the bureaucratic system for protecting privacy so often fails. The use restrictions and related limits are abstract. They make a kind of modest sense, but if they are enforced too strictly, they prevent new uses of information that may be critically important.

And often they are enforced too strictly. You don't have to tell a bureaucrat twice to withhold information from a rival agency.

Lawsuits, bad press, and Congressional investigations all seem to push against a flexible reading of the rules. If a use for information is not identified at the outset, it can be nearly impossible to add the use later, no matter how sensible the change may seem. This leads agencies to try to draft broad uses for the data they collect, which defeats the original point of setting use restrictions.

It's like wearing someone else's dress. Over time, use restrictions end up tight where they should be roomy—and loose where they should be tight. No one is left satisfied.

So what will work? Simple: accountability, especially electronically-enforced accountability.

The best way to understand this solution is to begin with Barack Obama's passport records—and with Joe the Plumber. These were two minor flaps that punctuated the 2008 presidential campaign. But both tell us something about how privacy really is protected these days.

In March of 2008, Barack Obama and Hillary Clinton were dueling across the country in weekly primary showdowns. Suddenly, the campaign took an odd turn. The Bush administration's State Department announced that it had fired or disciplined several contractors for examining Obama's passport records.

Democrats erupted. They remembered when Bill Clinton's files had been examined during the 1992 campaign, and Obama's lengthy stays outside the United States as a child had become a simmering underground issue in this campaign. It wasn't hard to jump to the conclusion that the candidate's files had been searched for partisan purposes. An Obama campaign spokesman called the records search "outrageous ... This is a serious matter that merits a complete investigation, and we demand to know who looked at Senator Obama's passport file, for what purpose, and why it took so long for them to reveal this security breach."[7]

After an investigation, the flap slowly deflated. It soon emerged that all three of the main presidential candidates' passport files had been improperly accessed. Investigators reported that the State Department was able to quickly identify who had examined the files by using its computer audit system. This system flagged any unusual requests for access to the files of prominent Americans. The fired contractors did not deny the computer record. Several of them were charged with crimes and pleaded guilty. All, it turned out, had acted purely out of "curiosity."

Six months later, it was the Republicans' turn to howl about privacy violations in the campaign. "Joe" Wurzelbacher, a plumber, became an overnight hero to Republicans in October 2008. After all, he was practically the only person who laid a glove on Barack Obama during the campaign. The candidate made an impromptu stop in Wurzelbacher's Ohio neighborhood and was surprised when the plumber forced him into a detailed on-camera defense of his tax plan. Three days later, "Joe the Plumber" and his taxes were invoked dozens of times in the presidential debates.

The price of fame was high. A media frenzy quickly stripped Joe Wurzelbacher of anonymity. Scouring the public record, reporters found that the plumber had been hit with a tax lien; they also found government data that raised doubts about the status of his plumbing license.

Reporters weren't the only ones digging. Ohio state employees also queried confidential state records about Wurzelbacher. In all, they conducted eighteen state records checks on Wurzelbacher. They asked whether the plumber owed child support, whether he'd ever received welfare or unemployment benefits, and whether he was in any Ohio law enforcement databases. Some of these searches were proper responses to media requests under Ohio open records laws; others looked more like an effort to dig dirt on the man.

Ohio's inspector general launched an investigation and in less than a month was able to classify all but one of the eighteen records searches as either legitimate or improper. (One search could not be traced because it came from an agency outside the jurisdiction of the inspector general.)[8]

Thirteen searches were traced and deemed proper. But three particularly intrusive searches were found improper; they had been carried out at the request of a high-ranking state employee who was also a strong Obama supporter. She was suspended from her job and soon stepped down. A fourth search was traced to a former information technology contractor who had not been authorized to search the system he accessed; he was placed under criminal investigation.

What do these two flaps have in common? They were investigated within weeks of the improper access, and practically everyone involved was immediately caught. That's vitally important. Information technology isn't just taking away your privacy or mine. It's taking away the privacy of government workers even faster. Data is cheap to gather and cheap to store. It's even getting cheap to analyze.

So it isn't hard to identify every official who accessed a particular file on a particular day. That's what happened here. And the consequences for privacy are profound.

If the lawyer's solution is to put a predicate between government and the data and the bureaucrat's solution is to put use restrictions on the data, then this is the auditor's solution. Government access to personal data need not be restricted by speed bumps or walls. Instead, it can be protected by rules, so long as the rules are enforced.

What's new is that network security and audit tools now make it easy to enforce the rules. That's important because it takes the profit motive out of misuse of government data. No profit-motivated official is going to take the risk of stealing personal data if it's obvious that he'll be caught as soon as people start to complain about identity theft. Systematic misuse of government databases is a lot harder and more dangerous if good auditing is in place.

Take another look at why government officials accessed these files. It wasn't to steal identities. (In fact, these would be pretty dumb places to go for identity theft. If you want to know what's in your passport file, get your passport out and take a look at the one page with printed data on it. It's got less sensitive information than your driver's license—a photo and your birth date and state. Not even an address, let alone a Social Security number or credit card number.)

No, the reason most of these people accessed the data was simple curiosity. Even the one access that may have been for more reprehensible reasons—the woman who checked confidential child support and welfare records for Joe the Plumber—was quickly caught and the data never leaked.

The speed and nearly complete effectiveness of the audit process in these cases tells us that network auditing tools can transform the way we enforce the rules for handling data in government. For example, if we catch every error, we can improve compliance and at the same time reduce the penalties for mistakes. Harsh penalties are not the most effective way to enforce rules. In fact, they're usually a confession of failure. When we can't stop a crime, we keep increasing the penalties, to make an example of the few offenders we do catch. But when we catch every offender, we can afford to lower the penalty. Parking fines are lower than tickets for driving alone in a car pool lane in part because parking violators are easier to catch.

Lighter, more certain penalties for privacy violations serve another purpose, too. We've talked a lot about the oddly protean nature of privacy. Not causing harm in unexpected ways is at the core of the concept, but it's nearly impossible to write detailed rules spelling out what is and is not a violation of privacy. Indeed, the effort to write such rules and stick to them is what gave us the wall, and thousands of American dead. So something must be left to discretion. Government employees must use good sense in handling personal data. If they don't, they should be punished. But if we are confident that we can identify any questionable use of personal data and correct it quickly, the punishments can be smaller. They can be learning experiences rather than penological experiences.

So why did we criminally prosecute the poor schlubs whose hobby was looking at the passport pictures of famous people? Everyone would agree that they shouldn't have done it and that they should have been disciplined. But a criminal record? How did that happen?

The election happened. Everything that touched on the election was put under a microscope. Evil motives were always ascribed to the other side. The State Department had to make a blood sacrifice to show that accessing the data was not part of an evil plot by one party against the other. Opening a criminal investigation was a way of condemning the access in the clearest possible fashion. That the poor schlubs probably only deserved demotions counted for little in the super-heated atmosphere of a presidential campaign.

That shows one of the problems with the audit approach. It is too easily turned into a phony privacy scandal. In both the Wurzelbacher and Obama cases, the audits did their job. With one possible exception, they caught the government staff that broke the rules. They prevented any harm to either Wurzelbacher or Obama. And they made sure that the officials who were responsible would never repeat their errors again.

The system worked. Privacy was protected. But that's certainly not the impression that was left by coverage of the affairs. Indeed, the chairman of the Senate Judiciary Committee, Senator Leahy, used the passport flap to tout new legislation strengthening privacy protections on government databases.

From a political point of view, then, the system failed. There were no thanks for the government officials who put the system in place, who checked the audit logs, who confronted and disciplined the wrongdoers, and who brought the solved problem to public attention. To the contrary, they were pilloried for allowing the access in the first place—even though preventing such access is an impossible task unless we intend to re-erect walls all across government.

How's that for irony? Audits work. But they work too well. Every time they catch someone and put a stop to misuse of personal data they also provide an opening for political grandstanding. In the end, the finger pointing will discourage audits. And that will mean less privacy enforcement. So, the more we turn every successful audit into a privacy scandal, the less real privacy we're likely to have.

That would be a shame, because the auditor's solution to the problem is the only privacy solution that will get more effective as technology advances. And we're going to need more solutions that allow flexible, easy access to sensitive databases while still protecting privacy.

If the plight of government investigators trying to prevent terrorist attacks doesn't move you, think about the plight of medical technicians trying to keep you alive after a bad traffic accident.

The Obama administration has launched a long-overdue effort to bring electronic medical records into common use. But the privacy problem in this area is severe. Few of us want our medical records to be available to casual browsers. At the same time, we can't personally verify the bona fides of the people accessing our records, especially if we're lying by the side of the road suffering from what looks like brain or spine damage.

The electronic record system won't work if it can't tell the first responders that you have unusual allergies or a pacemaker. It has to do that quickly and without a lot of formalities. The side of the road is no place for emergency medical staff to be told that they can't access your records until they change their passwords or send their medical credentials to a new hospital. No one wants to be the punch line in an updated surgeon's joke: "The privacy system was a success; unfortunately it killed the patient."

Auditing access after the fact is likely to be our best answer to this problem, as it is to the very similar problem of how to let law enforcement and intelligence agencies share information smoothly and quickly in response to changing and urgent circumstances. The Markle Foundation has done pioneering work in this area, and its path-breaking 2003 report on privacy and security in the war on terror recommends embracing technologies that watch the watchers. A unique mix of security, privacy, and technology experts managed to reach agreement in that report; they found that one key to protecting privacy without sacrificing security was a network that included "access control, authentication, and full auditing capability."[9]

The Markle report urges that large databases with personal information use emerging technologies that can identify all users of the system with certainty and then give them access that depends on their roles at any particular time. This includes "the ability to restrict access privileges so that data can be used only for a particular purpose, for a finite period of time, and by people with the necessary permissions."[10] The technologies they cited are not pie in the sky. They exist today: "smart cards with embedded chips, tokens, biometrics, and security circuits" as well as "[i]nformation rights management technologies."[11] The Markle task force later did a thoughtful paper on one of those technologies, which would preserve audit logs even if high-ranking officials seek to destroy or modify them later.[12]

These technologies can be very flexible. This makes them especially suitable for cases where outright denial of data access could have fatal results. The tools can be set to give some people immediate access, or to open the databases in certain situations, with an audit to follow. They can monitor each person with access to the data and learn that person's access patterns—what kinds of data, at what time, for how long, with or without copying, and the like. Deviations from the established pattern can have many consequences. Perhaps access will be granted but the person will be alerted that an explanation must be offered within twenty-four hours. Or access could be granted while a silent alarm sounds, allowing systems administrators to begin a real-time investigation.

There's a kind of paradox at the heart this solution. We can protect people from misuse of their data, but only by stripping network users of any privacy or anonymity when they look at the data. The privacy campaigners aren't likely to complain, though. In our experience, their interest in preserving the privacy of intelligence and law enforcement officers is pretty limited.

When I was general counsel of the National Security Agency, a well-known privacy group headed by Marc Rotenberg filed a Freedom of Information Act request asking the NSA to assemble all documents and emails sent "to or from Stewart Baker." Then as now, the NSA was forbidden to assemble files on American citizens who were not agents of a foreign power. Even so, Rotenberg was asking NSA to assemble a dossier on me. Since NSA and I were locked in a battle with Rotenberg over encryption policy at the time, the purpose of the dossier was almost certainly to look for embarrassing information that might help Rotenberg in his political fight. Indeed, Rotenberg claimed when I confronted him that he was planning to scrutinize my dossier for evidence of misconduct.

Had the FBI or NSA assembled a dossier on *their* political adversaries, it would have been a violation of law. In fact, it would have caused a privacy scandal. But Rotenberg saw no irony in his request. It wasn't a privacy problem, in his view, because government officials deserve no privacy.

I still think Rotenberg's tactics were reprehensible; he had singled me out for a selective loss of privacy because he didn't like my views. But I've come to appreciate that there's a core of truth to his view of government. Anyone who has access to government files containing personal data has special responsibilities. He should not expect the same privacy when he searches that data as he has while he's surfing the net at home. And now that technology makes it easy to authenticate and track every person, every device, and every action on a network, perhaps it's time to use that technology to preserve everyone else's privacy.

In the end, that's the difference between a privacy policy that makes sense and one that doesn't. We can't lock up data that is getting cheaper every day. Pretending that it's property won't work. Putting "predicates" between government and the data it needs won't work. And neither will insisting that they may only be used for purposes foreseen when it was collected.

What we *can* do is use new information technology tools to deter government officials from misusing their access to that data.

As you know by now, I think that some technology poses extraordinary risks. But we can avoid the worst risks if we take action early. We shouldn't try to stop the trajectory of new technology. But we can bend it just a little. Call it a course correction on an exponential curve.

That's also true for privacy. The future is coming, like it or not. Our data will be everywhere. But we can bend the curve of technology to make those who hold the data more accountable.

Bending the exponential curve a bit. That's a privacy policy that could work.

And a technology policy that makes sense.

Endnotes

Chapter 1. **Skating on Stilts**

1. Arthur C. Clarke, *Profiles of the Future*. New York: Henry Holt, 1962.
2. See, e.g., *Dictionary of Canadian Biography Online*, Vol. XV, 1921-1930 (Univ. of Toronto 2000), online at http://www.biographi.ca/index-e.html (search "Bell, Alexander Graham").
3. "Off for Paris in Jet Time," 45 *Life*, No. 19, Nov. 10, 1958, 113, online at http://books.google.com (search "Off for Paris in Jet Time").
4. Keith Reed, "Logan Troopers to Get Roving Database Access," *Boston Globe*, Jun. 22, 2004, online at http://www.boston.com (click on "Today's Globe," then search "Logan troopers to get roving database access").
5. Martin Finucane, "Wireless Devices Raise Questions about Crimefghting, ID," *USA Today*, Jun. 25, 2004, online at www.usatoday.com/tech/wireless/data/2004-06-25-wireless-and-id_x.htm.
6. Keith Reed, "Logan Troopers to Get Roving Database Access," *Boston Globe*, Jun. 22, 2004, online at http://www.boston.com (click on "Today's Globe," then search "Logan troopers to get roving database access").

Chapter 2. **Atta's Soldier**

1. Statement of Jose E. Melendez-Perez to the National Commission on Terrorist Attacks upon the United States, in *The 9/11 Commission Report: Final Report of the National Commission on Terrorist Attacks Upon the United States*. New York: W.W. Norton, 2004, online at http://govinfo.library.unt.edu/911/report/index.htm
2. Ibid.
3. Ibid.
4. Jose Melendez-Perez. Interview by author. Dec. 2009.
5. Ibid.
6. Ibid.
7. Ibid.

8. Ibid.
9. Ibid.
10. Ibid.
11. Ibid.
12. Ibid.
13. Ibid.
14. 8 United States Code §1225.
15. Melendez-Perez, Interview, 09.
16. Ibid.
17. Ibid.

Chapter 3. To the Wall

1. Memorandum to Attorney General Ashcroft from United States Foreign Intelligence Surveillance Court Presiding Judge Royce C. Lamberth (Mar. 9, 2001) online at http://www.historycommons.org/sourcedocuments/2001/pdfs/fisacourt20010309.pdf.
2. Stewart Baker, "Should Spies Be Cops?" 97 *Foreign Policy* 36 (Winter 1994-95).
3. Ibid.
4. Ibid.
5. Del Quentin Wilber, "Surveillance Court Quietly Moving," *Wash. Post*, Mar. 2, 2009, A2, online at http://www.washingtonpost.com/wp-dyn/content/article/2009/03/01/AR2009030101730.html.
6. Mary Jo Patterson, "A View from Inside the FISA Court," *Star-Ledger*, Aug. 21, 2005, 15, online at http://web.archive.org/web/20071019021504/www.nj.com/news/ledger/index.ssf?/news/ledger/stories/patriotact/insidefisa.html.
7. Barbara Grewe, 9/11 Commission Staff Monograph, "Legal Barriers to Information Sharing: The Erection of a Wall Between Intelligence and Law Enforcement Investigations," (Aug. 20, 2004), online at www.fas.org/irp/eprint/wall.pdf.
8. Royce Lamberth. Interview by author. Jan. 2010.
9. Frances Fragos Townsend. Interview by author. Nov. 2009.
10. Lamberth, Interview, 10.
11. *In re Sealed Case No. 02-001*, 310 F.3d 717 (FISA 2002), online at http://www.fas.org/irp/agency/doj/fisa/fiscr111802.html.
12. Lamberth, Interview, 10.
13. Ibid.
14. Ibid.
15. Judge Lamberth, who would not confirm or deny the story, says that the court liked Townsend but acknowledges that she was hurt by fallout from the faulty affidavits. Lamberth, Interview, 10.

16. Lamberth, Interview, 10.
17. Memorandum for Attorney General Ashcroft from United States Foreign Intelligence Surveillance Court Presiding Judge Royce C. Lamberth (Mar. 9, 2001), online at http://www.historycommons.org/sourcedocuments/2001/pdfs/fisacourt20010309.pdf.
18. Ibid.
19. Ibid.
20. Townsend, Interview, 09.
21. Lamberth, Interview, 10.
22. Ibid
23. Walter Pincus, "Judge Discusses Details of Work on Secret Court," *Wash. Post*, Jun. 26, 2007, A4, online at http://www.washingtonpost.com/wp-dyn/content/article/2007/06/25/AR2007062501901.html?nav=emailpage.
24. Ibid.
25. Ibid.
26. Report of the House and Senate Intelligence Committees Joint Inquiry into Intelligence Community Activities Before and After the Terrorist Attacks of September 11, 2001, S. Rep. No. 351 & H. Rep. No 792, 107th Cong. 2d Sess., 367 (Dec. 2002), online at http://intelligence.senate.gov/107351.pdf.
27. Ibid.
28. Memorandum for the Record (9/11 Commission Staff Interview of Larry R. Parkinson) (Feb. 24, 2004), online at http://www.scribd.com (search "Larry Parkinson").
29. Prepared Statement of a New York Special Agent Before the Select Committee on Intelligence and the Permanent Select Committee on Intelligence (Sept. 20, 2002), online at http://fl1.findlaw.com/news.findlaw.com/hdocs/docs/terrorism/ssci92002fbiagnt.pdf.

Chapter 4. **Never Again**

1. "Melissa C. Doi: Dancing Through Life," *NY Times*, Feb. 12, 2002, A12, online at http://www.nytimes.com (search "Melissa Doi," select "D" list in Portraits of Grief Archive).
2. Transcript of Melissa Doi's call to 9-1-1 operators, September 11, 2001, online at http://en.wikisource.org/wiki/Main_Page (search "Melissa Doi").
3. Formally designated as the Uniting and Strengthening America by Providing Appropriate Tools Required to Intercept and Obstruct Terrorism Act of 2001, Pub. L. No. 107-56, 115 Stat. 272 (Oct. 26, 2001), online at http://www.selectagents.gov/resources/USApatriotAct.pdf.
4. Associated Press, "System Will Assign Treat Level to All Passengers," *Eugene Register-Guard*, Mar. 1, 2003, A4, online at http://news.google.com (select

advanced news search, then select archive search, then search "system will assign threat level").

5. American Civil Liberties Union, Press Release, "CAPPS II Data-Mining System Will Invade Privacy and Create Government Blacklist of Americans, ACLU Warns" (Feb. 27, 2003), online at http://www.aclu.org (search "CAPPS II data-mining invade privacy and create government blacklist of Americans").
6. Naftali Bendavid, "For Conservatives, ACLU Now Has the Right Stuff," *Seattle Times*, June 8, 2003, A9, online at http://seattletimes.nwsource.com//html/home/index.html (search "ACLU right stuff").
7. Testimony of Stewart Baker Before the National Commission on Terrorist Attacks Upon the United States (Dec. 8, 2003), online at http://govinfo.library.unt.edu/911/hearings/hearing6/witness_baker.pdf.
8. Transcript of 9/11 Commission Hearing (Dec. 8, 2003), online at http://www.globalsecurity.org/security/library/congress/9-11_commission/031208-transcript.htm.
9. Ibid.
10. Known formally as the Commission on the Intelligence Capabilities of the United States Regarding Weapons of Mass Destruction.

Chapter 5. Europe Picks a Privacy Fight

1. Pub. L. No. 107-71, 115 Stat. 597 (codified as amended at 49 U.S.C. §40101, *et seq.*).
2. Pub. L. No. 93-579, 88 Stat. 1897 (codified as amended at 5 U.S.C. §552a).
3. Priscilla Regan, "Safe Harbors or Free Frontiers? Privacy and Transborder Data Flows," 59 *Journal of Social Issues* 263, 266 (2003).
4. Ibid.
5. U.S.-European Union Safe Harbor, Oct. 1998, online at http://www.export.gov/safeharbor/eu/eg_main_018365.asp.
6. European Commission Article 29 Working Party, "Opinion 6/2002 on Transmission of Passenger Manifest Information and Other Data from Airlines to the United States," Oct. 24, 2002, online at http://ec.europa.eu/justice_home/fsj/privacy/docs/wpdocs/2002/wp66_en.pdf.
7. Ibid.
8. Frits Bolkestein, "Resisting U.S. Demands: Passenger Privacy and the War on Terror," *NY Times*, Oct. 24, 2003, online at http://www.nytimes.com (search "passenger privacy and war on terror").
9. Ibid.
10. Directive 95/46/EC of the European Parliament and of the Council of 24 October 1995 on the protection of individuals with regard to the processing of

personal data and on the free movement of such data, *Official J Eur Communities*, L 281/31, Nov. 11,1995, online at http://ec.europa.eu/justice_home/fsj/privacy/docs/95-46-ce/dir1995-46_part1_en.pdf.

11. Ibid.
12. Ibid.
13. Ibid.
14. Ibid.
15. DHS Privacy Office, A Report Concerning Passenger Name Record Information Derived From Flights Between the U.S. and the European Union, Sept. 19, 2005, online at www.dhs.gov/xlibrary/assets/privacy/privacy_pnr_rpt_09-2005.pdf.
16. European Commission, Staff Working Paper on the Joint Review of the implementation by the U.S. Bureau of Customs and Border Protection of the Undertakings set out in Commission Decision 2004/535/EC of May 14, 2004, Dec. 12, 2005, online at http://ec.europa.eu/justice_home/fsj/privacy/docs/adequacy/pnr/review_2005.pdf.
17. Action brought on 27 July 2004 by the European Parliament against the Commission of the European Communities, *Official J Eur Union*, (Case C-318/04) (2004/C 228/67), Nov. 9, 2004.

Chapter 6. To the Brink

1. *European Parliament v Council of the European Union* (Joined Cases C-317/04 and C-318/04), Judgment of the Court (Grand Chamber) May 30, 2006,*Official J Eur Union* (Cases C-317/04 and C-318/04) (C-178/1), July 29, 2006.
2. Ibid.
3. Michael Chertoff,"A Tool We Need to Stop the Next Airliner Plot," *Wash. Post*, Aug. 29, 2006, A15, online at http://www.washingtonpost.com/wp-dyn/content/article/2006/08/28/AR2006082800849.html.
4. Statement by Homeland Security Secretary Michael Chertoff on Passenger Name Record Agreement with European Union, Sept. 30, 2006, online at http://www.dhs.gov/xnews/releases/pr_1159893986311.shtm.
5. Mark Ballard,"US and EU Stitch Up Airline Passenger Data Deal," *The Register*, Oct. 10, 2006, online at www.theregister.co.uk (click on Reg Archive (at bottom), click on Search the Site, search"US and EU stitch up airline passenger data deal").
6. Ibid.
7. UK House of Lords European Union Committee,"The Passenger Name Record (PNR) Framework Decision," Report with Evidence (Stationery Office Ltd, Jun. 11, 2008), online at http://www.statewatch.org/news/2008/jun/eu-pnr-uk-hol-report.pdf.

8. Eric Lichtblau and James Risen, "Bank Data Is Sifted by U.S. in Secret to Block Terror," *NY Times*, June 23, 2006, online at http://www.nytimes.com (search "bank data sifted secret block terror").
9. Byron Calame, "Can 'Magazines' of the Times Subsidize News Coverage?" *NY Times*, Oct. 22, 2006, C12, online at http://www.nytimes.com (search "Magazines of the Times Subsidize News Coverage").
10. Article 29 Data Protection Working Party, Opinion 10/2006 on the processing of personal data by the Society for Worldwide Interbank Financial Telecommunication (SWIFT), Nov. 22, 2006, online at http://ec.europa.eu/justice_home/fsj/privacy/docs/wpdocs/2006/wp128_en.pdf#7.
11. Article 29 Data Protection Working Group, Opinion 10/2006 on the processing of personal data by the Society for Worldwide Interbank Financial Telecommunication (SWIFT), Nov. 22, 2006, online at http://ec.europa.eu/justice_home/fsj/privacy/docs/wpdocs/2006/wp128_en.pdf.
12. Belgian Data Protection Commission, Summary of the opinion on the transfer of personal data by SCRL SWIFT following the UST (OFAC) subpoenas, Sept. 27, 2006, online at http://www.europarl.europa.eu/hearings/20061004/libe/background_commission_en.pdf.
13. Article 29 Data Protection Working Party, Press Release, Oct. 11, 2007, online at http://ec.europa.eu/justice_home/fsj/privacy/news/docs/pr_11_10_07_en.pdf.
14. Society for Worldwide Interbank Financial Telecommunication, "Distributed Architecture," online at http://www.swift.com/solutions/industry_initiatives/distributed_architecture.page.

Chapter 7. **Al Qaeda's Frequent Traveler Program**

1. Candy Booth Thomas, "The Flight Attendants: Courage in the Air," *Time*, Sept. 9, 2002, Special Section, online at http://www.time.com/time/magazine/article/0,9171,1003224-2,00.html.
2. Ibid.
3. Ibid.
4. Zolfan Dujisin, "Czech Republic: Washington's Trojan Horse?" *IPS News*, Apr. 14, 2008, online at http://www.ipsnews.net/news.asp?idnews=41974.

Chapter 8. **Privacy Victims in the Air**

1. David Leppard and Hala Jaber, "Human Rights Gagged MI5 over Abdulmutallab," *Sunday Times* (London), Jan. 10, 2010, online at http://www.timesonline.co.uk (search "human rights gagged MI5 over Abdulmutallab").

2. Ezra Ijioma, "Nigeria: Perverted Ingenuity," *AllAfrica.com*, Jan. 16, 2010, online at http://allafrica.com/stories/201001190302.html.
3. John Schwartz, "Debate Over Full-Body Scans v Invasion of Privacy Flares Anew After Incident," *NY Times*, Dec. 30, 2009, A14, online at http://www.nytimes.com (search "debate body scans invasion of privacy anew"). Rotenberg later told me that the *New York Times* misquoted him.
4. Letter to Representatives Bennie G. Tompson and Peter T. King, Oct. 23, 2009, online at http://epic.org/security/DHS_CPO_Priv_Coal_Letter.pdf.
5. Ibid.
6. Ibid.
7. Associated Press, "System will assign threat level to all passengers," *Register-Guard* (Eugene, OR), Mar.1, 2003, A4, online at http://news.google.com (select advanced news search, then select archive search, then search "System will assign threat level to all passengers").
8. Roy Mark, "TSA Books Data Mining Program," *Internetnews.com* (Mar. 4, 2003), online at http://www.internetnews.com (search TSA books data mining program").
9. Ian McCaleb, "Federal Agency Defends Itself Against ACLU Criticism of Terror Watch List," *Fox News*, July 15, 2008, online at http://www.foxnews.com/story/0,2933,382061,00.html.
10. Ibid.

Chapter 9. **Moore' Outlaws**

1. Bill Morem, "Internet Scam Victimizes the Gullible and Elderly," *Tribune*, San Luis Obispo, CA (Mar. 14, 2009),online at http://www.pharmacychoice.com/news/article.cfm?Article_ID=343578.
2. Regena Johnston. Interview by author. May 2009.
3. Husband of Regena Johnston. Interview by author. Feb. 2010.
4. See, e.g., Quotations by William Gibson, online at http://strangewondrous.org/browse/author/g/gibson+william.
5. Bill Gates, "Bill Gates Trustworthy Computing Security eMail," The itmWEB Site (Feb. 1, 2002), online at http://www.itmweb.com/f020102.htm.
6. Aaron Broverman, "Beware of Facebook Scams," *Bankrate.com* (Mar. 25, 2009), online at http://www.bankrate.com/brm/news/cc/Mar09_Facebook_scam_a1can.asp.
7. John Sutter and Jason Carroll, "Fears of Impostors Increase on Facebook," *CNN.com*, Feb. 6, 2009, online at http://www.cnn.com/2009/TECH/02/05/facebook.impostors/index.html.

8. William J. Clinton," On Keeping America Secure for the 21st Century," Remarks at National Academy of Sciences, Jan. 22, 1999, online at http://www.justice.gov/criminal/cybercrime/nas9901.htm.
9. Information Warfare Monitor, "Tracking GhostNet: Investigating a Cyber Espionage Network," Mar. 29, 2009, online at http://www.nartv.org/mirror/ghostnet.pdf.
10. Ibid.
11. Byron Acohido, "Cybercrooks Stalk Small Businesses that Bank Online," *USA Today*, Jan. 13, 2010, 6A, online at http://www.usatoday.com/money/industries/technology/2009-12-30-cybercrime-small-business-online-banking_N.htm.
12. George Ou, "Apple Keyboards Hacked and Possessed," *digital society*, Aug. 1, 2009, online at www.digitalsociety.org/2009/08/apple-keyboards-hacked-and-possessed/.
13. Elinor Mills, "Apple Suggests Mac Users Install Antivirus Software," *Cnet News*, Dec. 1, 2008, online at http://news.cnet.com/8301-1009_3-10110852-83.html.
14. Tarandeep Singh, "The Linux Kernel Bug, Vulnerability that Went for Eight Years Un-Noticed, Un-Fixed," *Taranfx*, Aug. 15, 2009, www.taranfx.com (search "Linux Kernel Bug").
15. Saul Hansell, "How Hackers Snatch Real-Time Security ID Numbers," *NY Times*, Aug. 20, 2009, online at http://www.nytimes.com (search "Hackers Snatch Real-Time Security Numbers").
16. Kim Wilsher, "French Fighter Planes Grounded by Computer Virus," *Telegraph* (London), Feb. 7, 2009, online at http://www.telegraph.co.uk/news/worldnews/europe/france/4547649/French-fghter-planes-grounded-by-computer-virus.html; "French Navy Surrenders to Conficker," *National Business Review*, Feb. 12, 2009, online at http://www.nbr.co.nz (search "French navy surrenders Conficker").

Chapter 10. Big Brother's Revenge

1. Maria Saminario and Margaret Kane, "U.S. Backs Off Private Monitoring," *ZDNet UK*, Jul. 29,1999, online at http://news.zdnet.co.uk/security/0,1000000189,2072871,00.htm.
2. Ibid.
3. Ibid.
4. Pub. L. No. 107-296, 116 Stat. 2238 (codified as amended at 6 U.S.C. §441).

Chapter 11. Invested in Insecurity

1. Pub. L. No. 100-418, 102 Stat. 1425 (codified as amended at 50 U.S.C. app. §2170).

2. Ted Bridis, "Arab Firm May Run 6 U.S. Ports," *Seattle Times*, Feb. 12, 2006, A12, online at http://seattletimes.nwsource.com//html/home/index.html (search "Arab firm may run 6 U.S. ports").
3. "Arab-owned American Ports?" *Wash. Times*, Feb. 14, 2006, A18, online at http://www .washingtontimes.com (search "Arab-owned American ports").
4. Paul Bluestein, "Some in Congress Object to Arab Port Operator," *Wash. Post*, Feb. 17, 2006, A11, online at http://www.washingtonpost.com/wp-dyn/content/article/2006/02/16/AR2006021602304.html.
5. Hearing before House Committee on Financial Services regarding "Committee on Foreign Investment in the United States (CFIUS), One Year After Dubai Ports World," 110th Cong. 1st Sess. Serial No. 110-2 at 47 (Feb. 7, 2007), online at http://ftp.resource.org/gpo.gov/hearings/110h/34672.pdf.
6. Compare H.R. 556 as introduced Jan. 18, 2007, online at http://frwebgate .access.gpo.gov/cgi-bin/getdoc.cgi?dbname=110_cong_bills&docid=f:h556ih .txt.pdf, *with* H.R. 556 as reported by committee, Feb. 23, 2007, online at http://frwebgate.access.gpo.gov/cgi-bin/getdoc.cgi?dbname=110_cong_bills&docid=f:h556rh.txt.pdf.
7. Pub. L. No. 110-49, 121 Stat. 246.
8. James K. Jackson, "Exon-Florio Foreign Investment Provision: Comparison of H.R. 556 and S. 1610," Cong'l Research Serv., Aug. 7, 2007, online at http://assets .opencrs.com/rpts/RL34082_20070807.pdf.
9. Exec. Order No. 13,456, 73 Fed. Reg. 4677 (Jan. 25, 2008).

Chapter 12. **Smallpox in the Garage**

1. Donald R. Hopkins, MD, MPH, "Public Health Then and Now—Smallpox: Ten Years Gone," 78 *Am J Pub Health* 1589, 1594, May 8, 1980 (restating World Health Assembly Resolution No. 33, declaring global eradication of smallpox), online at http://ajph.aphapublications.org/cgi/reprint/78/12/1589.pdf.
2. Kofi Annan, "Address of the Secretary-General on Accepting the Max Schmidheiny Freedom Prize," St. Gallen, Switzerland, Nov. 18, 2006, online at http://www.un.org (click on "Welcome," then search "Address Secretary-General Accepting Max Schmidheiny Freedom Prize").
3. National Security Council, "National Strategy for Countering Biological Threats," National Security Council, Nov. 2009, online at http://www.whitehouse.gov/sites/default/files/National_Strategy_for_Countering_BioThreats.pdf.
4. Ibid.
5. Exec. Order No. 13,527, 75 Fed. Reg. 737 (Jan. 6, 2010).
6. See, e.g., http://en.wikiquote.org/wiki/Robert_Oppenheimer.

Chapter 13. What's Wrong with Privacy?

1. Because the article owes much of its current fame to Brandeis's later career, I will from this point on discuss only his views without each time laboriously giving credit, if that is the right word, to his coauthor.
2. Samuel Warren and Louis D. Brandeis, "The Right to Privacy," 4 *Harvard Law Review* 193, 196 (1890).
3. Ibid.

Chapter 14. Privacy for the Real World

Chapter 14. Privacy for the Real World

1. Pub. L. No. 95-630, 92 Stat. 3695 (codified as amended at 12 U.S.C. §3401 *et seq.*).
2. Pub. L. No. 98-549, 98 Stat. 2780 (codified as amended at 47 U.S.C. §521).
3. An Act to Regulate the Collection of Duties, 1st Con. 1st Sess., Stat.1, Ch. V, Sec. 24 at 43 (July 31, 1789), online at http://books.google.com (search "Act to regulate collection of duties and July 31, 1789").
4. *U.S. v. Flores-Montano*, 541 U.S. 149 (2004).
5. *U.S. v. Arnold*, 523 F.3d 941 (9th Cir. 2008).
6. *U.S. v. Hampe*, 2007 WL 1192365 (D. Maine).
7. Karen Tumulty, "Snooping Into Obama's Passport," *Time*, Mar. 21,2008, online at http://www.time.com/time/politics/article/0,8599,1724520,00.html.
8. State of Ohio, Office of Inspector General, Report of Investigation, File ID Number 2008299, Nov. 20, 2008, online at http://clipsandcomment.com/wp-content/uploads/2008/11/oig-joe-the-plumber-20081120.pdf.
9. Markle Foundation Task Force, *Creating a Trusted Network for Homeland Security* (Dec. 2003), online at http://www.markle.org/downloadable_assets/nstf_report2_full_report.pdf.
10. Ibid.
11. Ibid.
12. Markle Foundation Task Force, *Implementing a Trusted Information Sharing Environment: Using Immutable Audit Logs to Increase Security, Trust, and Accountability* (Feb. 2006), online at http://www.markle.org/downloadable_assets/nstf_IAL_020906.pdf.

About the Author

Dupont Photographers

Stewart A. Baker was the first assistant secretary for policy at the Department of Homeland Security from 2005 to 2009. He now practices law at Steptoe & Johnson in Washington, D.C., and is a visiting fellow at the Hoover Institution. His law practice covers homeland security, international trade, cybersecurity, data protection, and foreign investment regulation. Baker has also served as general counsel of the Robb-Silberman Commission investigating intelligence failures before the Iraq war (2004–5), as general counsel of the National Security Agency (1992–94), and as deputy general counsel of the Education Department (1979–81). He clerked for Justice John Paul Stevens on the Supreme Court and Judge Frank M. Coffin on the First Circuit Court.

Creative Commons Attribution-NoDerivs License

The online version of this work is licensed under the Creative Commons Attribution-NoDerivs License. A Summary of the license is given below, followed by the full legal text.

You are free:

- To copy, distribute, display, and perform the work
- To make commercial use of the work

Under the following conditions;

Attribution. You must give the original author credit.

No Derivative Works. You may not alter, transform, or build upon this work.

For any reuse or distribution, you must make clear to others the license terms of this work.

- Any of these conditions can be waived if you get permission from the copyright holder.
- Your fair use and other rights are in no way affected by the above.

Creative Commons Legal Code:
Attribution No-Derivs 3.0
CREATIVE COMMONS CORPORATION IS NOT A LAW FIRM AND DOES NOT PROVIDE LEGAL SERVICES. DISTRIBUTION OF THIS LICENSE DOES NOT CREATE AN ATTORNEY-CLIENT RELATIONSHIP. CREATIVE COMMONS PROVIDES THIS INFORMATION ON AN "AS-IS" BASIS. CREATIVE COMMONS MAKES NO WARRANTIES REGARDING THE INFORMATION PROVIDED, AND DISCLAIMS LIABILITY FOR DAMAGES RESULTING FROM ITS USE.

Index